HOW TO BELIEVE

HOW TO BELIEVE

Teachers and Seekers
Show the Way to a Modern,
Life-Changing Faith

Jon Spayde

Random House New York

Published in the United States by Random House,
an imprint of The Random House Publishing Group,
a division of Random House, Inc., New York.

RANDOM HOUSE and colophon are registered trademarks
of Random House, Inc.

Grateful acknowledgment is made to Matthew George Epp
for permission to reprint excerpts from *Religion of Sand* and
Faith the Bow by Matthew George Epp.
Reprinted by permission.

LIBRARY OF CONGRESS CATALOGING-IN-PUBLICATION DATA
Spayde, Jon.
How to believe : teachers and seekers show the way to a
modern, life-changing faith / Jon Spayde.
p. cm.
ISBN 978-1-4000-6402-1 (alk. paper)
1. Christian biography—United States.
2. Spiritual life—Christianity.   I. Title.
BR1700.3.S63 2008
277.3'0830922—dc22   2007025841
[B]

Printed in the United States of America on acid-free paper

www.atrandom.com

2 4 6 8 9 7 5 3 1

First Edition

Text design by Laurie Jewell

To the memory of Ida Siljenberg Carlson,

and to all my fellow trudgers on the

road of happy destiny

CONTENTS

Introduction ix

Don't Think About God Richard Rohr 3

Hold On in Dry Times Elizabeth J. Andrew 8

Keep Faith Simple Kosuke Koyama 13

Enter into Relationship Victoria and Allen Queen 18

Don't Be "Churchy" Mary Forsythe 27

Throw Out Your Outmoded Ideas of God John Shelby Spong 34

Look for God Everywhere and in Everyone Matt Epp 43

Give Your Whole Self to God Cyndi Dale 50

Accept the Mystery Liz Kelly 56

Follow God's Promptings Wherever They Lead Matt Helling 61

Let God Heal Your Pain Larry Lee 66

Be Intimate with God Tina and Tom Engstrom 74

Find a Practice That Works for You James W. Jones 82

Be a Spiritual Explorer Joyce Rupp 89

viii • Contents

Expect Miracles Thien-an Dang   94

Be God's Partner Peter Gardiner-Harding   99

Accept That God Can Handle Anything Leonard Griffin   104

Stay Open to New Revelations Carie Gross   109

Go With God's Flow Cynthia Williams   114

Avoid Both Absolutism and Relativism Irving (Yitz) Greenberg   120

Unite with All Life William Bryant Logan   127

Be Honest About What You Don't Understand Leo Lefebure   133

Accept Where You Are Anna Bradshaw   141

Honor Other Paths Joan Kirby   146

Focus on the Good Chuck Robison   152

Find the Truth for Yourself George Bassilios   159

Understand Traditional Truth in Fresh Ways Aiden Enns   165

Cultivate Readiness and Willingness Helen Hansen   172

Ask: What *Did* Jesus Do? Jim Rigby   178

Trust That God Loves You for Who You Are Gerald Gafford   186

Let Yourself Be Crucified Gangaji   192

Don't Think About God Pier Giorgio di Cicco   198

Afterword   203

Acknowledgments   211

INTRODUCTION

This book arose from the realization, which came to me about twenty years ago, that I believe in God. To be sure, my first approaches to God were very deliberate and somewhat desperate acts of will—little leaps taken toward accepting a higher power in order to recover from alcoholism. But then, a little later, came the discovery that I actually did believe, and that was something of a surprise and a challenge.

I had the sort of spiritual and religious background that is typical of educated middle-class Americans of the baby boom–era. I got dressed up and went to church with my parents most Sundays, but the Congregational and Episcopal churches our family attended were so lacking in spiritual fervor, freshness, and challenge that our main reason for choosing or leaving a congregation was whether my father, a theater director, approved of the minister's vocal delivery. (He rarely did. "Why can't he look for the *operative words* and stress *those*?" he would mourn, prior to ditching a church.)

As for me, I endured the usual felt-board Bible stories in Sunday school, then joined a snooty Episcopal boys' choir (soon abandoned for the Boy Scouts) and underwent an Episcopal confirmation class whose curriculum consisted entirely of the rote memorization of the contents of a little green paperback catechism. The young priest who led us in this exercise was a puzzling combination of snazzy habits (he drove a candy-apple-red MG) and dust-choked theology.

Predictably, I revolted against all this smug dullness when I went to college, and by the time I was in graduate school, studying comparative literature, I had learned to file religion and spirituality within two big, and intellectually respectable, categories: Culture and History. I studied Japanese and Chinese classics, and viewed Buddhism as nothing more than a compromise between Indian and East Asian world views. I read European literature and philosophy, and noted that the demise of the Judeo-Christian God, at least as far as intelligent people like me were concerned, had occurred sometime between the late seventeenth and the early eighteenth century. I was an atheist (though not a very energetic one) and a cultural materialist, who considered all deities to be products of the human desire for comfort and order, emerging within specific cultures at specific historical moments.

At about the same time, without being conscious of it at all, I was giving much of my time and nearly all of my love to a personal god: alcohol—also known, with nice irony, as "spirits." The more dependent I became upon ten to thirty daily drinks to think, socialize, and even feel like a living thing, the more of a resolute, iconoclastic lone wolf I decided I was. Eventually, Stanford University kicked me out of its graduate school for inebriation and inertia; I then moved to New York to scrounge work as a writer. By the time I took my last six drinks—six bottles of Korean OB Lager beer from a downtown Korean deli, to be exact—I saw the brown glass containers for what they were: strange little spirit-idols, who knew me better than I knew myself.

· · ·

In the first weeks of my recovery, I latched onto the idea of a God to whom I could, and should, turn over the results of my efforts and the course of my life. Almost immediately this process of "letting go and letting God" gave me a powerful sense of relief and freedom. In the face of all the anxieties and feelings of worthlessness and confusion that tormented me in early sobriety, I kept on praying, kept on "turning it over," and kept on hoping that whatever giant disaster I was worried about (an IRS ultimatum, the loss of my apartment, cancer) would not come to pass. These calamities and many others that I imagined did not, in fact, darken my door, and I began to interpret powerful accidents and coincidences as acts of God.

The most dramatic of these came on a Friday night in New York, when I was depressed and sorrowful and certain I was going to drink again. I certainly wanted to, badly, and something inside me said that the time had come for me to fail at sobriety in just the same way I had failed at academia. I simply didn't have the discipline to stick with things or the self-respect to meet my responsibilities. Now, I felt sure, had come the moment when I would toss recovery into the toilet simply because it was too difficult. I was the sort of irreparably weak character who craved comfort above everything else, and on this particular Friday night, the ordeal of sitting inside my own skin was just too much.

So I made my way, sadly resolute, from my shabby apartment on East Seventh Street toward Astor Place with the idea of sitting down at one of the neighborhood's many Japanese restaurants, ordering a few cold sakes, and returning to my miserable but comfortable destiny as a good-hearted, weak-willed alcoholic screw-up.

As I turned from Avenue A onto Astor, a tall, middle-aged man in the brown uniform and peaked cap of New York's traffic police approached me. He was very, very drunk.

"Can you help me?" he asked.

I reached into my pocket for some coins to give the poor guy, but he shook his head.

"I gotta stop drinking," he said. And he stood before me as if waiting for an answer.

"Well," I said, staring into his watery brown eyes, "I actually can tell you a little bit about that."

I walked beside him along Astor, past the restaurants and bars, in and out of the throngs of NYU student revelers and bridge-and-tunnel tourists. I told him what I knew about alcoholism and what he could do if he really wanted to quit. At one point, we crossed the street, and he held on to me for dear life. When we reached the opposite curb, he looked at me strangely and seriously for a long moment, trembling and trying to focus his unblinking eyes—then he asked, "Are you an angel?"

I laughed, and he looked surprised. I offered to buy him coffee, but he pulled away from me. I told him I'd be happy to help him in any way I could, but he shook his head and began to run unsteadily up the street. Soon he had disappeared. I was frustrated by his retreat, but then I realized that my desire to drink had vanished, too.

Half an hour later, back in my apartment, sober and shaking with a combination of wonder and gratitude, I realized who the angel had been.

I've prayed for his recovery ever since, whoever he was and wherever he may be now.

If this experience was a coincidence, it was one that operated with something like precision: within minutes of my slipping into a mindset that had bedeviled me all my life—the certainty of failure and the futility of effort—I had had an encounter that lifted me completely out of that all-too-familiar bog. The moment I yielded to concern, even love, for a fellow drunk, I lost my sense of hopelessness—and my craving.

My recovery was not about self-discipline or strength of character. It was (I can see this now) an entry into a different world, a world of love. In that world, my weakness was strength if I could own up to it; my cluelessness was transformed into an openness that allowed a Spirit that I could not name to enter me; and if I was willing to leave the minimum-security prison of my ego long enough to help someone else, that Spirit would, in some mysterious way, go on changing me beyond recognition—beginning with this bewitching desire to drink, to which I had yielded every single day for nearly fifteen years and which was now quiet.

• • •

One night not much later, I lay on my bed listening to a tape of Ralph Vaughan Williams's "The Lark Ascending." The sweet violin music soared into the heights of the scale, and I suddenly felt an active, almost violent love stream in the window, eddy around me, and soak my whole body in its sweetness.

I laughed out loud and fell on my knees. I knew that I was protected, cherished, and forgiven forever. If I was not in the presence of God, I was at least in the grip of something too sudden, too strange, and too powerful to be merely psychological. This was far more than a mood swing; and in any case, my moods almost never swung in such a joyful direction.

This new world I had entered clearly held strange surprises for me, surprises that my tight-lipped, cultural-materialist view of the world could not account for. I decided that I believed in God—God as the force that had brought the traffic cop angel into my life, God as the wind of love that had fluttered my curtains that Friday night, God as the entity who, when I prayed to Him/Her/It, calmed me and gave my life a semblance of direction and hope. I felt grateful and wanted to thank God, not in isolation, but in fellowship with others.

For me that meant religion.

The "r" word, usually prefixed with the dreaded epithet "organized."

And for me, it meant the Christian religion. Not just because I had been (in a manner of speaking) raised in it, not entirely because it was convenient—churches on every corner—but because I had a rudimentary attraction to Christ. Whether or not he was God, he seemed to be somebody whom screw-ups could trust. He was a nobody who'd failed spectacularly, a homeless thirtysomething who had gone about with a band of illiterate blue-collar Jews declaring that the Kingdom of God was available to everyone, especially sinners. I believed that I had peeked into that kingdom, and he seemed like the right sort of guide to walk with as I attempted to explore it.

But this vague sense of solidarity with Jesus Christ was one thing, and the prospect of returning to church-in-America was quite another. I didn't want to join a chorus of believers for whom Jesus's name was a mantra. Oddly enough, it didn't occur to me to ask God what I should do. I was praying to God daily for the courage to get up, go to work, respond to unpleasant phone calls, deal with my aging parents, and survive a relationship that was headed nowhere. But the choice of how I was to express my feelings about God—in a church or not—was something I believed I needed to make all on my own, within the cramped confines of my brain.

One of the themes that emerges from my encounters with the Christian thinkers and doers in this book is that, while the modern tendency is to view religion as a matter of the head (what do I believe about God, about Creation, about sexual ethics, and how do I relate them to the rules and principles of religion?), religious *experience* is a matter of the heart. Had I been able to listen to my heart instead of my brain, I might have been able to open myself to all kinds of subtle signals of God's guidance. Instead, I tried to intellectualize my religious identity and so remained more or less immobile.

I eventually moved to Minnesota to work for the *Utne Reader,* a magazine that maintained a quirky mix of left politics, personal-growth self-help, green economics, hip trend-watching, and non-mainstream spirituality. I loved *Utne* and through it met and/or interviewed a number of spiritual heavyweights, from psychologist James Hillman to mystic Andrew Harvey, from meditation teacher Stephen Levine to sacred-text translator Stephen Mitchell. In the course of answering simple journalistic questions for my articles, these gurus helped me see that the best relationship with God is holistic. I began to feel God gently knocking at the doors of all my faculties—sight, smell, hearing, memory, desire—as well as my intellect. I began to be more intuitive as I sought a way or a place to worship God, and these intuitions led me to the most holistic church of all: Catholicism.

I found I liked the ritual of the church—even in its less esoteric post-Vatican II form since most of the changes in the liturgy had the effect of helping outsiders like me feel at home in the pews. I liked the spirit-charged objects and actions called sacramentals—candles, holy water, the rosary, the sign of the cross—and I liked the antiquity of the tradition, the unbroken line of saints, shepherds, and mystics reaching right back to the day when certain poor Jews experienced their rabbi as risen from the dead. Most of all, though, as I visited Catholic churches, I liked the feeling of belonging to a huge and inclusive group of very real people. Since Catholics tend not to dress up for mass, I found I was sharing pews with folks in bowling league jackets, Minnesota Twins jerseys, and wind-breakers advertising the owners' businesses: well drilling, pizza, plumbing supply—unthinkable in the Sunday-best Protestant and Episcopal churches of my youth. (Not that everyone came grubby: In one Vietnamese parish, I prayed with women in shimmering traditional *ao dai* dresses and lace-trimmed veils.) There seemed to be a niche for everybody in this vast, one-billion-strong church, from intellectual Jesuit theologians to elderly Minnesota Irish ladies to Basque farmers.

So in 2001, I joined a new-Catholic class at a large St. Paul parish, in preparation for what the church calls the Rite of Christian Initiation of Adults (RCIA). A little less than a year later, I was admitted to the sacraments.

Religious warfare had reached fever pitch in our country—a political-religious struggle between conservative Protestant evangelicals and their traditionalist Catholic allies on one side and, on the other, people like me: political and religious liberals. Tensions between these camps had been growing for thirty years, ever since the heyday of the Moral Majority in the seventies and the Christian Coalition in the eighties. The election of George W. Bush in 2000 represented the coming to power of a political alliance that spoke the language of these religious conservatives and declared itself in favor of their causes: an end to abortion, resistance to gay rights initiatives, and an overt Christian presence in public life. During the 2004 campaign, this cultural/religious struggle took on some of the savagery of real warfare.

The war shook me up. It didn't challenge my faith in God, but it made my identity as a Christian troubling. I saw an evangelical movement that seemed fanatically narrow, and while I knew perfectly well that there were many other kinds of Christians in America and the world, I found myself wondering if there was something in the Christian faith that naturally bred intolerance, some rogue gene that expressed itself as angry, us-versus-them legalism. I wondered about the near silence of the more moderate mainstream Christian denominations in the public debate. Why weren't they challenging the narrow theology and rampant judgmentalism of the evangelicals? Was their morale so low, were their convictions so tepid that they could do nothing but sit on their hands? What did that say about the liberal theology they, and I, embraced? Why were the suburban evangelical megachurches that supplied Bush's most loyal troops growing and thriving while the genteel liberal denominations lost members daily?

Meanwhile, journalists took to using "Christian" itself as a shorthand term for the conservative evangelical mindset and program. This made the term increasingly difficult for me to use about myself. And my reticence, in turn, made me wonder about the depth of my own Christian convictions. Shouldn't I be able to stand up proudly, utter the c-word without fear, and lay out my own beliefs about Christ's message: a message of inclusion, compassion, and the transformation of legalism into love? On a few occasions, I did so, but it felt furtive, and the great, old church to which I now belonged didn't seem aligned with those beliefs. John Paul II had overseen and approved the destruction of the great Liberation Theology current in Latin America and the censure or silencing of nearly every other contemporary Catholic voice that inspired me, from Swiss theologian Hans Kung, who, among other transgressions, challenged papal infallibility, to the forceful Sri Lankan priest Tissa Balasuriya, a critic of the church's claims to exclusive access to God through Christ.

I wondered whether my squeamishness about my relatively new faith—my sense that it might be wisest to become a secular person again or at least to disaffiliate myself from organized religion—was a natural response to the unsettling political and religious climate, a sign of my spiritual immaturity, or a signal that I was spiritual but not religious by nature. Or was I just getting sick of my latest commitment?

I had to ask myself another, deeper question, too: If I truly believed that Christ came into the world as a paragon of selfless love, and I was called to imitate him as best I could, how could I fight the evangelicals whose message I so disliked and distrusted? If I donned the robes of a liberal Pharisee and decided that all truth was on my side and none on theirs—or worse, if I dismissed them and failed to at least try to understand the human meaning of their yearnings, needs, blindnesses, and insights, I would fail to acknowledge my own arrogance, blindness, self-satisfaction, and general narrowness as I excoriated theirs.

• • •

I wanted to see if I could understand Jesus and the people who love him. I wanted to know how Christianity could make sense in the lives of intelligent, modern people. What about all the strangeness that seems to come with Christ—virgin birth, dual nature as man and God, redeemer of sinners? Is he best understood as a wise rabbi who lived a long time ago, or an ageless power alive in our hearts, or both? Is he God? How, for God's sake?

Where is the balance to be found between God's love and God's judgment? Does the evangelical emphasis on judgment close too many windows against the wind of God's forgiving love? Does the liberal insistence on the magnitude and power of this love let us "do what we will" to our detriment? Are other faiths equally valid paths to truth and union with God?

I vowed not to make the same mistake I made earlier when I tried to decide how and where to worship God. This time, I would seek the wisdom of others. I got out of the house and on the road, from Minneapolis to New York to Atlanta, from Missouri to New Mexico, from California to South Carolina, found interesting and forceful believers, some nationally famous, some eminent in their fields, some unknown to any limelight, and asked them to help me wrestle with these questions. I didn't want to hear sermons or speeches, to review dogma or set up a theological/political debate; I wanted to find out how real, breathing Christians came to their faith and lived it in the twenty-first century. Whether the Christian was evangelical or Quaker, gay or straight, a well-published author or a quiet Everywoman, I wanted to know what was most precious, most difficult, most changeable, and most certain about their faith. I hoped to move beyond doctrine and dogma, and to explore the realm of lived experience. That's where I figured the most authentic and compelling answers to these questions could be found.

Although this book was partly prompted by debates in our public sphere, it is not a debate. It is a series of portraits of believers, each one unique; I hope readers will be able to see that there is as much difference of style, spirit, and emphasis between two liberal thinkers as there is across the liberal/evangelical divide. (And some interviewees in these pages blur that line as well.) I have made no attempt to balance the sample by sex, race, age, politics, or theological flavor. I've simply included Christians (plus one Jew and one devotee of an Indian tradition) whose perspectives on Jesus Christ, God the Father, and the Holy Spirit invigorate me as I try to think, pray, and believe. If the sample skews toward the theological left, that's probably because I do and because I find so much necessary openness, vigor, and excitement there. But I would hate for this book to be read as a salvo in the left-right religious wars. I want to beg my readers to believe that people of faith on both sides of the progressive/conservative divide have much to teach us. I know this because I've been learning from them all.

I hope, too, that you will come to see possibilities for making your faith, whatever it may be, more alive, more honest, and more responsive to God, to your true self, and to the world. This is a Christian book because I have a Christian problem and because I believe the Christian faith presents many glorious, bizarre, troubling, and magnificent questions for anyone who takes it seriously. The people you will meet in the following pages won't necessarily answer these questions for you, but they all *live* them, every day of their lives.

How to Believe

DON'T THINK ABOUT GOD

Richard Rohr

When my wife, Laurie, and I entered the offices of the Center for Action and Contemplation (CAC) in Albuquerque in search of the center's founder and spiritual director, the Franciscan priest Richard Rohr, a woman at the reception desk smiled, tilted her head, and said, "I think I hear him coming."

What we heard was a child's laughter, and then into the reception area came a short, round, rubicund man in his sixties, wearing a baseball cap and carrying on his shoulders a little blond girl who could best be described as angelic. He smiled at us. The little girl giggled. It was what you could call a Franciscan moment.

"Okay, sweetie, I've got to talk to these people," he explained to the visibly disappointed little angel, helping her dismount. He explained to us that his companion was the daughter of one of the Center's staff members. Rohr established the CAC in 1987 as a retreat center and a launching pad for social activism, and the place has the friendly vibe of spiritual and social alignment among friends.

I had read a couple of Rohr's books, heard him speak at a church gathering in the Twin Cities, and listened to several of the tapes and CDs he uses to expound his generous, love-filled, socially alert take on the Gospels and on the Catholic faith. The experience made me a fan; Rohr presents a Catholicism that speaks of freedom, love, spontaneity, and openness rather than morbid self-scrutiny, tense moralism, and sectarian defensiveness.

Rohr's voice—musical, rhythmical, slightly breathy—is one of his most important tools. It can be heard on the hundred-plus audio and video recordings he has made since 1971, covering a wide and colorful array of topics: major themes of the Bible, the mysticism of the apostle Paul, the Holy Spirit and twelve-step programs, the nature of true religion, the stages of spiritual growth, the deeper significance of the 9/11 attacks. His voice brings a sort of buoyancy to the gravest topics, yet it is also insistent and impassioned. Rohr speaks easily and volubly, and yet there's the sense that he is struggling too—struggling to impart the idea that, despite all the pain and injustice of earthly life, everything is "okay." He gives the paltry word a strange dignity and resonance.

Born in Topeka to a farm family who'd fled the Dust Bowl, he was graced in his childhood with experiences he calls "unitive"—moments when he understood the oneness and beauty of the world and of God's love for that world and everyone in it.

"When these moments came, I would just be standing there, sort of gazing, and knowing that it was all okay," he told us. "I was a part of it, and it was good. And *I* was good. These experiences kind of protected me from fear-based religion. And later, whenever I was taught fear-religion in the seminary, by bad mentors and teachers—well, I just never believed it. I had good filters.

"It's okay. That's what I know. And I'm okay as a part of it. And everything is okay. Even though I simultaneously know that, more than ever, it's terrible! It's not okay at all! We're self-destructing. Just yesterday I heard a fighter jet go over, loud as could be—millions of dollars flying over us. It costs them two hundred thousand dollars just to takeoff. What could that money do for the world?"

The CAC is situated in the poorest neighborhood of Albuquerque, a barrio south of the city center that looks a good deal like rural Mexico. Through an internship program that combines work in low-income neighborhoods with social analysis and via an ongoing relationship with a poor barrio in Juarez, Mexico, the center seeks to raise awareness of the interlocking social ills that make for poverty and misery on both sides of the border.

The idea that our world can be both okay and wrong at the same time is just one of the sacred paradoxes that seem to fascinate Rohr. Some of the intellectual difficulties in Christianity that still irritate and confuse me, for example, are sources of delight for him. I remember the beatific smile on his face when, during his Twin Cities visit, he invoked the great strangenesses of the faith—a virgin mother, a man who is God, a God who is simultaneously One and Three. It was as if these were not problems to solve but glorious opportunities to escape from what he calls the "calculative mind" into the mystical realm where, he insists, religion really lives. As we talked in Albuquerque, he went even deeper.

"Those doctrines—the two natures of Christ, the Trinity, which really means the *flowing* nature of God—those are mystical insights," he said. "Once you pull them into the logical mind, you're dead wrong. God refuses to let Himself or Herself be *thought*. God can only be experienced. You can't think God, you can only be present to God.

"That's why religion at the higher level is always teaching you forms of presence. When you're present to God, you will know something. It's not a knowing that you can easily verbalize. It's not a knowing that you can prove, measure, control, or validate. That's why spiritual knowing is so wonderful, because it confirms you at the deepest level, and yet it makes you so helpless—because you can't prove it to anybody else."

Another paradox: The spirit confirms us *and* makes us helpless. That's not the sort of premise that sells self-help books, but it is a basic Christian insight, and it's characteristic of Rohr that he's as delighted by the helplessness as he is by the confirmation. For him, our helplessness before God, even our sinfulness, can ultimately be part of the vast "okay-ness" of everything. Why? Because if we understand the Gospels and the teaching of Jesus, we know that our frustrations, failures, defects, and sins—not our virtues—are the things that drive us into the hands of God.

Living a Christian life, Rohr believes, is not about assembling a laundry list of good deeds and ticking them off in order to get into heaven; it's the sharp realization that we cannot possibly be good on our own and our only chance is surrender to God, the One who can transform us. "Jesus actually *co-opts* sin," said Rohr, with a little laugh of astonishment. "As a moralist, I may claim I'm going to stop sin, or end sin, and go on and on about how we need to get rid of all these sinners. But Jesus says, I'm going to *use* your sin, whatever it is, to bring you to God, to me." And for Rohr, the presence of God is a joyous, safe, serene place.

Rohr's 2,000-year-old church is torn by angry debate between traditionalists and progressives. His emphasis on God's love over God's judgment, his insistence that a lot of Catholic practice is custom rather than ironclad rule, and his commitment to social action of a leftist stamp make him unwelcome in many of the precincts of Catholic conservatism. His work with male spirituality, including initiation rites that he carries out in natural settings, has even garnered him accusations of New Agery and paganism. But he insists that he has a deep love for Catholic tradition, the principles of authority, and the continuity embodied by the institutional church. It's all a question of when and how the conservative impulse is brought to bear.

In several books and tapes, Rohr has laid out a vision of how spirituality changes, or ought to change, over the course of a lifetime. "In the first half of life," he told us, "you need law, custom, tradition, authority, structure. You need to internalize values like patience, forgiveness, perseverance, love of God, love of neighbor. Those things have to be learned and practiced by standing still, loyalty to one group of people, one marriage, one system. I call that creating the container. Once you have the container, then you're ready for the contents"—the liberating message of God's love and the great freedom the Gospel imparts.

For Rohr, the frustrating thing about religious conservatism is that it proposes to extend the first-half-of-life program indefinitely, encouraging people to build and rebuild the container, even to worship it. He's often surprised at the tenacity with which some people resist the idea that Jesus's message for the latter half of life is one of freedom and joy. "It's almost as if the more I actually stick to the Gospel, the more attempt there will be from some people to disprove it. I talked about fear and grief recently in San Antonio, and a man stood up and practically screamed at me, 'We're *supposed* to be *afraid* of God!' Because everyone in the room could see just how angry he was at everything and everyone, I didn't have to respond to him."

Still, he's just as vexed by liberals who have no use for first-half values. "People who glibly pretend to have the contents—like so many of us in the sixties did—without internalizing any values, are just off the mark." And he told us that his biggest challenge as an implicit and explicit critic of the social order, the church, and even the Pope is dealing with the temptation to self-righteousness.

"It is a constant failure—who are you, Richard, to think you know better, to always have a better way to say things? Who are you to think that you know better than Benedict XVI? Yet it's a real dilemma to remain a Catholic when you know that so much of it is merely the container. I find it hard to teach young people today because they still need and want that container, and I don't have any patience with it. Discipline, structure, order, law; I know they've got to learn it. But my heart isn't into saying things like, 'You've got to go to mass every Sunday.' It's a wonderful custom. But it's nothing more than a custom. We used to call missing Sunday mass a mortal sin, like mass murder. Do you see how we ended up trivializing evil?

"So to maintain sanity, I just have to look in a different direction. I don't know how many days or months or years I have left; I don't have time for cynicism, anger, judgmentalism. This has led me to my teaching about nonviolence, which is at the core of Jesus's message. You have to learn a nonviolent attitude inside, or I don't think you can survive to an old age. My main conflict is how to keep handing my anger over to God, how not to take myself too seriously, how not to think I'm better than the church.

"Because at the end of the day, all the issues I engage, all the struggles I join—the sociopolitical ones, the ones about the church—they're really a larger mirroring of the conflicts, the gusts of arrogance, power, and violence, that go on daily inside of me."

• • •

Rohr's essential sweetness and his insistence that a real relationship with God is joyous and comforting is very Franciscan—and felt very liberating to me. His idea that God cannot be thought, on the other hand, came as something of a thunderbolt since I had conceived my basic religious problem, and even the major question of this book, as "how to think about God." In Rohr's thoughtful but impassioned presence, it became possible for me to imagine God as an enormous, loving presence rather than an idea. And his conception of the church as a means toward God (a finger pointing at the moon, as the Zen Buddhists say) rather than an end in itself, gave me a great deal to meditate on. If church could be a help toward a sense of God's mysterious presence rather than an intellectual faction defined solely by its rules, then I could go to church without feeling trapped.

I tried to hold on to Rohr's vision as I continued on the path, and his words returned to me again and again as I listened to others in this book and meditated on faith; but questions persisted. Was our relationship with God always a matter of joyous oneness? I'd read some of the Catholic mystics, and I knew there was doubt, trouble, even agony in their powerful faith. When I talked to Elizabeth Andrew, I got to hear about some of the trouble (and the joy) firsthand.

Hold On in Dry Times

Elizabeth J. Andrew

"The first time I heard the word 'bisexuality' spoken out loud was in an adult education session in my church—and my reaction was, 'Oh, so *that's* what I am!'" Thirty-six-year-old memoirist, writing teacher, and spiritual director Elizabeth J. Andrew was sitting across from me at a coffee table in her Minneapolis living room, explaining the intimate relationship between her sexual identity and her connection to the divine. She is a slender, graceful woman with the receptive demeanor of someone who knows how to listen.

"I knew my relationship to God would not stand still, and in order to grow, I had to come out. My conscious working on my spiritual journey really began then. Coming out was a process of reconnecting the pieces of my body and the pieces of my internal self. I was celibate and single at the time—so it wasn't like I was justifying a relationship with a woman. It was really about saying who I am."

Andrew has written about her struggle to name herself and her sexuality, and the powerful spiritual consequences of that naming in *Swinging on the Garden Gate: A Spiritual Memoir* (Skinner House). And she has helped many other writers in the Twin Cities put their spiritual lives on paper. In the process, she's come to a sense of storytelling that helped me listen to the interviewees in this book with a special kind of reverent attention. "When we relate our life experience, we have a sacred text," she told me. "In the same way as in a Biblical text, God is at work through our stories because God is at work in our lives. In our stories, there is always something to learn, some mystery, some miracle. When we enter into the process of writing that life story and we open to that mystery— well, it's amazing what kind of journey that can put us on."

Andrew's journey began in a devoutly Methodist family. Her father was a lawyer for IBM, but his roots were in the Italian-American working class; her mother had been educated in a seminary. In the family's home, Christian spirituality was always present but rarely discussed; as Andrew puts it in *Swinging on the Garden Gate,* "The origin of my relationship with God lurks in what went unspoken in my family. We kept quiet about the Sacred; words might endanger us by giving Spirit a substance or form we'd have to look at head on, unblinking. The act of naming was powerful, and so I was taught to shun it. Even today I hesitate, unwilling to choose words to describe God for fear I will, as is inevitable, fall short, or worse, defile something too magnificent for names."

Still, one of the most important things she learned when she came to the Midwest to attend college—at Carleton College in Northfield, Minnesota—was that it was, not only possible, but exciting to articulate faith. "At Carleton, there was all this lively dialogue about different beliefs," she said. "It was an amazing experience for me, a kind of a *conversion* experience. Suddenly I could take this undercurrent in my life that had been so important to me and talk about it, write about it, and learn about it in an academic way. My intellectual life and my spiritual life were the very same thing."

Andrew smiled at the memory and added, "The academic-intellectual buzz eventually wore thin, of course." For her sense of the divine to move from her head into her body—and for her to accept her body's real nature and real needs—took some more time and an epic trip to Wales.

A month's bicycle sojourn through the heartland of her beloved Arthurian legends seemed just the thing to reveal to Andrew—who had, she estimated, probably biked a total of forty miles in her entire life at that point—some necessary truth about herself. She had graduated from college and broken up with a boyfriend. She had a complicated, confused image of the woman she wanted to become—and it didn't seem to jibe with conventional ideas of love and marriage.

"I just somehow knew I had to create the space and time to be by myself and kind of wrestle with who I was," she told me. The trip was by turns harrowing and exhilarating. Her overpacked bike panniers some-times set her wobbling on heavily traveled roads, and she spent many nervous miles pedaling across lonely landscapes. She came across the un-responsive body of an injured, abandoned woman near Bangor—and was too frightened and confused by the experience to help her. Unseen, she gazed on two young women, intimate friends, in a hostel room in the town of Llanberis, as they spoke gently in Welsh, rubbed one another's backs, and shared what could only be called love. She inched closer to the truth about herself.

"I also developed muscles at a soul level," she said. "That's when I re-alized that the story I told myself about who I was wasn't true. That was the first time I had a real sense of listening to God. I was finally living in my body and, for the first time, listening to the sacred in my body. I knew what I had to do—that's when I think I fell in love with the Holy Spirit. I came back from that trip with a very strong image of being up on this green, lush ledge at the edge of a cliff, looking over the ocean—and what I needed to do was go over the edge."

The image recurred in her dreams and daydreams for three years. She found a spiritual director and finally managed to come out to her. She traveled to New York to tell her parents, then returned to Minneapolis to offer her coming-out as a prayer in the liberal Methodist congregation she attended. "There's no such thing as a private coming-out," she later wrote. "Truth-telling, like prayer, fuses the personal and public realms. It reconnects the fragments within us that are the result of falsification and joins us to others willing to risk similar positions of integrity."

Truth-telling also ushered Andrew into a period of blissful, sometimes ecstatic, communion with the Person of the Trinity that means most to her: the Holy Spirit. She took a job at the Action, Reflection, Celebration (ARC) Retreat Center north of the Twin Cities, began studying spiritual direction, and started writing *Swinging on the Garden Gate*. "It was this wonderful blossoming," she recalled. "I felt this dynamic, vital, personal relationship with God. I have memories of driving back and forth be-tween the ARC and the Twin Cities and having the window open and feeling I could just reach through that thin veil and touch the Spirit! It was almost unbearable but so *alive*."

Since leaving the ARC and relocating to Minneapolis, Andrew's fusion career—spiritual counseling, writing, and spiritual-writing-counseling—has lifted off. In 2005, she published two books, a collection of essays fo-cusing on her relationship with her house and what dwelling in a specific place means to her, and a guide to writing spiritual memoir. But she confessed to me that she has been living in a desert valley of spiritual dryness for quite a while now.

"I had had a visceral experience of God, vibrant and active," she said. "And then it just ended, abruptly." For a number of years she had been making an annual week-long silent retreat on the North Shore of Lake Superior—most years, "a glowing, amazing experience." "But this time I could barely stand it, barely stay there. For a while, I thought I was doing something wrong. I'm not a person who gets hung up about sin, so I didn't think God was punishing me—it was more like, well, everyone else around me was feeling connected, why wasn't I?" Her spiritual director struggled to help her, but nothing worked. She sensed that she had to find a way to understand what was happening to her. A handful of mystics, who understood negativity, darkness, and dryness, came to her aid.

"For a while, my only companions were Saint John of the Cross and to some extent Saint Teresa of Avila and Jean-Pierre de Caussade," she said. "Saint John is my particular hero because he experienced and expressed that sense of abandonment I've been feeling. He also has a lot of lovely androgynous and homoerotic imagery—he wrote about sucking on God's breast! I loved it—it absolutely spoke to me, and it gave me the courage to look for a new spiritual director."

The thirtysomething Methodist chose for her director a Catholic nun in her seventies, who suggested she pray the Hours—the daily prayers that Catholic clergy and members of religious orders say. When I spoke to her, Andrew was following through, and she was hopeful, but the going wasn't easy. "During my 'in love' period," she said, "it was so easy to see what I needed in order to grow: Read this next book! Join this next group! All these lovely synchronicities unfolded. I still am grieving the loss of that time, and I think that grief is going to be with me for a long time. I sit here and talk with people about their spiritual experiences, and often the people I talk to are fresh in their blossoming. It's just so beautiful to look at, and I'm in absolute envy and absolute awe. And then they leave, and I'm like, Grrr! Those people have *all* the luck, and I'm stuck with a dark night of the soul! It's not fun at all. It's not fun to sit down and pray and . . . nothing."

Andrew's serene sadness reminded me that, while so much contemporary spirituality, especially American spirituality, roots itself in experience more than doctrine or dogma, insisting that our own private discoveries about faith are more reliable than ancient, perhaps overfamiliar words, it's undeniable that experience can sometimes fail us as surely as misguided or dry dogma can. I had been taught by the sister who led our new-Catholic group that the spiritual life was essentially an up-and-down ride and to be ready for dryness and doubt. Stick them out, she told us. You may simply have abandoned a concept of God that once served you reasonably well in the face of the great Mystery but is now too small. You may be going through the wringer in order to learn that *any* concept of God is too small.

I've found this realization—which can come in the midst of the most crippling doubt—to be a significant entry point into faith. As odd as it may sound, a God perpetually beyond my full comprehension is much easier for me to accept than a medieval sovereign lord sitting somewhere in heaven making humanlike choices and expressing human emotions like wrath or self-satisfaction or anger. If God is real, I will never be able to reduce God to an idea that is small enough to reside in my brain. And if that is so, any feeling I may have of God's silence or distance is likely to be my own creation; God's supposed silence and distance are actually my categories and, thus, my problems.

"My life is a koan," Andrew told me. "I believe in God. For most of my thirty-six years, I've *experienced* God, and here I am, having absolutely no feeling of God and absolutely no proof, experientially, that any of this is true—and not really much confirmation around me of the spirit. I've got the love of books and that sister down in the monastery; other than that, I don't have a lot of people around me to mirror back that what I'm going through actually is a true experience of God.

"I know nothing else except to be faithful. I really don't *know* what I believe anymore; it's really about sitting with the mystery and figuring out ways to open my heart to it."

KEEP FAITH SIMPLE

Kosuke Koyama

"When I talk about theology," says Kosuke Koyama, "the bombing of Tokyo is in the background."

The seventy-six-year-old Japanese-born theologian and writer was in his mid-teens when his native city was pounded with incendiary bombs by American B-29s—on one hundred and two separate raids. Koyama and his family suffered through every one. "The war was a brutal encounter for me with what humans can do to other humans," he said. "Not only with what was done to us, but the terrible violence we Japanese did in China and Southeast Asia, and the violence that Japanese nationalism did to Japan. It's very much with me today."

These traumas determined the whole course of Koyama's life. The son and grandson of nondenominational Protestant Christians, he was more or less told by his siblings to become a minister—"to do my part so that none of this would happen again," as he put it—and he studied at Tokyo Union Theological Seminary and was ordained the youngest Church of Christ minister in Japan. Thanks to the financial help of some American military chaplains and their soldier-parishioners, he was able to travel to America for further study: a bachelor of divinity at Drew Theological Seminary in New Jersey, then a master's and doctorate at Princeton Theological Seminary.

It was the beginning of a remarkable career; Koyama taught in Thailand, Singapore, and New Zealand, becoming in the process one of the most important Protestant voices in the emergence of a new Christian theology for Asia. This theology broke with the paternalistic, convert-the-heathen model of earlier missions and opened itself to learning from Buddhism and the other ancient religious traditions of half the world's people, while finding Christian ways of responding to the complex needs of rapidly modernizing cultures. From 1980 until 1996, he taught at New York's Union Theological Seminary.

Koyama retired to Minneapolis–St. Paul, where he teaches part-time at Luther Seminary and attends a small UCC church. We met in a classroom at Luther—a classroom almost too small to contain his energy and volubility. The genial, white-haired Koyama is a man of passions, and the very issue of religious passion fascinates him. And despite a career notable for confronting cultural and social complexity, as we talked, Koyama kept insisting on the essential simplicity of his current beliefs.

"Looking back at what Japan did to herself and to Asia in the name of nationalism," he said, "I realized that there was a great theological theme running through it all: idolatry. Now the great prophets like Jeremiah, Isaiah, and Amos talk about idolatry—and so the prophetic literature became important to me. Their passion for justice moved me too—and at Union, I was right in the middle of the upsurge of feminist theology and black theology. These currents became a strong, stimulating part of my intellectual and spiritual life as well.

"You know, if you were to go up to Jeremiah and ask him what he thought of *monotheism,* he'd say 'What? I've never heard that word. But Yahweh commands us to care for the widow and the orphan.' " Koyama tapped the table for emphasis as he went on. "I want to ask, how can theology, how can our thinking, return to this command: *Care for the widow and the orphan,* which means, of course, care for the neighbor in his or her need and weakness?

"It's not liberal! It's not conservative! It's not fundamentalist or modernist! I'm sorry, it's just not!"

His words, delivered with an explosive laugh, hit me hard as both a relief and a challenge. They were another body blow to my idea of the Christian faith as difficult—by which I meant intellectually difficult. Beyond (or perhaps below) all the thorny questions of dogma, belief, and theological speculation, there's the ever-present opportunity to simply care for others. That's what Christ did, and when he said "follow me" (he never said "worship me"), that's probably what he meant.

What a healer of the rifts in contemporary Christianity these simple acts could be. They have nothing whatsoever to do with theological or doctrinal debate since it matters not a bit whether the man or woman who loves and helps is a liberal or a conservative. But for a selfish, leisure-loving, and bookish person like me, this simplicity isn't easy. Though I insist to myself that I want to find my way toward "a faith that works," I'd generally rather read a difficult 400-page tome about mystical spirituality than volunteer at a food bank, visit shut-in elders, or even phone a friend in trouble.

• • •

Koyama's emphasis on just and compassionate action as the touchstone of true religion also underlies his ecumenism. This word, which in the mouths of many clergy stands for dry chalk-talks about whether the Methodists can accept the Lutheran doctrine of grace or how to design a joint Catholic/Episcopal prayer service, is for Koyama a passionate and all-embracing issue. "I've lived lots of places, seen so many people, so many people who don't profess Christ but *do* what Christ said they should. And I know there are millions who profess Him who *don't* do what He said.

"When the unbelieving world is doing what Christ said to do, I say that's a matter for thanksgiving!"

Koyama actually lived the ecumenism he speaks of. By taking non-Christian modes of thought and belief seriously, he found himself not caught between faiths, but able to explore his own faith in new ways. His milieu in Japan and America was so Christian that it wasn't until he went to Thailand that he took up the challenge of understanding Buddhism. "In the Thai seminary where I taught, Buddhist monks came regularly to give lectures. As I learned about Buddhism, many of the Christian figures and concepts I had studied came back to me in different, and sometimes very sophisticated and subtle, ways," he said. "Take the issue of religious anthropology, the analysis of human nature. The Buddhists say, the human problem is desire. We want things, or we want things to be a certain way, and because life is inherently impermanent, we are bound to be unsatisfied and therefore feel pain—*dukkha*. These ideas shed light for me on Saint Augustine. He says of himself, in essence, 'I want to know God and know my soul. I want to be *settled* in God, but when I look at myself, I'm just a bunch of confusion.' For Augustine, one major cause of the confusion is concupiscence—sexual desire as disorder. For Augustine, order in the psyche brings tranquility; and in Buddhism, cessation of desire brings peace. These two somewhat comparable anthropologies, these two images of the cosmos, engaged me in a dialogue for many years.

"I am a Christian. But my understanding of Buddhism amounts to a tremendously useful commentary on the Bible and on my faith. I have no problem labeling myself a Buddhistic Christian. The translator and scholar of comparative religion Max Müller said that he who knows only one religion knows none."

He faltered slightly as he spoke and shook his head. "There are so many questions. American Christianity is a great communion of two hundred eighty million people. What is the real message of Christ to these two hundred eighty million today? Why is it that such a massive group within this two hundred eighty million is not supporting what Jeremiah said: that Yahweh commands us to care for the widow and orphan?

"Christianity has a difficult legacy, of course. For 500 years in Africa and Asia, it was in the position of a colonial master. Jesus came as a servant; he washed his disciples' feet! But the faith and theology became the tools of a master and a master mentality. In Asia and other places, the spirit of that master mentality continues today. How can we settle this account? How can we usher out the master mentality? What kind of language will do this?"

For Koyama, one answer is the language of history. For him, telling the full story of the Christian adventure, with all the imperial hubris, violence, and injustice included, may be—and he chooses his words carefully—"one salvation."

"Yes, to tell the story truthfully, this is the Biblical account, here's the historical account. Here is how the Western hegemony rose. Here is what happened in Latin America. Here's where we are. Perhaps our explanations will need to be brief and pointed, but we must make them. We must bring history into the sermon on Sunday. We need to educate our children in history.

"I would go so far as to say that it is through history that we must present the Gospel today. Tell me, if you don't know the story of the civil rights movement, how can you understand the Gospel?" Koyama's words were rushing out; in the small classroom on the tidy Lutheran campus, I was in the presence, not just of an elderly and distinguished theologian, but of prophetic passion, a prophetic passion originating from some of the most violent history of the last century. "All the negatives must be there, you know? My understanding of the Bible says: The truth! The *truth* shall make you free."

I asked him if his idea of truth, with the negatives an integral part of the truth, could apply to the individual human being's journey of faith too. Surely our personal problems and doubts, our hesitations and fears about the Christian life and faith needed to be addressed just as honestly as the dark sides of Christian history.

"Ah!" Koyama's face shone. "That's Paul Tillich! He taught at Union, you know. He was gone before I came there, but the halls still resounded with what he said. And one thing he said was: The moment you say 'I believe,' that moment and that saying always include profound doubt. Augustine, and Thomas Aquinas, too, always remind us that what they have said about God is unfinished. In Asia, we believe the same thing: as religious seekers, we are always on the way. We've never made it. We're always on the way.

"As for me, I would like to belong to a beloved community—a community where we share the words of Christ and the powerful *impression* he made. My focus will always be on that man, Jesus, and the beautiful impression of his personality. When I read the Bible, I am not exploring doctrine, I'm not so concerned with whether he said this or that; I am concerned with the *beautiful total impression of that life.*

"I'm not interested in whether I go to heaven or hell. I'm present-tense. After all, after I'm dead I will have no responsibilities! I don't even consider myself 'born again'—just someone who wants to belong to a beloved community."

He described the small UCC church he and his wife, Lois, attend in south Minneapolis; mental patients from a nearby group home worship there with the rest of the congregation. "We communicate not in words but in actions," he said. "We accept one another. In the parable of the prodigal son, the son who returned apologized and spoke of his misdeeds. He wanted to start an argument with his father, but his father simply welcomed him. Simply accepted him.

"How can we tell this truth today? How can we restore the atmosphere of that meeting?"

Enter into Relationship

Victoria and Allen Queen

I'll admit to feeling some trepidation about meeting Victoria and Allen Queen at the Victory Mission on the north side of Springfield, Missouri. So far in my quest to write this book, I'd kept myself more or less safe inside the cocoon of liberal Christianity—but the Victory Mission belonged to the Association of Gospel Rescue Missions and called itself nondenominational but evangelical. Not only that, but Springfield is the headquarters of the Assembly of God denomination, the largest Pentecostal group in America. The prospect of plunging into Holy Roller, hot-gospel country unnerved me, though I did have the spirit of my maternal grandmother, Ida Carlson, to call upon. Back in the twenties, she'd been a stalwart of the Full Gospel Church in Meckling, South Dakota, a tin-roofed tabernacle full of Swedish Pentecostal shouters.

The reality of Springfield was much more complex and interesting than my preconceptions. At first glance, it seemed like any other faded midland city—the hulks of long-abandoned brick industrial buildings shouldered up next to the stores and restaurants downtown, and downtown filtered out into modest residential districts along streets lined with boarded-up retail buildings, worn-looking old churches, and gas stations that had been converted into curio shops and pizza parlors. To the south, there was a gargantuan auto "strip" jammed with big-box chain stores and overfamiliar hotels and motels.

But the more time I spent exploring the city, the more surprised and delighted I became. I found a coffee shop as sophisticated and comfortable as any I've ever visited, a magazine store that sold a wonderful variety of publications, from bass fishing mags to sophisticated art journals, a bakery that offered beautiful artisanal bread, and everywhere, all kinds of intriguing outdoor art—clever murals, anarchist sticker and stencil art, and beautifully designed posters for cultural events at the local university, Southwest Missouri State.

The Queens rattled my clichés about evangelicals, too. Gracious, ebullient, and welcoming, they put me at ease right away in their spacious and comfortable home on the edge of Springfield. Allen is an ex-thief, ex-junkie, and ex-con. He's also such a warm conduit of spiritual energy and good nature that it takes about ten seconds to want to be his best friend. Victoria, who manages to be both stylish in her self-presentation and down-home in her manner, runs the culinary program at the Mission, a serious, upscale-oriented cooking school that helps homeless, often addicted or alcoholic men find, not just a trade, but a profession to be proud of. (A longtime food-service and restaurant pro, she knew every sushi bar and posh Northern Italian eatery in town.)

As we spoke, I was moved by the vitality of the Queens' faith, which seemed to be rooted in their conviction that "caring for the widow and orphan" goes beyond our contemporary understanding of charity as merely helping others. Unless we are willing to have a *relationship* with the widow, the orphan, the junkie, the lost soul, the homeless man or woman, we are in danger of missing the spiritual point of caring: the opportunity to open our souls, so that we may be transformed by the encounter. And the concept of a living relationship, as they understand it, extends to our connection with God.

The couple met when Allen was a Mission client going through the 12-step Christian Recovery Program there. Born in St. Louis, he grew up on the streets of the inner city. "I started running amok when I was fourteen or fifteen," he told me with a smile. "Went to prison two or three times." Like so many cons, on his release from his last incarceration, he had nowhere to go except bad places, both mental and physical. "I hadn't really been free, out of custody of some kind, since I was a teenager," he said. "I just couldn't get my life together. I couldn't find happiness, peace, joy. All the time, something was tugging at my heart. I was seeking some-thing, something in this world. I'd go after a job, a high, a relationship, anything to fill the void. I'd get a job, a car, and feel better—and then the feeling would disappear."

He called a friend in southern Missouri who offered him space in his farmhouse, but that association led to involvement in a meth lab and a "whole new realm of darkness," as Allen put it.

"One day, I just got tired of the world," he said. "I got a big sack of dope and a bunch of needles, crashed my truck, and said to myself 'I'm done.' I shot all the dope and said to God, 'If you're there, let me die.' I dug a hole to bury myself.

"I believe I was dying, spiritually. And then this light came down from the sky. What I said was 'Holy shit!' and fell back into the hole, and the darkness swallowed me up. I remembered something my sister had said about Jesus being the Light. So I began saying over and over again, 'Thank you, Jesus! I love you, Jesus! Thank you, Jesus! I love you, Jesus!' and I would stop falling and the light would return. I think this went on for days: I would fall into the darkness and beg Jesus to bring me back to the light.

"Eventually, the police came. They took one look at me and figured that there was no way this guy with the crashed truck and the holes in his arm wasn't involved in some kind of crime. But the thing was, I wasn't! Not right then. They didn't have anything to hold me on. I told them I had nowhere to go. I didn't want to leave. Everybody I knew was an ad-dict or a con, and nobody would believe this stuff about Jesus. So I just hung around in front of the jail until they said 'If you don't leave, we'll have to arrest you.' Well, that was okay with me."

Instead of arresting Allen, the police chief made contact with the Vic-tory Mission, and soon the latter-day Lazarus was enrolled in the Chris-tian Recovery Program. "I read the Bible for the first time," he said. "And it made sense. I believe that the flesh doesn't understand the word of God, but the spirit does; so when we make that decision for Christ, the eyes of the spirit open. It's no longer just a myth in a book; it's real. In me, the spirit that He gives all of us came alive, and that spirit hungered for the Word the way the body hungers for food. You see, because of what happened to me, I don't believe; I know."

"He had some trouble in the recovery program," Victoria added brightly. "He wanted everybody else to feel what he felt."

"Yeah," nodded Allen. "There was this guy one night who was resisting, and I wanted to beat him up and make him eat the Bible, you know? I told him, 'Buddy, you're gonna listen to the Bible or eat it, one of the two.' I don't exactly think that's what Jesus wanted us to do. The fellow who was running the program said to me—he said to me more than once—'Get out of my building!' I was bull-headed. I knew, see, what Jesus had done for me. But I was in the process of becoming a new creation, and I still am. The fruits of the spirit—like love, peace, and patience—don't just appear overnight."

Victoria laughed and added: "Allen was a real enabler. I was running the food service at the mission then, and when some of the guys who were disruptive were told to leave, well, they would hang around outside, and Allen would bring food out to them. I mean, somebody had to lay down the law to these guys, and here was Allen taking care of them like they hadn't done anything. He'd say, 'These poor guys out here!' Today we make a good team. I'm the tough one with the guys—he's the one that hugs them."

"Well, see, in the years I was in prison, submitting to authority wasn't even an option," said Allen. "So many people get in prison and start behaving. I said, why should I start behaving? What are they gonna do, lock me up? Now I believe that submitting to just authority is a law of God. Submitting to authority, humbling oneself, putting others first. It's a continual learning process, and we'll never figure it all out. I also believe that, whatever the issue or the action is, the answer is in the Bible. The Bible teaches cause and effect: If you do this, that will be the result. It says over and over and over how men love darkness. I think it's a proven fact that we do, because when we get in the light, we say, 'Oooh, that's too bright!' That's what the wrath of God means to me—and believe me, I have experienced the wrath of God in my addictions. He may not just zap you and strike you down, but you've got the consequences of certain actions you choose to take."

Victoria's story may have lacked the Dostoevskyan atmosphere of Allen's, but it had its own depth and drama. She was a preacher's kid, the daughter of a Pentecostal minister in Arkansas, and no stranger to fire and brimstone when she was growing up. "As a kid, I had a great fear of God," she told me in her soft and musical border-South cadence. "It was only as an adult that I learned about his love. The hymns we sang were about love, but all the preaching was about fear, and that's what I heard, that's what penetrated. I didn't feel like I could ask my dad about anything; what he said went, and nobody around him ever questioned him, nobody asked why. Looking back, I realize that those feelings affected my reaction to God the Father and the idea of the Father's love. I didn't have the kind of dad who hugged you. I mean, he only spanked me once in my life, but there was still this feeling of fear.

"I said to myself: According to them, I'm not doing anything right; I can never be as good as they want me to be. So I went and did my own thing for a while."

It's not as if Victoria plunged into a life of debauchery; she drank some as a teenager and, as she put it, "ran around." She attended Lyon College, a Presbyterian school in northern Arkansas, married at twenty-two, and was the mother of twins at twenty-eight. She worked for Lyon after graduating, then after a number of other ventures, including earning an MBA and running a restaurant, she landed a corporate plum: an executive position in the Marriott hotel and food-service chain. What she did not do—and from her current perspective this is a major source of regret—was worship God in any way or take her kids to church. "After I was saved, I felt a lot of guilt about that," she said.

For her, the issue of faith came to a head, as it does for so many people, at a moment of personal and professional change. She left Marriott in 2000 to start her own restaurant for the second time. She'd had partners in her earlier venture, but this time it was a one-woman show. And her eighteen-year-old son was about to leave for the Navy. "It wasn't any one event that led me to God," she said to me. "But I simply started to want to go to church. I was probably having a midlife crisis."

Victoria ended up in a Nazarene church near her home one Sunday, sitting in a pew and weeping. The preacher asked her if he could pray for her. "I kept saying 'no, no,' and crying," she said. "There was a woman sitting next to me, and I took her hand and told her my son was leaving for the Navy in just a few weeks, and I never took him to church. Well, she prayed for him. She prayed that somewhere, someone in the Navy would come to him and tell him about God."

As Victoria felt more and more connected to the church, her restaurant venture was losing steam. By the winter of 2000, it was on its last legs. At Christmastime, Springfield was hit with a blizzard and there was a spate of closings and cancellations around town. "That was about it," said Victoria. "I decided it wasn't going to get any better. I would close the doors.

"My friends came to help me shut down and take everything out. After that, I just stayed at home for a while, reading the Bible. And I found I was reading it in a whole new way. I mean, I knew the Bible. As a kid I memorized verses. At Bible camp in the summer, the counselors always chose me for the Bible competition. And at Lyon College, I had taken Bible—which they taught as a sort of history and geography lesson —and made the highest grade ever in that class! But after I closed the restaurant, I spent several weeks at home by myself, not going anywhere, reading the Bible and thinking, what am I going to do now? I've just spent all my money on the restaurant; what's next? I prayed, and read, and tried to search out what I was going to do. I'd read half the night."

This time, Biblical passages and phrases jumped off the page and spoke to her. " 'For I know the plans I have for you,' declares the Lord. 'Plans to prosper you and not to harm you.' " (Jeremiah 29:11) "Do not let this book of the Law depart from your mouth; meditate on it day and night, so that you may be careful to do everything written in it. Then you will be prosperous and successful." (Joshua 1:8) And lo and behold, Victoria soon got a job offer that solved her problem. Reverend Jim Herriger, the imaginative and charismatic executive director of the Springfield Victory Mission, had just decided to found a cooking school for the men he was rescuing from the streets, and he approached her to be its head.

She rolled up her sleeves and got to work at the Mission's facility on Commercial Street, the main drag of Springfield's gritty north side. She hoped to open the school by September of 2001, but building renovations pushed the project well behind schedule, and then 9/11 knocked the entire nation off-kilter. Meanwhile, she was struggling with some within the Mission who were resentful that a newcomer had taken over a prime position. It was a tough time. "I wondered if this was what I was supposed to do after all," Victoria told me. "I hadn't exactly heard an audible voice from God telling me to come here; I had made a decision to come here. After all, I'd had other job opportunities. I got physically sick and stayed sick for a long time."

Eventually the school got up and running, though, and Victoria found herself with a new, but by no means unique, spiritual challenge: the loss of her initial enthusiasm. "Sometimes I struggle with feeling guilty that I don't have that feeling I had right after the restaurant closed—sitting in bed, reading the Bible, and having those wonderful emotions. I remember going to church in those days and saying to people, 'There's so much uncertain in my life—I don't know where the money's going to come from—but I'm so happy!' And now when I don't feel that way, well, it makes me feel a little guilty."

I asked her if she felt guilty because she didn't think she was spending enough time praying and reading the Bible, and her response reminded me once again that my idea of all evangelical Christians as rigid caretakers of a do-this–don't-do-that moralism was a cliche. "I look at people doing all this perfect religious stuff," she said, "and I remember that that was the very thing Jesus went against—the Pharisees. It's not so much about laws and rules as, well, I'm depriving myself of that feeling because I don't do it—the reading and the prayer."

She looked at her husband. "It's a funny thing. Allen and I come from totally different backgrounds. I had this religious background but didn't really have it, you know, while he was brought up with none of it, but when he got it, he was all over it! He just glows with it. That's what attracted me to him in the first place; he had this light."

We talked about intellectual and other difficulties with faith. "When I sit down and read the Word prayerfully, I don't think there's anything in it I don't understand," said Allen. "I think the struggle is how to live the right way, not living the life so that the neighbor can see it, but living it as Christ would have. Our daily goal is to be conformed to His image."

"One thing I noticed," Victoria said, "is that my attitude changed. My attitude toward people. The first time I ever saw a homeless person was in San Francisco, when I was at a conference. I absolutely freaked out as I walked past these people living in boxes down by the Civic Center. I'd never experienced anything like that. But by the third day, I'm just walking over them. They were nothing to me. I didn't know these people. I had no feelings one way or the other. But in the Mission, I began to see people as people, not as he's the president of this or that, or the governor, or a senator. That's what I learned in that year and a half when I was trying to get the school open. They're all just the same. They simply have different experiences. Some of the men here are very intelligent and have learned a lot from what they've done in life. The idea is that everybody, no matter who, has something really interesting and exciting about them. And that's something that had never crossed my mind: if somebody wasn't successful or powerful, they could still have something of interest to me. But I discovered that there were fascinating people who didn't have anything but themselves. And those are the people Jesus loved."

I asked Allen how he helps people find faith. His response was immediate: "I don't think there's a lot we can do—no one comes to the Father except those He draws. We just have to love people and allow them to see that love in us, no matter who they are and what they've done because that's the way Christ sees us. Now, if we have a seed of faith, we need to tend it, to water it, with the Word of God. But we have a lot of other things to take care of too, and we can't go around with the Bible in our face day and night. That's what I used to think—Hey, I haven't got time for you, I've got to go read the Word. I was on my way to becoming . . . well, a Pharisee. Laying down these laws and rules. Now, those rules may have been right for me at the time but not for that person over there.

"Some of the churches come up here to Commercial Street, and they see a guy with long hair, not too clean, with holes in his jeans, and they get him to come to their service some Sunday—then they expect that next Sunday he'll be all cleaned up, hair cut, acceptable. But that's not who that guy is. I think we have to stop looking visually at people and start looking inside."

"Some people say, 'I'll give to the mission, but I don't want to get to know them,'" Victoria put in.

Allen nodded "If you come down here and build a relationship with these men, that's what's real. It's the same in marriage. If you're working the day shift and I'm working the night shift, well, the relationship is going to go in the wrong direction. It's the same with Jesus, with God—we're supposed to be building a relationship.

"We say, 'Care for the homeless and the widow and the orphan,' and I believe that. But it's not just them; it's our neighbors who look like they're okay, but are they? Our ultimate purpose is to reach people but not beat them down with our message—'Hi, I'm Allen, I'm your new neighbor, and if you don't repent you're going to hell.'"

"Sometimes the trade school guys say 'If I only had money,'" said Victoria. "I tell them, 'Look at some of these people with a ton of money or power who can't stand their lives and commit suicide. You can be happy whatever your circumstances. Sometimes, when you're in crisis and you have to ask, and go to prayer and to the Bible, you become happier than when you're leading a safe, uneventful life.'"

"It's in our desperation that we turn to God," added Allen. "But at the same time, I don't want to have to get to the end of my rope before I connect with Him. My prayer is 'Lord, don't let me be in that position where I'm running around in the woods, trying to kill myself to find that closeness with You. Let me find that in my situation today. Let me seek after You today, as I sought after You then.'"

"It's like with any relationship," said Victoria as we ended the conversation. "Have I called my mother? Have I contacted that friend? Here's somebody called Jesus, he's my best friend, and I haven't talked to him in three weeks! But I try to remember too that sometimes you're closer to a friend than at other times. The closeness comes and goes and comes back again, and that's natural. It's the kind of relationship God wants with us. We're not yes-people or slaves, but human beings."

Don't Be "Churchy"

Mary Forsythe

Another conservative evangelical Christian who challenged me to live in relationship, not mere intellectual or moral agreement, with God and my neighbor was Mary Forsythe. She began teaching me this truth by establishing a caring relationship with me right away. "Jon, I'm just a train wreck for Jesus," she said in a phone conversation with me before we met at a coffee shop in the Dallas suburbs. She laughed; I laughed. And then she gave me some good advice about hotels, restaurants, and highway navigation in the Dallas–Fort Worth area. That combination of forthrightness and kindness turned out to be characteristic of this glamorous, voluble, and very serious evangelist, who spent five years in prison for white-collar crime before deciding to help others experience the Holy Spirit who had transformed her. Today, as the head of Kingdom Living Ministries, she preaches and teaches in venues that range from suburban Dallas churches to seminar rooms in Ukraine.

Not even her help, though, could clarify Dallas's insane freeway system, in which constant, confusing off-ramp exiting and on-ramp entering is required simply to remain on the same numbered highway. When I finally arrived at our meeting place, Forsythe came on strong. "Jesus is so *after* us, Jon," she said. "He wants us to be totally inundated with his love. But there is spiritual warfare going on too, and it goes on 24/7. There's an enemy, and we all have that enemy. I didn't even know I was in a war until I was already taken captive."

She was referring, not only to the circumstances that earned her five years in prison—and three more years on probation—but also to her whole life before she found God. She had a troubled childhood and adolescence in Kentucky, followed by business success that at first seemed like a sort of redemption. Forsythe owned a thriving pharmacy, was engaged to a handsome, prominent, and well-off man, drove a Mercedes 560 SL, and took off on weekend trips to Europe for high-end shopping.

At the time—the late 1980s—the federal government was releasing the brand-new anti-retroviral drug AZT through state programs that selected certain pharmacies as dispensaries. Forsythe's pharmacy in Dallas became the largest dispenser of AZT in Texas. She was at the cutting edge of HIV/AIDS therapy, but the frantic demand for the new miracle drug and the complexities of the federal program and the health-care insurance system made the keeping of inventory records uniquely complicated. Forsythe, with classic entrepreneurial restlessness, was spending more time traveling and looking into possible new ventures than overseeing the paperwork. Some of her overwhelmed employees couldn't cope and began to cut corners. State regulators, aware that fraud was rampant around the drug, sniffed out the irregularities in Forsythe's records, and a lengthy investigation followed. After two and one-half years of nail biting, she was convicted on fifteen felony counts.

Mary Forsythe received the promise of a pardon from George H. W. Bush's White House in 1993. "I still have the letter, on Camp David letterhead," she told me. She and her fiancé, Mike, calculated that the ticket out would come in the traditional flurry of last-minute pardons as Bush left office, about fifteen days after she entered jail. "Entering prison was like being tossed into a blender. I was scared to death, but I was arrogant too. I figured I could do *anything* for fifteen days," she said. The pardon never came through.

The former high roller worked in a warehouse for seventeen cents an hour, baiting rat traps, driving a fork lift, and mopping floors. "I was living with these *people,*" she said. "I was better than any of them and determined not to make friends." She had plenty of time to look back on a life that, despite its surface sheen, had been riddled with trouble from very early on. There was, for one thing, alcohol. "I was first drawn to it when I was five years old," she said. "I was in my grandfather's closet, and he had a lot of liquor bottles there. And I can remember my little five-year-old heart saying, 'I'm going to have those someday!' Well, we lived in a dry county in Kentucky, but when I was sixteen and got my license, somehow I found a bootlegger. The demonic realm got hold of me very early and got me started on that lifestyle."

My theology is pretty resistant to the idea of demons and their realms, and I asked her if her urge to drink could have been simply a natural urge to explore life and what it held—good and bad.

"Well, that's the issue of the flesh," she said, "and it does get combined with the enemy that comes from the spiritual realm. But I never want to discount the activity that's going on in the spiritual realm. That would be to live one-dimensionally."

Whether you accept demons as living realities or not, it's hard not to feel the power of darkness in Forsythe's young life. She drank heavily from adolescence on, was raped in her second year of college, and, as she said, "stuffed the pain, stuffed the rejection. Went on stuffing all the feelings right up until the time I went to prison. My brain was in captivity, my personality was in captivity, my emotions were in captivity. And then God set me free when I was behind bars."

As is often the case with people who undergo conversion, she had had glimpses of God's grace beforehand. At age twelve, she had even been "born again" at a Methodist youth revival in her hometown, Greenville, Kentucky. "I heard in my heart, 'Mary, you need to repent of your sins; you're a sinner, and I want to save you tonight.' I went up and shook Jesus's hand. But then I turned my back, went off, and lived my own life. No one really taught me how to incorporate meeting this man Jesus into my life in a practical way. I didn't know. So I turned out religious and in pain and bondage. I had *religion* but no *relationship*."

Her second encounter was in Carmel, California, after her conviction and before sentencing. She and her fiancé, Mike, were burdened, not only with the thought of her impending jail time, but with the aftermath of Mary's miscarriage of a child she had originally intended to abort. They visited a Catholic cloister whose mother superior was allowed to meet the public to receive prayer requests.

"Mike turned to me and said, 'Let's go up for prayer.' In everything we'd gone through, we had not understood prayer. I mean, we both went to church. We were very religious people. We paid our tithes, we took communion, but we really didn't follow God. We had form but no power. Again, religion and no relationship.

"When Mike introduced us to the mother superior, I shook her hand and all of a sudden it was like electricity or a fire—a power that started traveling up my right arm to my shoulder, hit the top of my head, and went through my body. There was this electricity going all through my body, and I begin to tremble and cry. Cry! I didn't cry when I lost the baby. I didn't even cry when I returned the silver to Neiman-Marcus! But all of a sudden these tears started to flow. So they sat me down in the pew, and for forty-five minutes I'm shaking and trembling and crying.

"Mike picked me up and took me to the car, and for two-and-a-half hours I was struck dumb. I didn't talk, and trust me, that is a miracle! After I could speak again, Mike, who was studying in a seminary, started trying to tell me about the cloistered nuns and all this theological information. That did not help at all. I needed somebody to explain what had happened and nobody could. I now believe I was touched by the Holy Spirit to help me handle the things that were coming on the journey I had in front of me in prison."

The reality of that journey hit hard after she had begun her sentence and a tearful Mike told her on the telephone that Bush senior had left office without issuing the expected pardon. She would have to do her time—all of it. "The next morning," she said, "I rolled out of my bunk and hit my knees and said, 'God, I can't do this anymore.' And for the second time since my salvation at twelve, I felt I heard something in my heart from God. I heard this: 'Mary, that's what I've been waiting to hear.'

"Now, nothing changed on the outside. The warden did not rush into my cell and say, 'Mary, you're a good girl, and you can go home now.' But everything began to change on the inside."

Her faith was awakened by these surrenders, but Forsythe needed a further push into a passionate relationship with Jesus. It came in a mysterious way. She was sitting in a chapel service without feeling much enthusiasm—"It got me out of my cell," as she said—when a guard called to her and told her she had a visitor. She had four people on her approved visitors list: her parents and sister, who were far away, and her fiancé. It had to be Mike. She arrived in the visiting room but didn't see him.

"I'm looking around," she said, "and this man walks up to me and says, 'Are you Mary?' Now, I hadn't got rid of my pride and arrogance at this point, so I put my best hand on my best hip and said 'Yeah. And *who* are *you?*' He said, 'My name's Gary, and God sent me. Can we talk?'

"What do you say to that? I said something like 'Uh, yeah, I've got a little time.' We went out to sit on a bench. Families are talking, guards are everywhere, there's no privacy. He sits to my left and he looks at me, and this is his next question: 'Do you want to receive the baptism of the Holy Spirit?' Now, I'm Methodist, and I'd never heard that phrase before. But about a week earlier, I had come upon a little booklet, which I now know was a tract, and it had said, 'When you don't know how to pray, pray in the Holy Spirit.' I didn't know how to pray, and I thought I ought to do that sometime. So when Gary said what he said, it connected in my brain with the words I had read. I pointed to heaven and said, 'Did *he* ask you to ask me that?' He just looked back at me very calmly and said, 'Yeah, he did.' And all I said was, 'Okay. I'll take it.'

"He told me to stand up, and I did, which was against all the rules; the guards should have been all over us. He touched me with one finger, and it was like when an ocean wave catches you and you lose your balance. The next thing I know, I am lying down under this oak tree in the prison visiting yard. Gary gets down on his knees and begins to pray for me. And that absolutely changed my life. I got delivered, I got filled with the Holy Spirit.

"Visiting hours ended, I'm back in my cell thinking, okay, I'm crazy. I've lost it. This is it. They're gonna come in white jackets and get me. I'm a pharmacist, so when the white jackets take somebody away and bring them back, I can pretty much tell you what drugs they gave them. And I know that they are no longer the same person. I figure I'm next. But the next morning, I woke up with a hunger for something I had never eaten before. I got into my locker and pulled out a Bible that Mike had sent me. I took that Bible to a shower stall, and the Holy Spirit began to teach me the word of God from that day on. My seminary was prison, where God trained me by the Spirit and by the word. When I started reading the word, I felt that I got in touch with unconditional, unexplainable, almost surreal love."

Forsythe soon became known as "the inmate who prays." Women began to come to her for help with the devastating pain of broken lives and incarcerated hopes. Her cell was next to a mop closet, which became her spiritual-direction "office." She would take the women into the closet, pray for them, and urge them to repent of their sins. "God trained me to help other people," she said. "It was a strenuous boot camp of the spirit. I would ask the Holy Spirit to help me help them. I would be praying for someone and God would give me an impression, a vision, a dream, a scripture verse—something that would help unlock the pain. I would pray for them, and they would pray for other women. That's how discipleship works, even though I didn't know it at the time."

It was the beginning of her career as an evangelist, though it took her some time to realize it. The freedom that followed her release from prison was, to put it mildly, a mixed blessing. Her fiancé had married someone else, and she had no money, no friends, and no prospects. She struggled to return to pharmacy, but the state board of examiners refused to re-license her. "At that moment," she said, "I knew that God had another path for me, and I began to look. I started sharing my little testimony at a breakfast at my church; the next thing you know, I'm speaking at meetings, I'm doing the 700 Club on television. God encouraged me to write my book, A Glimpse of Grace, which tells the prison story. I saw people's lives being changed; people would come out of addiction; I'd see emotional healing by God; people reconciled with one another.

"As for me, there's been so much restoration, but I'm still a work in progress. I wish you could have met me six years ago—there's been such a change since then. I can look you in the eye without being ashamed. I'm not bitter, I'm not angry. And I feel like there's still more restoration to come.

"One of the things I most diligently seek is to hear His voice. I don't want to speak me, because I got me in trouble. The ways I tried to live my life got me incarcerated, for heaven's sake. I want to stand behind the cross. I want Jesus to be seen and not me. I want the Kingdom of God to be seen and not me."

Forsythe was unfailingly gracious, even when we disagreed on points of theology and spirituality. She expressed her convictions with passion but without arrogance or any attempt to force them upon me, an attitude that struck me as evidence of the genuineness of her conversion to what she calls "kingdom values," otherwise known as the fruits of the Spirit. Love, joy, peace, and gentleness head the list.

Above all, her insistence on relationship feels like a gift for all believers, wherever they may be on the theological spectrum. For Christians, the relationship with Christ is something that may be furthered by, but goes beyond, doctrine, dogma, piety—beyond religion itself, just as Jesus's relationship with his Father in heaven stretched his own tradition. Several times, Forsythe said things like, "I don't mean to sound religious. I don't want to seem churchy . . ." and in these words, which I never expected to hear from an evangelical Christian, I could feel how far her faith went out into the enormity of the Kingdom.

THROW OUT YOUR OUTMODED
IDEAS OF GOD

John Shelby Spong

To call John Shelby Spong's reputation formidable is a bit like calling Hurricane Katrina a rainy day. The retired Episcopal bishop of Newark, New Jersey, is practically a force of nature in the world of liberal religion. He calls for "a new Christianity for a new world" and is the author of eighteen books, many which support the radical reform or abandonment of elements of the Christian faith that many thousands of believers of various stripes consider foundational. Among other things, Spong would jettison the virgin birth of Jesus, his physical resurrection, and his very divinity. He'd even junk the "theistic" concept of God—the idea that God is, as he puts it, "a being, supernatural in power, dwelling outside this world and invading the world periodically to accomplish the divine will." His most recent book, *The Sins of Scripture,* arraigns certain "terrible texts" in the Bible for anti-Semitism, misogyny, homophobia, and religious chauvinism.

One traditionalist Christian website slams him as "a rogue 'priest' who has made a career of bashing the Son of God." More responsible critics have accused him of hypocrisy in accepting a bishop's mitre (and salary) while refusing to do a bishop's job—that is, to teach the orthodox doctrine of his denomination. Thousands of readers, however—and I include myself among them—have welcomed Spong's willingness to address pretty much everything that makes us squirm about the Christian religion, from Biblical violence to physical anomalies, such as the virgin birth, to sexual attitudes that seem out of touch with human reality.

On many points, Spong is securely within the orbit of postwar liberal religious thinkers like the late Paul Tillich, who strove to translate traditional Christian concerns into the vocabulary of contemporary thought, particularly existentialism, and who was even bold enough to declare in one of his sermons that Christ came to free us from religion altogether. Another important influence upon his thinking was the martyred German Lutheran pastor Dietrich Bonhoeffer, who called for a "religionless Christianity." Spong has, however, consistently refused to give up, or give up on, the church. He has declared many times that much of what he believes and teaches has been common coin in advanced seminaries for decades, and that he is mainly bringing up-to-date thought out of the academic cloister and into the pews.

I'd read several of Spong's books, but for the purpose of this one, I wanted to get at least a glimpse of the donut rather than the hole—not just what he opposes, but where his positive faith lies. For decades he's been clearing the ecclesiastical attic of what he considers to be white elephants; what set of experiences and developing convictions has made that necessary, and what has the clearing out left him to live by?

Despite Spong's reputation as a firebrand, the man himself is courtly and soft-spoken, a youthful seventy-five-year-old whose speech retains the melody of his native North Carolina. And like many other Southerners, he's an inveterate storyteller. As we sat in his living room in leafy Morris Plains, New Jersey, and snacked on cookies, he launched into the tale of his life with gusto. It's a story he has told many times to other interviewers and in autobiographical sections of his books, and it's important for understanding how his sense of justice—racial, sexual, and social—evolved alongside, and entwined with, his image of an ideal church that does justice to both God and the modern mind.

Spong's alcoholic father was a mostly non-observant Episcopalian, his mother a strictly-brought-up Presbyterian. The young Jack Spong took to church from the beginning, singing soprano in the boys' choir and donning the bright red robe of an acolyte. The elder Spong died when the boy was twelve, but within a year Jack had a surrogate father: the church's young and decidedly glamorous new pastor. Father Bob Crandall wore white bucks and drove a convertible, and his gorgeous Georgia-born wife used a silver cigarette holder. Spong's teenage piety, rooted in acceptance of pretty much everything he heard or read in church, was charged with excitement and emulation, and it wasn't long before he'd decided to become a priest himself. Father Crandall was an Anglo-Catholic, the sort of Anglican who is very close to Roman Catholicism in his beliefs and style of worship, and young Jack followed suit. "From being a Biblical fundamentalist, I became an ecclesiastical fundamentalist —that's what an Anglo-Catholic is," he told me. "I didn't say 'the Bible says'; I said 'the *church* says.' "

College at the University of North Carolina shocked him by assailing his settled beliefs—he had persuasive professors who identified themselves as atheists—but his church-centered orthodoxy held. When he went to seminary, though, Spong was, without realizing it at first, setting forth on the road to unconventional Christianity. He studied sophisticated Biblical criticism and read avant-garde theologians such as Tillich and, as a thoroughly modernized young cleric, was assigned to a church at the edge of the Duke University campus in Durham, North Carolina. He preached sharply intellectual sermons, introduced modern methods of Bible study to the congregation, and generally impressed the mostly-academic churchgoers with his intelligence and ambition. But it was not until he moved to a small town in eastern North Carolina—Tarboro— that he became Jack Spong the iconoclast.

"I moved to Tarboro in 1957, and when the court ordered the town de-segregated in 1961, I was right in the middle of it, and it was fascinating," he said. "There was a small black Episcopal congregation in town, and they couldn't begin to afford a rector, so I served that church as well. I baptized black babies, married black couples, buried black people. I soon became known in the white community as an *untrustworthy* white. A black youth group got going in town, and a black dentist ran for the town council, and I was accused of being behind both, which was ridiculous. The kids organized themselves very well—I would have helped them if they'd asked me, but they didn't—and the dentist ran a smart campaign all on his own. But the prevalent idea was, if blacks did anything successful, a white had to be behind it.

"I had the vigilantes on me, the Klan calling at night, threatening to force a black man to rape my daughters. I got dropped from my golf foursome. People wouldn't speak to me. I kept my congregation, though, because we were the only white Episcopal church in town; Episcopalians are funny—they won't change churches because it's a step down socially.

But they started going out the side door. If they could have fired me, they would have, but the Episcopal church doesn't allow that. It was a tough time, but I learned a lot about what you have to stand up for and that there's no integrity in trying to please people if you know what's going on is wrong."

After this social-justice baptism of fire, Spong was transferred to Lynchburg, Virginia, a posting that allowed him to combine his advanced-theology teaching with activism. Lynchburg was a conservative town (Jerry Falwell was just getting his start there when Spong arrived), but Spong's church was near the campus of Randolph-Macon College, and the congregation included a number of faculty members.

"I started an adult Bible class on Sunday morning," he told me. "I taught it the same way you would teach at Union Theological Seminary or the Harvard Divinity School. Many of these people had never heard anybody say that the Bible didn't drop out of heaven fully written, that Noah's ark is really a fable, that the Adam and Eve story is an old Babylonian tale reframed for Jewish use, and that the virgin birth is not history. And a whole lot of other stuff that's just commonplace in the academy. It scared that town to death, but they wanted to be there because it was exciting."

Things got a little too exciting when Martin Luther King, Jr., was assassinated. Tensions ran so high in Lynchburg that Spong was called upon to mediate a number of black/white disputes. The fact that his brother Bill had been elected to the Senate from Virginia gave him some credibility with the local elites, although it didn't keep the local newspaper from labeling him a communist. ("A communist was anyone who favored labor unions or the rights of women or blacks," he recalled.)

Spong's last assignment in Dixie was to Saint Paul's Church in the old capital of the Confederacy, Richmond, Virginia. He came on strong, all his values blazing. The church's vestry was in the habit of flying the Confederate flag two weeks every year—the weeks of Robert E. Lee's and Jefferson Davis's birthdays. Spong wouldn't hear of it. "It was a 70 percent black city," he said. "I told them if they flew those flags, I was taking those two weeks off." He agitated for open housing in Richmond as well.

Even more consequential, however, was his theological teaching. He set up the same kind of up-to-date Bible study classes he'd taught in Lynchburg. "Every Sunday morning, I would teach the Bible in a radical way—not radical in the sense of *liberal,* but radical in the sense of *schol-*

arly. We usually had three hundred people, and the class was even on the radio. It was out of the class that all my books started growing. I just turned these lectures into books."

One of his earliest books was *This Hebrew Lord,* a study of Jesus and the New Testament in the light of Jewish values. Rabbi Jack Spiro of Beth Ahabah Congregation in Richmond happened to pick it up, read it, and immediately phoned Spong. "He told me he'd never read a book by a Christian that paid such homage to Jews. 'Of course I disagree with your conclusions,' he said, and I said, 'Well, of course you do, or you'd have to get baptized.' He asked if I was interested in debating the book in his synagogue. We met over lunch to mull it over, and after talking for four hours, we decided that we wanted to do a dialogue, not a debate."

The dialogue stretched over three Friday evenings at Beth Ahabah (when Spong visited to discuss Christianity) and three Sunday mornings (when Spiro talked about Judaism with Spong's parishioners). It was, to put it mildly, a media event. The local papers covered it on their front pages. The Richmond PBS affiliate broadcast it. And the Spong-Spiro tag team attracted some fifteen hundred people to each discussion. "I think we broke down some barriers between Jews and Gentiles in Richmond," said Spong. "It was also the first time I felt real hostility from the Christian right. My church was picketed by a Baptist church. They didn't like it that I didn't try to baptize the rabbi. And orthodox Jews began to attack Jack for engaging me in dialogue."

Spong's growing notoriety and lengthening shelf of books (five by 1976) was making him bishop material. Dioceses nominated him in Kentucky, Mississippi, South Carolina, West Virginia, and Delaware. But the call he finally answered took him out of the South for good—to the struggling industrial city of Newark, New Jersey. "I had no intention, originally, of ever leaving the South," he said. "But Newark had always been a forward-looking diocese. My predecessor had been with King in Selma, and my predecessor twice removed had been one of the first voices raised against the Vietnam War. They sort of expected that kind of leadership from a bishop."

It was from this bully pulpit that Spong became a national figure, taking a stand on issues of gender, sex, and marriage. He helped lead the fight for the ordination of women (the church accepted the policy on January 1, 1977, and Spong ordained his first woman on January 3). He advocated the creation of a liturgy for divorced people—"To come back to the church and say, look, we took our vows for life but we can't make it," as he explained it to me. "We ask forgiveness and we ask you to recognize us as single people again." He refused to categorically condemn sex outside marriage. "I argued that the idea of marriage as the only container of sex had developed in a world when kids came to puberty at fifteen or sixteen and got married when they were sixteen or seventeen. But we live in a world where puberty has been pushed down to twelve and marriage up to twenty-five. There's a ten- to fifteen-year gap there. And then we say that there's only one way to deal with sex during that time and that's to repress it. That makes for some really weird people. If you're serious about containing sex in marriage, I said, then move marriage back to twelve and thirteen. But nobody thought that was a good idea."

But the biggest issue by far, within Spong's church and outside it, has been homosexuality. Spong didn't always accept gay clergy or gay marriage.

"I must tell you," he said to me, "that when I was elected bishop I was as homophobic as anyone I have ever known. I told people that we just didn't *have* homosexuals in the South—I had never met one. If I thought about gays at all, I probably thought that there were only two ways to see them: a kind way—they're to be pitied; they're mentally sick and they can't help it—and a harsher view that they are morally degenerate people who choose to live in an immoral way. I chose to be kind to them.

"When I came to Newark, I confronted gay and lesbian people who were not ashamed to be gay and lesbian, who were fully out and made no bones about who they were and were living their lives with an enormous amount of integrity. They didn't fit my stereotype. I realized if I was going to be an effective bishop, I had to know something about the homosexual issue, so I made a friend at the Cornell School of Medicine and asked him if he would take me on as a pupil and teach me everything he could about sexual orientation. I actually researched what it meant to be gay. And I'm a left-brain person, so I got my brain converted and that took care of my heart."

Spong's book of 1988, *Living in Sin?,* crystallized his sexual concerns. In it, he firmly supported gay marriage—about a decade before the issue became front-page news. "I suggested that the sacred commitments of gay and lesbian people are as sacred as anybody else's commitments," Spong told me. "But even if you want to be moralistic, you either bless gay and lesbian relationships or you encourage gay and lesbian people to be promiscuous. On this issue, the right-brain religious folks think the choice is between no sex and promiscuous sex—and they're in favor of no

sex. I think the choice is between responsible sex and irresponsible sex."
Living in Sin? stirred the media—Spong appeared on Oprah Winfrey's
and Phil Donohue's talk shows and on *Firing Line* with William F. Buck-
ley. A debate with Spong's old Lynchburg rival Jerry Falwell heated up
Good Morning America, and Spong's next book was a rejoinder to Falwell's theology called *Rescuing the Bible From Fundamentalism.*

Meanwhile, Spong was staunchly supporting the cause of women and
gays within the conclaves of the Anglican Communion. He advocated
the election of women as bishops at the 1988 Lambeth Conference, the
every-ten-year worldwide council of bishops. At the 1998 conference, he
supported the election of gay bishops, and he took a beating. Much of
the opposition to the proposal came from conservative clerics in Africa,
and when Spong called their understanding of homosexuality ignorant,
he was accused of racism. "It was a dreadful experience," said Spong. "We
lost badly. The vote was something like 550 to 72."

Since then, of course, the diocese of New Hampshire has chosen an
openly gay bishop, Gene Robinson. "That could not have happened if
we had not done the work we did back in the eighties and nineties," he
said. "I'm very proud of him and of my church, but there is enormous
hostility still out there. And I still get hate mail."

Spong retired in 2000, but he's kept busy since lecturing, writing, and
communicating with supporters and critics via a website, www.Bishop
Spong.com. When I asked him what effect his eventful and combative
life has had on his Christian faith, he responded immediately and vigor-
ously. "I'm more deeply committed to my Christian faith now than when
I started this career," he said. "But it's very different because I'm not committed to a lot of the ways we used to define the Christian faith. I'm not
committed to the idea that Jesus is a sacrifice that had to be offered to
overcome the sin of the world—I think that's barbaric. I'm not committed to a whole lot of the definitions of the past—I don't deny them, I just
think they're irrelevant to the world I live in. So I keep trying to find a
way to communicate what I think the essence of the Christian faith is in
the language of the twenty-first century. What I am suggesting is not a
threat to what people already believe; it's a new dimension of what they
believe. People say to me, 'You're articulating what I always believed but
didn't have the courage to say out loud.' Or 'I never believed all that stuff,
and I thought there was something wrong with me. You've given me permission to think about it in a way I never have before.'

"I try to talk about God in what I call non-theistic terms. To get away from seeing God as the supernatural man upstairs, the Mr. Fix-it of the Universe. I go back to the Bible and find definitions of God that aren't familiar such as: God as the wind, a life-giving wind—a very fascinating image. God as a rock, and on this rock I stand. In the epistle of John, God is simply described as Love—and if God is love, then I think love is also God. If I look at the Jesus story through that lens, then Jesus is not so much a divine invader as he is a human life so open to God that he is infused with divinity.

"There's nothing radical about that; that's exactly what Tillich was saying in the thirties, forties, and fifties. But most people have not put that together with their Sunday school religion.

"The theistic God is either impotent, evil, or He doesn't exist. If God hasn't got the power to stop the tsunami, then He's impotent; if He has it and doesn't, then He's malevolent. That kind of God doesn't live very long in the thoughtful minds of people. A lot of what people call prayers to the theistic God are letters to Santa Claus—dear God, I've been a good boy. God's in my employ, and God's going to pay me off. There's a very ancient connection between my behavior and making God serve me. And yet most people have so identified God with that sort of image that, when they hear you critique the theistic God, they think you are saying there is no God. But theism is a human definition of the holy, and all human definitions can change.

"If you give up the familiar God-idea and clear away things that have grown irrelevant to our lives, such as the virgin birth, physical resuscitation as the meaning of resurrection, and the idea there is only one way to God, well, you give up a lot of the security that religion is created to enhance. But I don't think Christianity gives us security—I think it gives us the courage to live with our insecurity. A big difference."

For all of Spong's conviction, persuasiveness, and charm, I couldn't help wondering if he wasn't jettisoning a little too much. For me, mysteries such as the virgin birth, the divinity of Jesus, and even physical resurrection are powerful reminders of all that we can never fully understand about the divine—perhaps not literally true but valuable and profound pointers to a mystical reality that is finally unknowable.

On the other hand, Spong has lived a long life on the boundary of belief and social justice, and in his struggles with fundamentalism, he's seen just how literal-minded conservative religion can be, how unsubtle, unmystical, legalistic. His whole life's effort has been to dislodge the airtight religious certainties that have gone hand in glove with unjust social structures. A literally true, inerrant Bible seen as divine word can be used as a pseudo-law code condemning blacks and gays to pariah status; a theistic God can have a gender and encourage a bias for the masculine; the pre-medieval and medieval ideas that many tradition-bound believers cling to can turn the world into a closed place—a cosmic Tarboro, North Carolina, circa 1950.

I found theological fearlessness bracing too. In his rejection of much Christian doctrine and tradition as outmoded symbolism, he calls attention to it *as* symbolism and challenges us to go past it to a living mystery. In the process, he helps us decide just how important religious symbols are for us and in what ways they are alive or dead, meaningful or misleading. This very critical path is one clear way for a modern person to remain in the church with intellect intact.

I find a great deal of joyful mystery *in* the symbols as well as beyond them, and that may be why I'm a Catholic. But as a believer who isn't interested in a holy lobotomy, I am grateful for someone who will hold on to God while he fearlessly interrogates all the ways in which we represent a reality that is finally beyond our comprehension, as well as our power to symbolize.

As our conversation drew to a close, Spong underlined the importance of the relationship between religious belief and the social justice that he's steered his life by when he described the sort of local church he supports —and finds in many different denominations around the country. "They're open to interpreting the Bible outside the box, open to people of color, to varieties of religious experience, to gay and lesbian people, open to full participation by women. Frankly, if you aren't open on *all* those things, you tend not to be fully open on any of them. It's one of the things we've learned. The homosexual battle is the same battle we fought over segregation and women's rights. The same people who didn't want either one of those don't want gays to participate fully as gays. They just keep moving the battlefield."

Spong paused and smiled. "I understand why people want to hold on to the old conceptions, because I once held them. They finally got cracked open for me in theological seminary, and I became more or less what I am, which is a sort of mystic wandering in the wilderness, convinced of the reality of God, not convinced of any formula that purports to describe what God is. I am always on a journey into the mystery which is bigger than any of the creeds can possibly contain."

Look for God Everywhere and in Everyone

Matt Epp

The CD is called *You'll Find Me Alone.* Singer-songwriter Matt Epp's right eye is on the cover, and the eye is very large, very blue-green, and very pensive. On the back, Epp wears a black T-shirt and poses with a guitar. He's seriously handsome, Versace-ad handsome, but with that twentysomething look of trying to figure out too many of life's persistent questions *right now.*

The title cut is the first one on the CD, a melancholy, tuneful ode to post-adolescent isolation. Guitar, tenor voice, and fiddle blend for that high-lonesome Canadian-folky sound. "Boy Ought to Be in New York" is about bailing out of the prairie provinces, "Kissing and Drinking Wine" is as innocently libidinous as its title, and "We Can Be in Love" is a duet in which the wonderful voice of fellow Winnipegger Julia Kasdorf adds just the right sweet-rough touch.

And then comes "Religion of Sand." Epp, a little hoarse, addresses Jesus: "Lord help me see it's not about me/Or what I can do to deserve you. I go in your name all over the land/But is my faith a religion of sand?" In "Faith the Bow," he sings about being "allowed to grow/into feeling what we know/Knowledge the arrow/faith the bow." And he turns Saint Augustine's formula for faith into folk-rock with "Got a hole inside of me for you, my God/for you created me so."

In our popular culture, deep self-doubt and serious questioning of ultimate reality is a secular business, but Epp brings his questions to God. And they're real questions, not the rah-rah affirmations that Contemporary Christian Music (CCM) superstars provide for the Jumbotrons of suburban megachurches.

"Yeah, my contempt for CCM comes out pretty strongly sometimes," he said with a smile as we sat in a coffee shop on Winnipeg's Corydon Avenue, a gentrifying street with few reminders of its heyday as the center of the prairie city's Little Italy. Epp, with tousled blond hair and a many-zippered leather jacket, looked like a sort of angel-headed bad boy but exuded a simple friendliness and openness that made me wish I had a younger brother just like him. He'd played a downtown Winnipeg pub the night before, kicking off a tour in support of *You'll Find Me Alone* that would take him east to Toronto and other Ontario cities, then back through the prairie provinces to British Columbia, then home. The stops along the way are a sort of index to his complex identity as both music-scenester and committed Christian: saloons and church basements, alternative coffee shops and Mennonite youth centers.

He's on a roll. He made the CD in two five-hour sessions—"everything just flowed," he told me, "and even the mistakes turned out great"—and now he's on his first national tour, a mere two years after he first picked up a guitar. But the twenty-four-year-old musician is thinking more about getting re-centered in his faith than taking a heady ride. "When things get really busy, it's hard to connect," he said. "God's the one who lights the creative fire for me, and I hear Him saying, 'You've been doing some things, going some places, but now we need to talk.' After the tour, there is going to be some quiet time. The point I'm at now is *seeing* God but feeling dissatisfied with the lack of personal relationship with him. It's almost like we've been business partners. I'm surrendering to Him, and He's working in what we're doing. But what about our friendship? I'm really questioning that."

Epp struggles with promoting his business and himself. "You have to put yourself out there and say what's good about you, but I hate talking about myself. First of all, I'm cautious about the pride issue, and second of all, I don't really know anything; it's just my pilgrimage, and all I want to do is show somebody something big and beautiful."

Epp's background is Mennonite—the Anabaptist-descended church is very strong in Manitoba—but his family practiced a form of the faith that was barely distinguishable from mainline Christianity. He told me that he has always believed in God, but as he grew up in several small towns in Manitoba, he found the institutional church more and more disillusioning. "I saw the eternal difference between religious activity and a real connection with the Creator," he said. "The reverence and the joy and the freedom; the simplicity of loving God and loving and serving people was lost in a lot of legalism. As soon as you focus on that, *religion* is your god. I found so little real devotion and so much really atrocious behavior in the background of all the piety. If you're too young to know that there *is* truth behind all of it, that it did start out as truth, well, you say to yourself, 'What *is* this?' "

After high school in Steinbach, Manitoba, he was hungry to figure God out and ready for practically any kind of adventure. "I always wanted to know the truth, the absolute truth," he told me. "It didn't matter if it wasn't easy, it didn't matter if I liked it or not. I wanted to know the truth and align myself with it. I always knew there was a creator. You see storms and you know he's a powerful God. You see a woman and you know he's a beautiful God. You see people and you know he's a personal God. It's too bad, but it can sometimes be easier to see all of that outside the church than inside it. I just wanted to strip everything away and see and experience all kinds of things for myself."

He made hitchhiking forays all over Canada and down into the United States, putting his fate in the hands of strangers and a higher power. He stumbled into a two-week stay with the family of a high government official in Quebec, swam in an idyllic hidden lake in Ontario, helped a slightly sinister-looking pilot repair his floatplane in exchange for a long ride, accepted a knife from another hitchhiker with the proviso that he pass it on to yet another knifeless wanderer. "Hitchhiking brought me seriously closer to God," he said. "I was starting from scratch. Without saying it in so many words, I was doing this forced-dependence thing. I refused to believe things just because I was told them, and the only person I could trust was God. The truth has to come from the Truth, you know? Because I had been conditioned, I couldn't trust my own ideas. Hitching, I trusted God for food and safety and everything. And I opened my mind to talking to other people wherever I was, and I saw God in them."

In 2001, Epp moved to Winnipeg, the hard way. He lived in his car and worked two jobs, scrambling to save money for a rent deposit before Manitoba's murderous winter set in. And, in a modest prairie version of the Hollywood dream, he was discovered—by a small-time talent agent who handled the casts of made-in-Winnipeg B movies. Epp soon found himself in an interesting corner of schlock cinema; he was cast in *The Brotherhood III: Young Demons,* a tale of high-school kids conjuring up the devil. At the helm was David DeCoteau, one of the few openly gay B-movie directors and something of a camp-horror cult hero for often replacing the scantily-clad sorority girls of traditional exploitation cinema with hunky young men in their underwear. It was a lark for Epp and the other local actors involved—shooting took all of five days—and everyone expected the movie to die quietly on rental racks. But *The Brotherhood III* became a giant direct-to-video hit; Blockbuster bought the rights, and dubbed and subtitled versions appeared around the world. "It was everywhere," said Epp with a smile. "I started work at this group home in Winnipeg, and one of the kids had it there. I show up for my first shift, and my DVD is staring at me! I'm on the cover in my prosthetic demon eyebrows."

Epp did some modeling and continued to act. He appeared in a comic-horror short called *Cannibalism: A New Taste in Style* directed by David Zellis of the Winnipeg Film Group, Manitoba's innovative indie-film collective. And he learned how to party with the film, video, music, and fashion folk who now made up his world. Like a hero in a picaresque novel, Epp had come to the big city (or at least the sizable regional city), tasted some very worldly pleasures, and couldn't figure out why he was still bewildered and unsatisfied. "I had a couple of friends in that scene who were Christians," he said. "We'd get drunk and talk endlessly about God. But it was basically a void. I had lost my foundation, and felt lost and totally without motivation. But God came and met me, and his timing was perfect.

"In the mall one day, I met an aunt of mine whom I hadn't seen forever, and she said that one of my cousins was getting married. She asked me if I wanted to come and offered to pick me up and take me. 'We're going to church first,' she said. 'Do you want to come?' I was like, 'Yeah!' But once I got to the church, I was feeling pretty cynical, you know, about the church thing, organized religion. I walk in, and I'm totally disarmed. God takes my cynicism, takes my negative awareness away. I see God working in all these people. It was actually like God taking the scales off my eyes. I see these people, and I'm connecting with the Body of Christ."

Epp went back to the church to speak with a pastor about his doubts, his distance from the church. "The pastor said, 'Well, you know God, right? Just pray to Him.' The next time I came to church, at some point in the service, I heard this voice that asked me to kneel. I knew it was the voice that people say they hear. Audible or not, it was there. I said to myself, this is your chance to just obey. This was the thing I'd been waiting for. I went to the edge of the aisle and really just lay down. I felt that I had Jesus's head on my shoulder. I could feel it. I wept and wept and wept. It was phenomenal.

"From that point on, I dropped everything in my life except for writing and going to church. Simplifying. Church became, not just an institution, but a place where I could meet God."

• • •

Epp, newly full of emotions that he could barely name, found an outlet in playing the violin—"the most emotional instrument I could think of," he said. He then gravitated to the guitar and toyed with composing songs based on the poetry in his notebooks.

He often wrote in a Corydon Avenue restaurant not far from the coffee shop where we were talking. A waitress there suggested that they go to hear a rising Manitoba folksinger named Dan Frechette. "I went and heard him, and it fell on me like a brick," said Epp. "I just sat there in awe and knew that for the rest of my life I'd be writing songs. I didn't know then if it would be how I made my living, but I knew it would be how I expressed myself. At seven in the morning, I phoned my job, this dollar-ninety-nine breakfast place where I was a server, and said, 'I can't come in.' The guy asked, 'Are you sick?' and I said, 'No, I'm inspired.' There was this long silence, and then he asked, 'Well, will you be inspired tomorrow?'

"Good question. But I just kept churning out songs, mostly about my faith."

In Matt Epp, I had found another believer who was not merely believing —not merely, or even mainly, assenting to intellectual or moral propositions about God, Jesus, holiness, or redemption. Epp was *living* in a way that was faithful to a vivid experience of a power greater than himself.

Like me, he had started with a tiny mustard seed of faith—he'd prayed to a God he barely understood but sensed was there. And that had been enough to shift his way of seeing, so that now he can find God everywhere. He refuses to draw a firm line between the holy and the mundane, the energies of earthly and divine love. I find this inspiring and refreshing: after all, a dualistic Christianity, which considers the world and the spirit, the secular and the sacred, as permanently opposed, is not traditional Christianity, and it's not modern Christianity either. God is present everywhere and in everything; we can turn away from God—that's sin—but no structure of life, not even contemporary secular, materialist culture, can keep God out.

Epp's faith has matured in the short but busy time that he has been a professional musician. If faith infuses the songs, the songs can also rekindle the faith. "I'll notice sometimes when I'm playing, it's just empty," he said. "Sounding brass and tinkling cymbals instead of music, right? Then suddenly I'll be playing a song like 'Religion of Sand'—and what a wakeup call that is. Like—no kidding, I have to pay attention. When a song is inspired, it will teach me over and over. Some lyrics I didn't know why I wrote, they just kind of fit and felt right at the time—but then later on, they teach me something new. In 'Faith the Bow' I wrote:

> We must read the Word
> Finally hear what we haven't heard
> See what we haven't seen
> Find out how we're now who we will be.

Only now am I learning what that last line means—that my character is what it is, that I will have to deal with myself, good and bad, as I am, for the rest of my life."

A lot of Epp's appeal, as a person and as a musician, comes from the unique way his spirituality blends with his artistry. While he's committed to a lifelong, intense relationship with God within the Christian faith, he hasn't settled into a pew or a position; he's not preaching, and he's not trying to convert anyone. If God is everywhere, then God can be in a sexy love song or a chord change too. "It's not like it's some kind of missionary thing," he said. "Some people once called us a 'stealth ministry,' and I found that hilarious. See, we might get a glimpse of God in *anything* creative we do, whether it's a purely romantic song, or something that's good musically, or lyrics that are directly about God—whatever. We want to say to our audience, we love you, we want to share something beautiful so that you can see it too.

"We go in those clubs and have amazing talks with people. We're open to everybody, and we try to stay in touch with them too, with e-mails or whatever. I sometimes feel uncomfortable in church, and sometimes I sense that some dark club, full of lust and bad energy, is not cool either. But I feel I *can* be open to just about anybody in those places because I've never exactly fit in myself. My friend John Parks, who plays on the album, has a song called 'Sunday Morning' about being caught between the haves and have nots, the believers and the doubters. He's got a great line that I love: 'Please let us wanderers in, too. We all may be lost but we're searching for you.' "

GIVE YOUR WHOLE SELF TO GOD

Cyndi Dale

When I learned that Cyndi Dale, a Twin Cities psychic and author of *New Chakra Healing* and three other books with *chakra* in the title, considered herself a Christian, I was intrigued. I wondered how a New Age shamaness experienced Christ.

So I signed up for a psychic/healing session at her pleasant, and in no way exotic, suburban home. We discussed my insomnia, and she impressed me as someone with a solid grounding in physiology and health. We didn't talk chakras or auras much but concentrated on endocrine glands and vitamin supplements. She was blond and a bit glamorous, as well as focused, intense, talkative, and kind. She seemed far more anxious to actually help me than to dazzle me with occult power-projection or spiritual fireworks. And we didn't touch on Christianity at all.

It was at our second meeting, in a bustling St. Paul Starbucks, that I asked her to talk to me about her sense of Jesus, which is entwined with the paranormal perceptions and presences she experienced through much of her life.

"I grew up a white-bread Lutheran, as basic as you could be," she said with a smile. "Stoic, prim, and proper. Go to the church potlucks, be absolutely quiet in the pew. Jesus isn't going to talk to you." Other entities *were* talking to Cyndi. At three, she was having parties for the boy and girl angels who visited her, serving them cookies and little cups of her mother's perfume. She could see colorful lights shining around people and dark, vaporous spirits emerging from some of them. "Particularly from my mother," she said. "When she was angry or depressed, gray ghosts or demons projected from her."

While her mother dismissed these visions as imagination or fibs, they frightened her father and he regularly forbade her to talk about them. "I know that my dad's mother saw spirits," said Dale. "I think that his experience of her visions spooked him."

In any event, her second sight abandoned her when she was around twelve years old, as family troubles, including abuse and alcoholism, came to a crescendo. One of the last visions she had for many years came when she went to bed and decided to die. "I wrote a farewell note to my parents, and then I got ready to go. I got violently ill, and nobody knew what to do. I left my body, but I only got so far. There was no great light, no chorus, just a voice that said 'You haven't done anything. You have to go back.' And so I started to get well, and I was *furious*."

So began her grim teenage years. She grew lethargic as her creative spark abandoned her. She struggled with anorexia and bulimia. "I was miserable and probably made everybody else miserable, too," she told me. An impulsive marriage when she was twenty turned bad. And all this time, the spirits were silent.

Then Dale went into therapy, and things changed. "I heard voices at night, saw colors again, thought I could tell what people were thinking. At first I thought, 'Great. I've been compulsive and codependent and now I'm crazy.' But one of my therapists said to me, flat out, 'Cyndi, you're ill, but I don't think you're *just* ill. I think you're psychic.' And my response was, 'What's that?'"

Dale was to find out what that was over the next few years. She got a divorce, traveled to Europe, Latin America, and Asia, and found herself gravitating to, and attracting, traditional healers, shamans, and other spirit-filled folk. "People in England and Ireland were very receptive to what I am about," she said. "They'll look at you and ask, 'Do you have *the sight*?' Or 'The hotel is haunted; I hope you don't mind.' And, of course, in Latin America it's everywhere." Dale's interest in perceiving, and healing, beyond the limits of the strictly rational grew and grew, until she was traveling in order to seek out *caranderos*, "wise women," and the like.

"That was about the time that Dolores Krieger came out with her technique of Therapeutic Touch," she said, "and nurses were using it in hospital settings. When I was twenty-eight, I took a class with a woman who taught the technique, which involved auras and the chakras, the vortices of energy in the body. I said to myself, 'So *that's* what I'm seeing. The colors around the bodies. Auric fields and chakras.' " The class was made up of a varied crew of very ordinary people—stockbrokers, corporate managers, housewives. Dale herself was nearly 100 percent corporate; alongside her program of exotic wanderings, she'd developed a mainstream public relations and fundraising career. But as she took more classes from Twin Cities-based healers, including the nationally known Echo Bodine, she inched closer and closer toward a full-time commitment to "energy work." And then a voice—God's?—spoke to Dale again.

"It said, 'Quit your job'," she said, laughing. "I was like, 'Hello? How will I pay these bills?' But all I heard was 'Quit your job.' It didn't tell me how I was going to manage.

"Well, just for the hell of it, I had these pink cards printed up at Kinko's that said 'Psychic Healer.' I didn't even really know what I was going to do with them; it was an impulse. As I picked them up, I got embarrassed for myself. I couldn't do this. I mean, my family is all doctors! So I was going to go home and paper the bathroom walls with them or something. But this woman at the copy shop saw the cards, grabbed a handful, and said, 'I'll send you clients.' She did what she promised, and before too long, I was making enough money to get by."

"As a New Ager," she said, "I believed that the world was full of spirits, and we could talk to any of them; Jesus was just one of the masters. And then, when I was about thirty-three, I had a couple of dreams with Christ in them, and he said, 'I'm coming.' Well, I *have* these visions and dreams, but I'm not always responsive to them, you know? I sort of said, 'Oh. Okay. You do what you have to do.' "

A couple of years passed, and Dale was back in a dark valley. Her second marriage was dissolving, and she was taking it hard. "This was a good, good man," she said, "but he was straight science and rationalism, and he just couldn't come to terms with what I was doing. And as for me, well, I was full of shame and sick of being so weird.

"I was writing my first book, *New Chakra Healing,* and taking time off now and then to drive to some land I owned on the Mississippi near McGregor, Iowa. I was coming back after one of those trips—it was maybe eight o'clock at night—and this huge light came in through the front windshield. I knew it was God. He said, 'I am love.' I freaked out. I pulled off the road, and my heart was pounding. I felt like saying, 'Do you have to communicate with me this way? I could have wrecked the car.'

"I pulled back onto the road, and I thought I was going to be fine. But then—and I can't really explain it—Christ came from inside my heart, from *in,* and it was like I saw the world through his eyes. And it was all light. It was beautiful. Then he said: 'Heaven is on earth. I love you.' "

The experience was shattering, and it set a very confused Dale on a new course. She immersed herself in a doctrinally strict Pentecostal sect, dated and then married a man from that world—"I felt directed to," she said— but suffered from round-peg-in-a-square-hole syndrome almost from the start. Her new community was suspicious of her New Age background— doubly so when her chakra-healing book came out from Llewellyn, a St. Paul-based New Age publisher. Everybody—her husband included— insisted that she give up what she considered to be her gifts and her purpose. "I mean, I was *helping* people. They were healing. And as for these supposed Christians, well, I didn't really want to go where they said they were headed.

"And as soon as my New Age friends found out I was a Christian, they didn't want to see me. Some clients canceled. I felt like I was nothing. But I just went on doing what I did, because I had to make a living; I wasn't about to go corporate again—who would hire me, the chakra lady?"

Dale felt abandoned and alone, but she didn't take it lying down; in an effort to figure out what and who she was and where she stood, she took a serious plunge into the Christian side of her life, enrolling in a master's program in theology at Bethel University, an evangelical Baptist institution in suburban St. Paul. She got straight A's, but she couldn't shake the New Age stigma; a delegation of her fellow students went to Bethel administrators and declared that they didn't want to share classrooms with anyone of her ilk. "So I was hauled in for an inquisition," she said. "My then husband, the evangelical, said 'Don't blow this; it would really embarrass me.' Thanks for the support! Anyway, I went in there and laid out on the table who I was and what I had experienced. And do you know what they said? They said, 'You're on a path, Christ has called you, and we will completely support you. Stay here, do what you need to do.'

"So now my question became not where do I fit, but how do I Christian and psychic fit together?"

She took a trip to Wales with friends to tour some sacred sites. Her father was ill with lung cancer, and she was feeling prayerful and concerned—"I called him every day, once from this phone booth in a cow pasture," she said. As she stood beside an ancient Celtic cross, she saw Christ, in body, approach her. "I was crying about my dad, and he looked at me with incredible compassion and never said a word. There was no dogma, just his presence, just a feeling that said 'I love you, and I love your father. I wish I could take this away from you, but it is what it is.'

"Later, I was in Glasgow with three friends: a pagan, a Jew, and a Hindu-Buddhist. We represented the whole spectrum; these were women who totally accepted me as a Christian and loved me for who I was. We went into a museum of religious art, of icons from around the world. I stood with my back to this painting by Salvador Dali, *El Mundo*—The World—an image of Christ on the cross, hanging over the entire world. I felt Christ leave the painting, come down from behind me, and hold me; and he said in my ear, 'Isn't it wonderful how many ways there are to worship God?' "

Another time, Dale was in church, a little bored and preoccupied, and wondering what Christ would think of the liturgy, the building, the pastor, the hymns. She suddenly had a vision of him carrying his cross.

"I asked him, 'Do you really *want* to be carrying that?'

"He looked at me, and he said, 'In two thousand years, no one has ever asked me that question.' He came out from under it, and it stood there, still leaning, just as he left it. It was just fine; it didn't need him. He sat next to me and asked, very kindly, 'Do you want me to walk with you?' 'Yes,' I said, and that was it."

Experiences like this led Dale to a resolution of her psychic-or-Christian dilemma. When it came to her, it was childishly simple: "I'm both," she said. "I mean, in the Old Testament, Joseph did divination with a cup. The Levites threw dice that they kept in their breastplates to see what God had to say. The Hebrew prophets, especially the early ones, were shamans who lived apart, behaved very strangely, and were possessed by the Spirit of God. I read Morton Kelsey, an Episcopal priest whose book *Healing and Christianity* called Jesus the greatest of all shamans. Kelsey looked at the New Testament from a Jungian perspective.

"Paul, in Colossians and Ephesians, speaks of the gifts of the Spirit. What is Christ's healing but the channeling of energy? These things are all revelations—the question is do you bring them under God or not? I think we all have psychic gifts—I consider psychic perception to be nothing more than the receiving of very fast-moving information—but we need to bring it, use it, under God.

"I don't think of the New Age as spiritual at all, but as a beginning point in being conscious of psychic energy, in learning how to consciously manage it. The New Age has to do with mind only and with focusing, sending, and receiving this kind of energy. I think of spirituality, on the other hand, as saying, 'I'm now going to bring these psychic gifts under God and let God use me. When I used my gifts as a New Ager, it was very egotistical. *I* could do the healing, *I* could figure out mysteries. *I* could talk to spirits and manage everything. But being in charge makes a mess. The truth is, I was conflicted. I didn't know if I was sending the right energy to people—really, whether I was doing good or doing bad. It wasn't under God, so it was out of control.

"But to do this with Christ as my instructor is different. Not that everything I do comes from Christ, not that I do it the right way every time, but making that decision has been the humbling step I needed to be more in receipt of God's help than trying to figure it out all by myself. Now I ask God to work through me, to use my gifts so that I can help someone. With his help, I'm clearer about what I know, what I don't know, what I can do, and what I can't."

· · ·

I think of Cyndi Dale's life as a particularly trustful surrender to God because she was willing to give to God experiences and powers that many Christians think of as unorthodox at best and demonic at worst. Rather than cut off part of herself by turning against her psychic gifts—labeling them evil or irrelevant to faith—she presented her whole self to God, confident that God loved her for who she was and would sort out the useful and the useless in her life.

This seems to me a particularly realistic and God-honoring way to proceed. I know that I am a bundle of contradictions, with talents, powers, weaknesses, blind spots, obsessions, gifts, and manias jostling each other. When I am willing to let God have all of me, not just the elements of my life I judge (or the church judges) to be good, I can be reasonably certain that I am not trying to manipulate God into loving me, which is just about the most pointless process I can imagine.

Accept the Mystery

Liz Kelly

My first encounter with Liz Kelly was in an old-fashioned Catholic-goods store in St. Paul—the kind of place that sells agonized Italian crucifixes, tiny First Communion gowns, and figurines of Jesus helping a kid catch a football. A new Catholic, I was looking for a book on that most Catholic of devotions, the Rosary. One stood out: *The Rosary: A Path Into Prayer* (Loyola Press). While most of the other rosary books were written by austere-looking Father So-and-So from some enormous diocese in New Jersey, the author photo on the back of *A Path Into Prayer* showed an attractive woman, dramatically lit, who was a jazz singer with an MFA in fiction from the University of Alaska and, at the time, worked for Harvard University. I was intrigued, to say the least.

Kelly's text was special too—it went beyond the usual history-and-homily pattern to show the rosary as a living, even life-saving, reality for her and for many others, not all of whom were Catholics.

A bit of research revealed that Kelly had two CDs out: *It Seems to Me,* a set of standards ("Corcovado," "Caravan," "They Can't Take That Away From Me") and *Anima Christi,* which could best be described as Catholic devotional jazz. "All-Consuming Fire" is a steamy, R & B-spiced love song to God, while "Doxology" transforms "Praise God from Whom All Blessings Flow" (which my childhood congregation sang unsteadily to the accompaniment of a tinny piano) into a pulsating jazz samba. Kelly had appeared at the Montreux and North Sea jazz festivals and gigged in clubs from Lawrence, Kansas, to Anchorage, Alaska, to Nashville, Tennessee.

To meet Kelly, I returned to Cambridge, Massachusetts, where I had gone to college. Kelly suggested that we connect at Saint Clement's church in Boston's Back Bay, where she attends mass and spends a lot of time in meditation and prayer. Having missed the subway stop, I had to find an unoccupied cab (not easy) and so reached the church a little late. I knelt in a pew, decompressing and asking God, as usual, to help me with the interview by helping me be less self-conscious.

The woman in the pew behind me was Kelly. I suppose I expected either a smoky jazz siren, an austere contemplative, or a strange amalgam of both, but she turned out to be something else—an open-hearted woman with a ready and frequent laugh, the sort of person who puts you at ease by being profoundly at ease with herself.

As we rode in her Volkswagen New Beetle to her home in Watertown, we talked about Harvard. I had both loved and feared the place when I was there, and it had done me both great good and a certain amount of damage. I had loved the sense of being connected to traditions of the American intellect, from Emerson to John Kenneth Galbraith, but I had also learned to measure people (including myself) on a punishing scale that ran from "brilliant" to "super-brilliant" and made no provisions for any other qualities of mind—or any qualities at all of heart. And since I secretly knew that I didn't belong on the scale, I felt like a fraud. I started drinking seriously while at college—though only in the summers. I managed to stay sober during school terms to stay afloat.

For Kelly, Harvard represented a challenge too. She loved her job, writing profiles of professors holding endowed chairs. (Her singing career was on hold for the moment, she explained, while she enjoyed a job with benefits—but she wanted to restore the jazz/writing balance as soon as she could.) It exposed her to a range of brilliant men and women in many fields, and it kept her on her toes as a researcher and writer. But she could see conflicts looming. Her heartfelt and rather conservative Catholic faith wouldn't allow her to profile anyone involved in embryonic stem cell research, for example, and just such a profile was waiting on her office's to-do list. And as a person who accepted spiritual mysteries as a part of life, she found the university's exclusive focus on rationality a little forbidding. Kelly struck me as far too well-adjusted to be deterred by conflicts like these, but as we talked at her sunny dining room table, I learned just how hard-won her serenity and cheerfulness were.

She'd grown up in south-central Minnesota, a pious little girl who loved Jesus and the Holy Family. "They were as real and natural to me as you and I sitting here," she said. "Little kids don't have that crap in their heads about the physics of the world!"

She'd shown a love of writing very early on—"I was very rarely without a Big Chief writing tablet in hand," she recalled—but her talent for music was a surprise to everybody, including herself. A high-school acquaintance enrolled her, without her knowledge, in a community choir in the town her family had just moved to. Soon, the director was giving her solo parts, and Kelly, who had had no idea that she could sing, became something of a standout. "It saved me, because it gave me something to put my lonely little, just-moved, got-no-friends heart into," she said with a smile. "It was actually a little miracle."

Kelly sang in a jazz vocal group as an undergrad at the University of Kansas at Lawrence and discovered that she was a natural improviser. When she went off to Anchorage for her writing MFA, she kept the jazz bubbling as featured vocalist with the University of Alaska faculty jazz band and with gigs at Anchorage watering holes like Bernie's Bar and Grill and Elevation 92. After Alaska, she moved to Nashville to focus on her music, though she also taught writing at a film school in the city and freelanced for religious publications.

On the outside, it was the story of a talented, ambitious young woman building a respectable, if unconventional, career blending two callings. Inside, Liz Kelly had been slowly coming apart for years. She had been raped—and had told no one. She was overeating—and sometimes starving herself too. In college, she'd abandoned her childhood faith under the influence of a pair of Protestant acquaintances who'd convinced her that Catholicism wasn't Christian. In grad school, she explored secular feminism, Buddhism, and other ways of life but didn't find a home in any of them.

"My main problem wasn't my exploration of other ideas and faiths; that's a necessary venture," she said. "The temptation I felt was trusting my intellect more than my spirit. Like at Harvard, I was in a place that worshipped the intellect, and to even suggest that we are spiritual and physical beings as well as intellectual beings just seemed ludicrous to a lot of people. And what I didn't realize at the time was that I was reacting more to other people's discomfort with faith than any real alienation from it that I felt. I was just really insecure—overweight, unhappy, and obsessed with what other people thought."

Still, Kelly doesn't regret her struggle. "God is very efficacious and merciful, and He brought me back around to Him," she said. She began to reach out for help with her eating disorder and to understand that recovery was also a profoundly spiritual process. She read the Catechism of the Catholic Church and recovery literature, and became convinced that it was beyond her own power to remove the habits and defects of character that had kept her so miserable so long. "I knew *I* couldn't do it." She was relieved to release the burden. "And everything changed after that. I fell into the arms of my Beloved, who's perfectly capable of picking up the pieces, putting me back together, and making me useful in the world."

A friend in Nashville gave her the door-lock code to a Catholic chapel, and she began visiting it at odd times of the day and night. At first she couldn't pray in her own words, but she could manage the familiar prayers that went with the rosary beads: Our Father and Hail Mary. And the simple, very physical rhythm of touching bead after bead soothed her soul.

For Kelly, elements of the faith that had seemed odd, perplexing, or off-putting at first—and can seem doubly so to an outsider—were transformed when she patiently and peacefully gave herself to them. Praying the Rosary of the Holy Wounds, a devotion in which Christ's wounds before and during His crucifixion are invoked, once seemed a classic case of Catholic morbidity to her. But as she prayed the wounds, she slowly found her own psychic wounds healing, her own vulnerabilities becoming transformed.

The same went for the transubstantiation. Transubstantiation is the complex idea that, during the mass, the substance of the consecrated bread and wine—the part of them that is independent of their "accidental" characteristics, such as their color, taste, and texture—is transformed into the body and blood of Christ. The elements still look like bread and wine but have become truly (not just symbolically) the substance of Jesus—and you eat them.

"I wasn't sure I believed the transubstantiation, and it seemed kind of creepy," Kelly said. "I could give you a textbook definition of it, but I don't think that would do the job. It's like getting a heart transplant. You had a heart that thumped one way, and now it thumps another way. It's as if Jesus's heart were manifest inside you, body and soul. That's not something I can study and then say, 'I get it!' Really, my mind can barely scratch the surface of it. As a Catholic, I'm called to live a life within mystery. Once I accept that, I don't have to figure out all the answers.

"Reason is vital. You don't check reason at the door. But it's only a part of the *truth*. The truth isn't just in a book, it isn't just in my brain or in the feelings I have at any moment. If I took my feelings for the only truth, I'd be eating my way back to two hundred pounds and misery. Truth is a combination of these things and more: a mystery; I can take part in it, but it's not for me to solve. I don't get to have God's view; I get to have my partial view of this great mystery."

Kelly's struggle is a struggle to live a unified life in line with an explicit, connected set of values. And any temptation on my part to pigeonhole her as a rigid "conservative Catholic" was blown away by the generosity of her personality and her insistence that she goes to God, not as someone who has "got it right," but as a struggling, flailing, failing human being who, without God's love, will always get it wrong.

"Before I met you today," she told me, "I had gone to noon mass at Saint Clement's and then just sat there for a while, thinking, Thank God, I can just come here and fall apart. I don't have to have any answers here. I come as I am, just as I am, and fall on my face—and God doesn't kick me out! In fact, He says: 'Come closer! Oh, daughter, I'm just so glad you're here.' Now, really taking *that* in will even change the way you walk across the street."

FOLLOW GOD'S PROMPTINGS
WHEREVER THEY LEAD

Matt Helling

Matt is a quiet, honest man in his early forties whom I've known for a number of years now—we both belong to an informal writers' group that gathers every Tuesday evening in a Minneapolis bar. He works as a psychiatric social worker, and if I were coming out of psychiatric hospitalization, I can assure you I'd want him on my case. His calm, deliberate manner inspires a lot of confidence, and yet he's far from solemn—little flashes of wit and irony, often directed at himself, light up his conversation.

For a long time, I knew in a general way that Matt was a "believer." I knew that he attended an Episcopal church in St. Paul and was interested in learning how to do religious counseling, a form of therapy where it's okay to talk about God. But it was his way of living that suggested to me that he'd had a genuine encounter with God. He's an ascetic, and he's been one for close to twenty years. He lives in conditions of great simplicity—in a basement apartment in St. Paul, as his building's caretaker. He drives a beat-up Volvo, works only three days a week at his social work job, and spends a lot of time writing.

Fiction writing is a profound calling for Matt. He's working on a novel that could best be described as Christian science fiction, and he's organized much of his life around completing the book. But he also takes time to play the electric bass—not very well, by his own cheerful admission—to care for his mother, who lives in an assisted living facility thirty miles away, to keep in good shape with regular laps in a local university pool, and to spend time with his friends, many of whom are artists, writers, underpaid helping-professionals, and others who have missed or jumped off the approved career tracks.

When Matt talks about his decision to, as he puts it, "let go," and give his life to Christ and to God as he understands Christ and God, he displays none of the triumphalism that tempts some people who've discovered their path in life. Instead, he's wistful.

"I've given up a great deal," he told me. "Things I would have liked and which might have been a better fit for me than what I'm doing now. I've given up opportunities for money. I'm not in a relationship now and haven't been for a long time. You can be surprised, even a little shocked, by what can happen to you when you *let go*—you just don't know what's coming."

For Matt, letting go meant abandoning two careers in widely different areas of academia, careers for which he was talented and qualified and which would have provided him with a better paid, more stable mode of life than social work and religious science fiction. But Matt didn't feel called to them, and responding to calling has become his *modus operandi.*

The son of academics (his father was a sociologist, his mother an educational psychologist), Matt grew up in Omaha, Nebraska, and Northfield, Minnesota, with an interlude in rural Turkey, where his parents did fieldwork.

Church meant little to Matt until he went to college at Saint Olaf in Northfield, where his parents taught. There he found himself more or less adrift, drinking a little, using drugs from time to time, seriously involved with a woman, but uncertain of his future. He felt both aimless and under pressure. "I used to drop in to the Saint Olaf's chapel from time to time," he recalls, "just to get a little peace of mind. Sometimes I would begin a sort of conversation with God. But then I would leave and go get myself mixed up in more confusion."

Matt married his college girlfriend, but the relationship didn't last. After the divorce, he drifted, working minimum-wage gigs and living in rundown apartments in Minneapolis. He fell in love with a woman who didn't return his interest, and the more he struggled to make his life cohere, the less sense it seemed to make.

"Anybody could see that my life wasn't working—anybody but me," he says. "Growing up in my family, there had been sort of an assumption that there was a certain path I would take—and things would work out for me because of who I was. And somehow the path had faded into nothing. I didn't really have, inside myself, any basis on which to choose a new path. The things that motivate a lot of people were never big motivators for me. Careers had passed me by several times by this point. I had spent a lot of time saying, 'No, that's not it,' not knowing where to go but not being satisfied with what was being offered."

And then one night, alone in his apartment, Matt fell into what he describes as "a strange mood . . . a very strange place in my own mind. I was able to kind of let go, to lose control, and to say to myself, what if there were some kind of higher power? And then I had a really strong feeling that there *was* a truth, that there *was* something outside of me. I went to church the week after that."

Matt's first visits to the UCC church he decided to attend weren't affirming or comforting. "I was *scared*," he recalls. "I had to hook my foot around an inner leg of the pew I was in because there was a strong force, something outside me, pushing me out, and I felt I just had to hang on." The fact that he *did* hang on had a lot to do with his upbringing. "That would never have flown in my family," he recalls with a smile. "To show up and say you're going to stay, and then get up and bail halfway through a church service or anything else—well, it just wasn't done."

Once he had mastered the temptation to flee, he found himself responding almost viscerally to the familiar words of Christ from the Gospel according to Matthew, repeated by the pastor at the beginning of every service: "Where two or three are gathered together in my name, there I am in the midst of them." The words moved Matt, and he decided to trust that Christ was present there. "I took my issues to church and waited for answers. Amazingly, I would get those answers."

One of the biggest questions Matt brought to church, and to God, provoked a decisive turn away from a conventional career. He had been accepted into a University of Minnesota graduate program in neuroscience. The program provided him with a fellowship, a stipend, an identity, and a future. "I had been looking around pretty desperately for something to get me out of my drift," he recalls, "and this practically fell into my lap." His parents were happy. He should have been happy too—but something told him that his path lay elsewhere. He attended a summer seminar with other program members and enjoyed it but couldn't shake the sense that he was being called in another direction. So he took the issue to church.

"On that particular Sunday, the Gospel passage was the one about the rich young man who wants to be Jesus's disciple," he says. "Jesus says, 'Sell all you own and follow me.' The young man can't do it. It hit me hard. I had never brought the issue of doing neuroscience to church in the first place. It had been *my* decision, in isolation; now I felt like the rich young man—called to a different life but uncertain if I could give up my new advantages to follow that call."

Unlike the rich young man, Matt struggled with the question, praying that his way be made clear. And he was led about as far afield from neuroscience as a modern American can be: to the Greek and Latin classics. He had no background in the field, not even much undergraduate coursework in literature, and no idea where classics would lead him. But he felt compelled, so he applied to the graduate program in classics at Minnesota. The faculty told him that he would need to learn Greek and Latin as quickly as he could, then pass a translation exam. So Matt set to work. He took demanding, accelerated language courses while still working long hours at minimum-wage jobs. When the time came for the exam, he didn't just pass it, he had the highest score in the room, earning a "PhD pass" with which he could begin doctoral work immediately.

Matt opted for an MA instead and spent a year teaching high school Latin in North Dakota before returning to the Twin Cities to train as a social worker. What classics gave him, he contends, wasn't a career, but a way of believing in himself. "I had never really mastered anything before I learned Latin," he says. "I'd always sort of gotten by on being a good talker and a good test-taker. But in Latin, you learn tenses and declensions and cases, systematically, and then you can figure out the text. There's no big mystery if you are willing to follow a certain procedure. By doing well in Latin, I realized I can do well in other forms of endeavor. It's going to be hard in the beginning, and I'm not going to know what I'm doing, but eventually it'll clear up."

So if Latin wasn't "the path" for Matt, it was prime preparation for living the sort of life he now feels called to: a life in which he regularly challenges himself. He deals with bipolar people and schizophrenics every day, struggling to find places in our fraying social fabric where they will be safe and happy. His Christian science-fiction novel is his first venture into creative writing, but unlike most writers I know, he seems unfazed by self-doubt; he writes and rewrites industriously, never complaining about the frustrations of the writing life. He's active and energetic, caring for his clients, his parents, his friends. "There's nothing wrong with meditative being-ness," he says, smiling. "But I just don't get it. I would rather be doing the next right thing."

Which is not to say, as I noted earlier, that Matt is living happily ever after. He's deeply aware that "letting go" has brought him uncertainty and regret as well as satisfaction. And at the time we talked, he told me that it had been quite a while since he had been able to feel God's guidance on a daily basis. "I still go to church seeking the presence of Jesus there," he says. "But a lot of times now, I come out as unclear as I went in. Maybe I'm not as open as I used to be. If you believe God is going to let you know what to do, you have to be ready to really open up and listen. To have your mind made up before you pray is defeating the purpose. It can be very scary, very difficult to do. That may be why I am not getting answers right now—I may have gotten too hooked up with my activities and my plans."

For Matt, more uncertainty, more asking, and another, deeper "letting go" may be the next phase of an evolving life. For me, his willingness to be absolutely faithful to God's voice within him was a challenge. I have always looked at worldly opportunities—fellowships, job offers, writing assignments—as life preservers on life's stormy sea, to be seized at once and at all costs. No matter how much my inner voice may rebel at some inappropriate opportunity, it's difficult for me to say no to anything that appears to offer me security, money, or some form of socially approved identity: successful writer, big earner, real man.

Matt appears to have lost all interest in any specific identity, and instead, fills his life with actions in aid of others and in aid of his faith. He seems to have turned over to God the question of who he is and who he is supposed to become. For me, this is a daunting and yet liberating way to live, without conventional signposts and markers of "progress," yet within an intoxicating kind of freedom: the freedom of no longer having to run the show.

LET GOD HEAL YOUR PAIN

Larry Lee

The Georgia Diagnostic and Classification Prison (GDCP) is an underground bunker linked by a tunnel to a "sally port," an entrance area that's a labyrinth of electronically operated doors. Despite its awe-inspiring security structure, its main function is more bureaucratic than punitive. It's the processing center and gateway to the entire Georgia prison system, through which all state prisoners pass on their way to other lockups—a sort of revolving door.

In one part of the prison, however, the doors close with finality. That part is the dwelling place of everybody convicted of a capital crime in Georgia. Death row.

I visited the GDCP in September of 2004 with a friend from St. Paul, Adam Gordon. We were on the visitor list of a forty-six-year-old Catholic convert named Larry Lee, a resident of death row for no fewer than eighteen years. Larry had been corresponding with Adam for the better part of a year, thanks to connections set up by Adam's Minneapolis parish and by Sister Mary Jude Jun, a nun who's been deeply engaged in a death row ministry for years. Convicted of a brutal triple murder in 1986 on the testimony of his sister-in-law and a convict who claimed that Larry confessed the crime to him in prison, Larry has steadfastly maintained his innocence, and his lawyers have been struggling to get the Georgia courts to admit new evidence that they claim will exonerate him.

When Adam and I arrived at the GDCP, we had to clean out our pockets, prove our identities to the guards' satisfaction, and clear the various doors of the sally port, which left only about a quarter hour of visiting time. We entered an ordinary common room with chairs scattered here and there. No Plexiglas barrier, no telephone handsets. The short, polite, sandy-haired man in the blue-and-white, pajama-like prison uniform who identified himself as Larry might have been the guy across the counter at the video store, the quiet co-worker in the next cubicle, the dad in the next pew. We shook hands all around.

Prison-visit conversations in the movies are usually about lawyers, revenge, escape plans, or the smuggling in of contraband, but Larry and Adam talked about crocheting. Using only the bent-over end of a Bic pen cap, Larry had been practicing the art for the entire eighteen years he'd been at GDCP. In those years he'd made, as he put it, "a bit of everything," including stuffed animals (which Sister Mary Jude sold for him), a curtain with an openwork image of Jesus's face for the backdoor of his sister's house, and an entire baptismal gown for Adam's parish. I'd seen the lovely piece on Adam's baby son, Ian, at his christening; it looked like the chef d'oeuvre of an elderly French lacemaker.

I knew that Larry was more than an artisan. Irreligious all his life, he entered the Catholic church in 2000 under the guidance of a local priest and deacon. He began attending mass in the prison barbershop, and since then, he had become a spiritual presence on death row; even the prison administrators knew it. Four months before we met him, the authorities moved him into a cell next to Robert Hicks, a mentally retarded inmate whose execution date was fast approaching. Larry's gentle counsel and his prayers had, he was sure, helped bring Robert peace at the end.

The rules didn't allow me to bring any sort of recording device into the prison, even pen and paper, and our time was running out anyway. All I could do was register Larry's profound peace of mind, his gentle cheerfulness, and his courtesy. ("Can you believe he asked us how our flight to Atlanta was?" Adam marveled later. "A guy on death row wanted to know if we'd been comfortable on our bloody airplane.")

Larry and I corresponded by mail after our visit, and Sister Mary Jude let me look at the trove of letters she received from him, beginning in spring 2001. Larry writes fluently and well in a small, precise, almost old-fashioned hand, and he is a powerful storyteller. His personal story rivals anything by Dostoevsky.

Larry Lee grew up in the housing projects of Savannah, the beautiful, notorious coastal city that has a reputation as the scapegrace sister of the more respectable Charleston. His alcoholic dad abandoned the family when Larry was six. "My father never came around, never paid child support, never even sent a birthday or Christmas card," Larry wrote me. His waitress mother struggled to support her five kids. "She loved her children, and she did the best she could with what she had," he wrote. "She didn't drink or take drugs or bring lots of men home. Most of my friends' mothers were drug addicts, alcoholics, and prostitutes."

Even though his mother had fewer mouths to feed when Larry's older brother, Bruce, got locked up and Elaine, his older sister, ran away from home, times stayed hard. "Some months we had no heat, other months no electricity," he wrote. "Because we moved so much (to avoid bill collectors), I don't remember ever spending a full year at any one school. Two things I did learn to do at an early age were to fight and to steal. I had to fight to protect my younger brother and sister. I began to steal so we could have candy and board games."

By fifth grade, Larry was a pot smoker and a "huffer," sniffing airplane glue for the high. "I was eleven when my friend's sister suffocated while sniffing spray paint with us," he wrote. "I had seen people shot and stabbed before, but this was my first experience with death. Instead of shocking me into being a good kid, the experience caused me to believe I was going to die before I reached eighteen. This was a common belief among my friends.

"I began stealing everything I could get my hands on, and I took every drug that came around. I told myself I was having fun, but I was just hiding from the pain of reality as I knew it. I ended up going to reform school twice for theft and drugs."

At fifteen, after his second reform-school stint, Larry settled down, relatively speaking. He dropped out of high school, worked "a thousand different jobs," and used and dealt dope. "I managed to stay out of jail until I was twenty," he wrote.

His first adult prison term was the climax of a botched adventure in 1980. He and a friend took off for southern California on a lark. When their money ran out, they held up a liquor store in Ontario and were promptly caught. During his three-year sentence, Larry learned the baking trade and worked in a San Bernardino bakery after his release. He also got married—to a woman who had sold him speed. "In March, 1986, we moved to Savannah to get away from the drugs and fast life in California," Larry wrote. "By June she had had enough and moved back there."

Then Larry's downward spiral picked up speed. His brother Bruce proposed that he join Bruce and Bruce's wife, Sherry, for a burglary in Brunswick, Georgia, a small coastal town south of Savannah. The plan called for Sherry to drop the two men off at the house, whose occupants were away, and return a half-hour later. "While we were in the house, the owner came home with a friend," Larry wrote. "Bruce shot the owner, and the friend shot Bruce. Then he ran off. I wasn't in that part of the house, and when I got to Bruce, it was all over: he and the owner were dead. Not knowing what else to do, I ran. I ended up in Flagstaff, Arizona."

Terrified and exhausted, Larry eventually phoned his mother and told her the whole story. She advised him to turn himself in, and he agreed. "As much trouble as I had been in," he wrote, "I had never been in this sort of mess before. I knew I had not killed that man, but I felt very remorseful for what had happened. Nobody was supposed to die. I didn't even know Bruce had a gun with him."

While Larry was in jail awaiting trial, he was charged with a crime that had occurred two months before the abortive Brunswick robbery: the murder of restaurant owner Clifford Jones, his wife, and their fourteen-year-old son in the town of Jesup, about forty miles northwest of Brunswick. His accusers were Sherry (who implicated Bruce as well) and a prisoner who knew Larry in the lockup. "Sherry had a made a deal for immunity and, in return, told them whatever they wanted to hear," Larry said. "There was no evidence other than what she said and the testimony of a jail informant who said I 'confessed' to him while he was reading a Bible passage about confessing sins. A blatant lie. I was tried and convicted in November, 1987." Three months later, he pled guilty to the Brunswick crime and was sentenced to life—on top of being sentenced to death.

Larry's bitterness about the verdict had a religious dimension. "By the time my trial in Jesup ended," he told me, "I had a very negative feeling about Christians in general. The informant had used the Bible against me. During the opening and closing arguments, the DA spoke to the jury as if he were a Baptist preacher—hell and damnation if you don't convict, etcetera. And most of the jury were God-fearing church people. I pretty much decided it was all a fraud or God really hated me.

"When I reached death row, I was so bitter, angry, and hurt it was unreal. I railed against God and anyone who dared to mention him around me. To me, religion was all a big lie created by rich people for their own benefit. Over time I calmed down outwardly, but inside the hate was eating me alive. Deep inside of me I felt this need for something, anything, to quiet the rage. By the time I read an article about Pope John Paul II taking a stand against the death penalty, I was very close to committing suicide.

"That one article planted a seed of hope in me. It was several years before I actually went to my first mass. But that one article caused me to rethink my view of Christians and their faith."

When the Pope visited the United States and Mexico a number of years later, Larry was impressed to see that the pontiff was walking his talk; John Paul convinced the governor of Oklahoma to save a condemned man from execution. "And it wasn't just that," he wrote. "It was the sincerity and dignity with which he spoke and carried himself." Larry decided to look into Catholicism.

Larry began attending mass in the barbershop. He explored his growing faith with the mass celebrants, Father Austin Fogarty of Saint James's church in nearby McDonough, Georgia, and deacon Tom Silvestri, the GDCP Catholic chaplain. "They were very open and warm and made me feel like I belonged there," wrote Larry. "I expected them to try to pressure me into becoming Catholic or accepting Jesus as my savior or something, but they didn't do that." Instead they patiently answered Larry's many questions. Silvestri lent Larry "a ton of books about Catholicism and church history, which led to more questions. What I was asking, I considered to be educational stuff, but somewhere along the way (after *hundreds* of questions), I started to believe what I was learning." Larry was accepted into the church on December 7, 2000.

Larry's last question for Silvestri was the big one: "If God loves me so much, why was I allowed to be sentenced to death for a crime I did not commit?" Of course, Tom couldn't speak for God, but he explained how all humans are given free will in this life, and while God does love us, he wants it to be our choice to love him. Humans—being very hardheaded—sometimes have to get themselves into very difficult situations before they realize they need help and turn to God. And God is willing to forgive us at a moment's notice because of what Jesus did long ago.

" 'Remember, Larry,' he said, 'Jesus was condemned and executed for something *he* didn't do. He never committed *any* sort of crime.'

"Granted, my situation is extreme, but you know, Jon, it almost had to be for me to call out for his love and forgiveness. My faith is still a work in progress, but the absolute, terrible fear of dying and all the bitterness and hatred it fueled are gone now."

It's clear that one of the main reasons Larry has been able to escape the death grip of his darkest emotions is his active love for others, particularly other death row inmates. His letters to Sister Mary Jude Jun are full of concern for the lives and souls of those about to die and those whose lives the state has taken. Nowhere was this clearer than in his ministry to Robert Hicks. Larry's letter to Sister Mary Jude chronicling Hicks's last hours is worth quoting at length:

Dear Sister Mary Jude,

Greetings to you, my dear friend. I hope this letter finds you and all the sisters there doing well.

It is with a sad heart that I have to tell you that my mentally challenged friend, Robert Hicks, was executed by the state on July 1 at 5 P.M. . . .

As you know, I was moved over here to this cell block to spend his final two weeks with him. It was the only mercy the state showed toward him, but he was so happy to see me when I came in the door! We just sat around and talked about our seventeen-year journey together—the good and the bad.

He told me on his final day that he had been watching me since I became a Catholic, and he decided that he liked how I had changed, and he believed that my God and my faith were real. He asked me how he could get to heaven so he could be with God, and with me when I got there. So I asked him if he had ever been baptized. . . . He is covered there, thank God. I was in a bit of a panic because there was no time to arrange for him to see a priest. So—Lord forgive me if I did this wrong—I prayed and talked to him about the church, and I told him how Christ came to Earth as a man to preach the gospel; how he was crucified and raised from the dead by God, and how, because of this sacrifice, we could all receive salvation through repentance of sins and God's merciful grace and forgiveness. But you have to repent and open your heart and let this love in. . . . I asked him to say a silent prayer and tell God how sorry he was for all the bad things he had ever done, to ask God to forgive him, and claim him as his child.

After he was finished, I told him: Robert, before they put you to sleep over there, they are going to ask you if you have anything to say. . . . The girl's family will be there, and don't you think it would be a good idea to tell them how sorry you are? He said Yes, God would want that too. I told him: After that I want you to ask God again to forgive you and ask him to come and get you. Then close your eyes and go to sleep.

He told me he would do that too, Sister.

And that night, on the TV news, he did exactly what I asked. . . . His victim's family said they were thankful he apologized to them, relieved that it was over, and they took no pleasure in his death.

That was the hardest thing I ever had to do, Sister. I can only hope that my humble fumbling around was enough to get my friend Robert to God. . . . I think God touched his heart because I could see it in his eyes—he was not afraid anymore. . . .

It has been a couple of days now, and I have been grieving his loss, Sister. After seventeen years of living with him daily, it has been difficult not seeing him anymore. However, my grief is, not for him, but for myself and the horrible society that could kill a man like Robert and call it justice. Forgive them, Lord, they know not what they do. . . .

Well, I need to close and catch the mail. Please know of my deep gratitude for your support and all the prayers. Lots of love.

Larry

When I find myself nursing regret for the fifteen years that my active alcoholism stole from my life and bemoaning the late start of my career as a writer, I try to remember Larry Lee's graceful, grateful way of accepting the circumstances of his own deeply troubled life. He sees those circumstances as probably the only way that a hardheaded young man could have found the grace of God. I try to remember that arrogance, selfishness, isolation, and fear of life ruled my thoughts and actions before alcohol brought me low. The wound alcohol inflicted was a sacred one that enabled me to find the humility to open myself, however hesitantly and intermittently, to life's beauty and God's truth. I don't believe that there's a single person on Earth who doesn't bear a sacred wound. We all carry the pain we need to humble us and open us to joy.

And as for Jesus of Nazareth—well, I certainly can't think of anyone who better understood that failure and brokenness are the keys to the kingdom of God, that the lost and sinful are closer to God than the successful and virtuous—simply because the lost and sinful have a greater need. As I spoke to the people in this book, it became clearer and clearer to me that my *need* for God is more convincing than any argument for God's "objective" existence. God is that finality which my soul seeks, the safety net into which I can cast my fears. I believe that the way I found God was by casting those fears—experimentally—into the hands of some greatness I called God and then finding those fears transformed into an inner strength, a strength not my own.

It may have been nothing more than a psychological trick, a sort of auto-hypnosis. But the tenor of the experience, the feel of it, was different from a simple change of mind or mood. It went deeper, and it has lasted far longer. At the very least, my early encounters with the Power I call God felt like closeness to reality, nearness to the ground of Being. And that nearness has transformed me, as it has transformed Larry, from a lost soul into a useful human being.

BE INTIMATE WITH GOD

Tina and Tom Engstrom

"If you had told me ten years ago how rich my relationship with God would be today, how much that relationship would bring into my life," said Tina Engstrom, "I would have told you that you were crazy. In those days, I wondered, is God really 'close to us,' or is that just a phrase? I couldn't have guessed then how *intimate* my relationship with God would become."

Tina is bright-eyed, a bundle of energy, eager to speak. Her husband, Tom, has a more deliberately-paced personality: a quiet voice, a reticent manner. "Yes," he said. "I'm amazed at the specific ways God has directed me, the corners He's taken me around, the specific things He's put in place."

The young couple work for the evangelical organization Campus Crusade for Christ in Ashland, Wisconsin, a cheerfully bohemian small town on Chequamegon Bay, an inlet of Lake Superior. Ashland is home to two campuses, the four-year Northland College and Wisconsin Indianhead Technical College, a two-year institution. Tina and Tom counsel students in both schools.

We met in the Black Cat Coffee House just off the main drag in Ashland. It's well-known among alternative types in the Midwest for its made-from-scratch organic food and its countercultural-but-community-friendly atmosphere—the former blue-collar bar still serves beer along with cappuccinos and lattes. While children played, writers tapped away at laptops, and tables full of mainstream and bohemian locals chatted, we talked about God. The God who animates and directs the Engstroms' lives is very much a God of love, acceptance, and intimacy, and you can sense it in the peaceful energy they exude.

Tina's "walk with God" (a metaphor they both use often) began in college—University of Wisconsin-Eau Claire—and with a dilemma. Confronted with the brand-new freedoms of the college freshman, she found that the decisions she was making were making her miserable. "I was in the driver's seat, and I was out to make myself happy," she said, "whatever that meant: the party scene, dating. I was trying to fill an emptiness in my heart. But the more I tried to fill myself up with those things—pleasures of the moment—the more emptiness and loneliness I felt."

Tina was a well-adjusted girl with the support of a loving family. Her father is Cliff Smith, the skillful personal coach who helped my interviewee Cynthia Williams find her way (see p. 117). Before Tina's departure for college, Cliff had given her a ring to remind her of her childhood love for God and her need for a spiritual life. "I think he had lost touch with his faith for a while in college and he didn't want me to," she said. "But I turned my back. And I remember thinking, if this is all there is to the world, well, it's not so good, and I don't like it.

"I had a friend who was an atheist. He took me aside one day and said, 'Now Tina, I don't know what this means, and I don't believe this for myself, but I know you are happier when you have God inside you.'

" 'I don't know what to say,' I told him.

" 'I don't either. I'm still an atheist, and I don't want to talk about God, but for you, it's different.'

"Well, I knew enough to realize that God must be speaking through my friend, that God was trying to get my attention. I had a roommate who was more or less at the same stage of being broken-hearted about the world, a woman who had had a hard life and suffered from depression. We talked about the Bible, how some people opened it at random and got guidance for each day that way. We were sort of on the outskirts of faith looking in."

Then Tina's roommate left school, Tina got pneumonia during finals week, and, as she put it, "I hit rock bottom. I got on my knees, and I said,

'God, I don't want to take control of my life anymore. I'm sick of trying to make myself happy. I give you my whole life. I don't know what that means, but would you please come here and come into my heart?'

"Up to that moment, I had never felt God's presence, but I did then. It was like a huge hug. The hopelessness was gone; my despair lifted. I wondered if it was my imagination."

Tina tested the truth of her experience by working at a Christian youth camp that summer and found that she enjoyed being around people of faith. Returning to Eau Claire in the autumn, she roomed with a woman she knew from her partying days but who had had a conversion experience over the summer. The pair attended a huge return-to-campus party, then did a sort of check-in with each other.

Tina and her friend realized that neither one of them really wanted to be at the party. "My friend said, 'I guess my eyes were opened to the despair and hopelessness that was there. I didn't have much of a desire to go back.' With her and with other people from the Inter-Varsity Christian Fellowship, I prayed for the people around us and on our dorm floor. We prayed that they would experience forgiveness and the love that God had for them."

Another person Tina knew in the Inter-Varsity group at Eau Claire was Tom Engstrom. "I had a crush on his best friend," she said with a smile. "But then, after Tom graduated, we started e-mailing each other. For three or four years we were friends, until people we knew said, 'Come on, why don't you just call it *dating*?' "

The man Tina was just-about-dating was a convinced Christian who, nonetheless, was reticent to share his faith with others. Born in the Ashland area, Tom grew up in a devout home. During his college years, he struggled "to decide that my faith was *my own*. I was exposed to many different belief systems, and more and more I realized I was choosing the Christian life for myself, not because of my parents. And then I started asking God what he wanted from my life. What *I* wanted was a daily relationship with Him; I wanted to walk with God."

When he graduated in 1996, he was at loose ends. He told me, "I said to God, 'I just want to follow you, but I don't know what that means.' "

Then, like many a restless American youth, he took a trip to Mexico with a friend. Needless to say, tequila and magic mushrooms were not on the agenda; for these born-again kids, the trip was about holiness, not hedonism. They hooked up with a group called Youth in Mission and worked at one of the group's churches, which was part of the burgeoning evangelical Protestant movement south of the border. It was Tom's first taste of bona fide mission work, and it set him wondering whether that was his calling. "After I came home, I checked out some mission options," he said, "but nothing fell into place. I was back in Ashland, working this factory job. It was the last place I wanted to be. I wanted to experience other places in the world. But I also wanted to do what God would have me do. So I told God, 'I feel like you've put a burden on my heart to do ministry in some way. But if you just want me to do this job, right here, I'll stay. I want to be content with where you have me.' "

This kind of radical acceptance of one's situation as God's will is one of the most authentically "countercultural" elements of Christian spirituality (and of other spiritualities too, of course). A particularly frustrating product of our secular culture, with its fixed idea that the autonomous individual should invent his or her own destiny, is a perpetual anxiety about making something called the right choice. The incessant bass note of actual or potential dissatisfaction that runs under all our choices can drive us crazy.

There's an odd alchemy in being content with where God has you right now and choosing what you already have: it actually makes changing your life easier when the time comes. It can be easier to leave something you accept than something you resent, especially if you invest so much energy in that resentment that the bad thing starts to become a fixture in your psyche. This Christian acceptance has given Tina and Tom an ability to change the course of their lives without the angst and confusion that plague most of us who have abandoned Life Plan A for B, C, or D.

On a trip to Eau Claire to visit Tina during their non-dating dating period, Tom ran into Darryl, a guy he knew from his Mexico sojourn. Darryl, a youth pastor, was organizing a group of men to return to Mexico to do church construction and evangelical work. He invited Tom along, and the group spent a week building a church bathroom and handing out food and Bibles. Darryl and the trip had a lasting effect on Tom.

"He challenged me," said Tom. "At the end of our trip, he took me aside and said he felt that God wanted him to pass something on to me—that God might have plans for me to become a youth minister." Tom was shocked at the suggestion. "I was really impressed with the way Darryl worked, and I was sure I couldn't do it. But he planted a seed."

By this time, Tom had fallen in love with Mexico, and it wasn't long before he was putting together a group of high school–age kids from his own church, Salem Baptist in Ashland, to go south of the border. "We prayed for just one to sign up, and we got twelve," Tina put in.

"When the trip was over," said Tom, "I found that I had gotten to know these kids, and I wasn't too happy to say good-bye. I wondered if there was some way we could keep in touch." He began volunteering at Salem as a youth worker, and when the church's youth pastor position opened up, Tom took the job. A few years later, Campus Crusade contacted him to be their representative in Ashland, and he added that commitment to his life. Eventually, he went full-time with the Crusade.

Tom is a quiet and reserved man, the antithesis of the glad-handing, booming-voiced evangelist. He had to overcome a spiritual shyness in order to become a minister. "I really did sort of tiptoe into ministry," he said. "For a long time, I had a hard time speaking with others about my faith. I just wanted to live my life to please God—and not talk about it! I had a fear of what others would think of me. I didn't want to stand out. But there are so many people around me who don't know God and are struggling because of that. So many are seeking and wanting to know. They have certain perceptions of Christianity, and unless someone takes the time to tell them what the Gospel is really all about, they may never hear it. Is it right, I asked myself, to sit back and wait until they ask me? Is sharing my faith as important to me as it needs to be?

"I had to ask God to give me more of a passion to share with people, to make it more of a real and daily thing. I asked God to put a burden on my heart. And God did stir up that desire in me."

The Engstroms' conviction that their paths through life have been guided by clear messages from an intimately present God was tested when Tina had two miscarriages. "I knew that others experienced hard things—much harder things—but I had been *so* protected, and my heart had been so set on a child," she said. "I would cry until I felt I had no more tears left and then cry some more. It made me question what it meant to be a Christian. I thought that, if you were really faithful, God would keep you safe from these major mishaps. I was wrong about that, but what I learned during that experience was the depth of God's love. On a daily, even an hourly basis, we felt God's closeness."

I asked Tina how she sensed His presence.

"In a lot of ways," she replied without a pause. "I would happen on a passage of scripture or a song that was just what I needed. 'You understand sorrow because you went into the depths of sorrow for us. But sorrow doesn't last forever.' "

"During the worst of it, I would just feel peace at certain moments," Tom added. "And God would send people into our lives to be with us, to walk with us."

Tina suffered complications during her third pregnancy but gave birth to a healthy son, David.

"While I was carrying him," Tina told me, "in the fifth or sixth month, I prayed, 'Lord, if this child is not going to come into the world, it's okay with me. I know you are in control.' And then I got this picture of us baptizing him, and I heard God say that this child was not our own but a gift from Him, and He would show us how to raise and love him.' Now, maybe it was my imagination, my way of dealing with my fear— but I felt Him speaking to me, just as He had sent people, images, and scripture passages into our lives.

"Having gone through my own pain has helped me help others. So many people have undergone something hard or hurtful in their lives, and they're *stuck* there. One student I talked to was very angry and bitter over a situation in her life, and all of her decisions came out of that anger and bitterness. She needed someone to walk beside her and say 'I'm sorry you had to go through that; it must have been awful. But God doesn't want you to live in that pain.' She thought that God wanted her to suffer. But God created us and loves us and wants to be with us. He isn't surprised or taken aback or angry when we make mistakes. So many people have this warped picture of God as *distant,* and it keeps them from embracing him.

"Another girl I knew said: 'I can't become a Christian because it means I have to give up some of my friendships and lose drinking and smoking.' I told her yes, God might challenge you on some of those things, but He's not out to get you."

"He challenges you," said Tom, "because He wants the best for you, and He knows that those things are not going to be fulfilling for you. People think that being a Christian is nothing more than having this list of do's and don'ts. But, as parents, we know that there are certain things we don't want our son to do—not because we're mean parents, but because we love him and want the best for him."

"People believe in a legalistic God who is pointing a finger, and they try to prove to Him that they're doing the right thing," said Tina. "There was another student I talked to, a young woman who was super quiet and shy; when she spoke, you could hardly hear her. She was from the South and didn't know anyone at school. She joined our group, at least partly, to make some friends, and she soon did.

"But I could tell she was wrestling with something, and one day she told me what it was. She had this phrase in her head from childhood: 'Give God your best, and He'll do the rest.' What she heard that to mean was: You need to be almost perfect before you can ask God's help. 'Tina,' she said, 'I try and try, and I can never get there. So I can't ask for God's help.'

"I said, 'Honey, that's not what it means! Jesus went to the cross so that you could know forgiveness. He knew you weren't going to be perfect.'

" 'Do you mean I can ask Him at any time, any moment?' she asked. Tears were running down her face.

" 'Of course,' I said. 'You haven't disappointed God. God loves that you ask for help. That's what He lives for, for you to cry out His name.' "

The loving intimacy of the Engstroms' relationship with God and Christ contrasts vividly with what I consider to be one of the biggest misunderstandings or distortions of Christian belief, both inside and outside of church: the idea that we are in the world to earn God's love by being good.

Most of us who were raised within Christian culture in America, whether we were Catholics or Protestants, got the same message: original sin, that taint passed down from Adam and Eve, meant that we were bad little boys and girls who needed to struggle to be good little boys and girls in order to please Jesus and earn our eternal reward. A popular personality on the conservative Catholic television network EWTN recently put this doctrine succinctly: "No holiness, no heaven."

But Jesus blessed and healed without checking the sufferer's moral or religious credentials. (About half of the people he healed in the four Gospels weren't even Jews.) On those occasions, he usually told the healed that their faith—not their moral goodness—had made them whole. And Saint Paul articulated the forbidding-sounding but actually joy-bringing idea of justification by faith: we are all sinners, that is, all separated from God, and our perverse wills increase and prolong the separation. (My foibles, manias, and inabilities, including the inability to pray when I most need to, are all the proof I need of that.) But far from holding that we ought to, or could, close the gap between God and ourselves by our own efforts, Paul says that it is the crucified Jesus who has, once and for all, justified us—that is, acquitted us of our guilt. An ebullient gospel song, "Jesus Dropped the Charges," summarizes the doctrine in its title and chorus.

We're too weak to be good on our own, at the mercy of our vacillating minds and inconstant hearts, and we can't earn God's forgiveness and love because, wonder of wonders, they have already been granted. We can only let the bizarre and wonderful truth into our hearts and lives: we're hopeless screwups, but we are deeply loved anyway, and everyone else is too, including everyone we don't like. Our job is not to try to get what has already been freely given, but to respond in deep gratitude and live according to this miraculous situation: forgiving again and again as we have been forgiven, loving tirelessly as we have been loved. Anybody who thinks this is a cop-out, or too easy, or not enough of a challenge, should try it for two hours.

Find a Practice That Works for You

James W. Jones

One of the things I keep relearning as I wander on and off the spiritual path is how tricky the matter of the intellect is. In any effort to come to terms with the true immensity of What Is—which for me necessarily includes God—the intellect is both a necessity and a hindrance. While most religious traditions assert that the Divine is somehow beyond rational thought, no one recommends irrationality, the complete sacrifice of the mind, which, if it were possible, would probably be madness. For most orthodox Christians, the idea of mystery marks the frontier between what the intellect can and can't do with propositions like the Trinity and the dual nature of Christ.

Episcopal priest, theologian, practitioner of Tibetan Buddhism, and psychologist James W. Jones suggests a novel way to approach these mysteries. Professor of religion and adjunct professor of clinical psychology at Rutgers, he's written nine books, most recently *Waking from Newton's Sleep: Dialogues on Spirituality in an Age of Science* (Wipf & Stock Publishers, 2006). We met on a raw, windy day in late February in Long Branch, New Jersey, where he lives in a seaside condo. Over coffee we talked about his life and faith, and his conviction that the life of faith is more a series of actions than a mere pattern of beliefs. Any pattern of belief will weaken and die if it isn't supported by disciplined action: prayer, liturgy, service to others.

When it comes to mysteries of faith, Jones suggests that their effect on the believer is more important than whether or not the believer can fully understand them. "In Tibetan and other forms of Buddhism, when you reach a certain point, you take a set of vows called Bodhisattva vows," he said. "And one of them is that you will not teach about Emptiness, one of the most difficult Buddhist concepts, to the spiritually immature. I wish we took a vow in Christianity that we wouldn't talk about the dual nature of Christ or the Trinity with the spiritually immature because these are not philosophical concepts, they're contemplative strategies.

"They're not intellectual Ping-Pong balls to bop back and forth. They're things to contemplate, to think about in a meditative state of mind, not constructing an argument in a linear sense. The creed is not a philosophical statement. It's a liturgical statement. A contemplative strategy. If you put yourself in a contemplative state of mind and you focus on the two natures of Christ or the opening chapter of the Gospel of John—"In the beginning was the Word"—and you do that for a while, what thoughts come into your mind? What feelings are generated? When you're done, twenty minutes later, do you feel different physically?"

Jones is a tall man who combines three qualities not always found together: an obvious physical vigor, the fluent and articulate speech of a well-trained intellectual, and an openness to others. As spiritual inquirer and therapist, he is a skillful question asker and was as interested in this book as I was in his views of God and faith. Our interview was more like a wide-ranging, free-form conversation.

Jones had a paradoxical childhood. Born and raised in the Detroit area, he entered adolescence as a problem kid. Expelled from junior high for hitting a teacher who was attempting to discipline him, he ended up in a strict private academy with high academic standards. Genuinely challenged at school for the first time, he shone academically—but hung out with the hoods too, drag racing and partying on the weekends to the beat of Chuck Berry and Elvis. Despite his stellar school record, the academy eventually kicked him out as well—and the result was a catastrophic blowup at home. Jones, in classic Beat-era style, hit the road. He worked odd jobs and lived in his car. For a while he stayed with a friend's family in northern Michigan, working as a mechanic in a gas station. His hosts insisted that he reconnect with his family, and he did, though he still refused to return to Detroit. Instead, he toured college campuses across the Midwest, determined to get back on an academic track. His eventual choice, Earlham in northern Indiana, turned out to be perfect for a smart kid with personal problems: it was a rigorous school with a caring and approachable faculty.

It was also the perfect place and time to experience the sixties. Quaker-connected Earlham was a political campus, and it wasn't far from Ann Arbor, Michigan, where Jones had friends. He was present at the founding of Students for a Democratic Society (SDS) in Ann Arbor in 1960 and took part in New Left conventions and demonstrations around the country. He also went south to visit the Highlander Folk School in Tennessee, one of the seedbeds of the Civil Rights movement.

After two years in this heady political atmosphere, Jones realized that he was spending a lot more time on the barricades than in the library, and he wanted to reclaim the academic side of his education. And something else was going on too. "I felt a certain dissatisfaction that I can only articulate in retrospect," he told me. "I felt that the politics I had been involved in were not going to produce the kind of change I was wishing for. Some kind of deeper transformation was called for. It was a questioning of my own personal history and also whether politics was a real vocation for me. So, partly because I was pretty debilitated emotionally, I didn't go back to college that year. I decided to take a year off and go into psychotherapy for the first of several times—and I lived in Detroit and worked in a library."

He may have left Earlham, but Jones wasn't about to stay out of politics or the classroom altogether. He made contacts with politically active people in Detroit and took some night-school classes, including one in philosophy that was to have major consequences for his spiritual life. "The professor was a very angry skeptic, on a tear about religion all the time," he told me. "And there was this coterie of students—they were probably evangelicals—who just rose to the bait again and again. They weren't his intellectual equals, especially when it came to knowing how arguments are put together, and it was sort of like watching somebody shoot skeet. I had no stake in this—I was neither a militant atheist nor a devout religious person—but it did hit me that the professor's skeptical arguments weren't all that well grounded either and that if he examined his own premises with as much fierceness as he examined everybody else's, they probably couldn't stand up. So that got me thinking."

At around the same time, Jones met the Episcopal priest, playwright, and author Malcolm Boyd, who would later write *Are You Running With Me, Jesus?*, a book of prayers in modern language touching on contemporary concerns that was to become a minor spiritual classic of the sixties. At the time, Boyd was serving as Episcopal chaplain at Wayne State University in downtown Detroit and doing civil rights and other social-justice work in the city. "Originally, I had no religious connection with him," said Jones. But the two were frequently at the same political meetings. "And so, when I was taking this philosophy class and having these doubts about secularism, he was there at hand, willing to talk. He wasn't a philosopher, but he was a bright guy with a lot of integrity." Jones also began talking with a Catholic chaplain from Wayne State. It was the beginning of his reversed version of the classic tale of the young person brought up in a tradition of faith who begins to doubt it in college. Raised agnostic, Jones began to wonder about the foundations of the strictly secular world view.

"It was a sort of figure-ground shift," he said. "I realized that, if you assume certain skeptical premises, you'll come out with a skeptical conclusion—there's no great surprise there. But why start from those premises? Why not at least examine them? In my mind, the burden of proof suddenly shifted from the religious frame of reference to the skeptical frame. I realized that the professor in my class was just assuming this frame because, well, he was the professor, and I knew it wouldn't do. I started to read philosophy of religion and church history."

When Jones returned to Earlham to finish his degree, it wasn't long before he underwent a full-blown spiritual crisis. You could call it an intellectual crisis too since he was simultaneously losing his grip on the intense intellectuality that had characterized his thought-life for many years. Jones was groping for a way to live at a deeper and truer level. "The student political movement was still going on, but I was much more marginal to it," he said, "not because I didn't believe in its goals, but because I was ambivalent about whether this was the best way to do things. It was also a period of tremendous ferment—I was in this religious quest mode, taking courses in religion and reading things I had never known existed. The power of the purely cognitive began to weaken—and that really did feel like a crisis. I had had the false expectation that all the important issues in life were intellectual. But now I was sensing that the mind can't carry the weight of your whole life."

What might have been a liberating realization was, for Jones, a dark night of the soul. "I just felt myself sinking into this despair," he said.

"Nowadays we don't necessarily differentiate between despair and depression—the clinical word has taken over the other senses. But as someone who knows something about depression in the clinical sense as well as the classical sense of despair, I can tell you that what I was feeling was not depression! It wasn't something that Prozac or psychotherapy would have done much for. I felt myself sinking down and sinking down, and I reached the point where I said to myself, I don't know if I am going to get out of this. It wasn't like I was going to kill myself—I just felt I wanted to sit down and let myself dwindle down to one point. I was at the end of my rope and there was nothing to be done.

"It was then that I suddenly had this experience of some vitalization, some energy, some life, coming into me from outside of anything I could possibly have constructed or willed or made happen. It was a kind of energizing of things. It was very transformative. I suddenly popped up and things looked different and felt different; *I* looked different and felt different."

It was the ego-deflation at depth that precedes the first light of a spiritual awakening. It made all the difference to Jones; in its light, he completed college and enrolled in theological school. But looking back on it today, he realizes how fragile and ephemeral the pure experience was because, at the time, he had no sustaining spiritual practice to keep reminding him of its power, and he didn't know where to seek guidance. "Nobody I knew had heard of anything like spiritual direction," he told me. "There were classical texts on it, but very few of them were in English translation—and this was also long before the great influx of Buddhism and its practices into America. So a discrete spiritual experience, like the one I had, just dissipated because there was no way of nurturing it."

As a student of theology, though, he discovered a set of devout men who were able to meld a vigorous spiritual discipline with sophisticated philosophy and theology: the Church Fathers, those writers and preachers of the early Church who struggled to forge Christian doctrine and create a distinctive Christian spirituality. "One of the things that was appealing to me about the early fathers was that they were both spiritual practitioners and brilliant philosophers and theologians," he said. "They saw no conflict. One of the problems in our post-Enlightenment age— one that's done a lot of mischief in religion—is the separation of theory and practice. That's partly because of the hegemony of the physical sciences; science really separates what you know from who you are. And both philosophy and theology have taken a scientific turn too—toward abstractions.

"You read books of theology or the philosophy of religion and they are pretty 'experience-distant,' to put it mildly; really abstract. Or you can go to a Pentecostal church or a New Age gathering and there's a lot of experience but it's not very digested, it's not very reflected-upon. And one of the things I saw in the fathers is their conviction that you have to keep experience and theory together. Years and years later, I encountered the Tibetan Buddhists—they also have a very long tradition of very sophisticated philosophical reflection, but it's very tightly rooted in their spiritual practice. What I saw through looking at Buddhism was that *practice* is the missing piece in our religious lives."

But Jones's critique of contemporary religion goes deeper. In the last three or four decades, he feels, North America has secularized so rapidly that millions of people have lost touch with what a genuine religious tradition is all about.

"So the field of Christianity is left to the noisiest and the most media savvy to define," he said. "Many people are doing this noisy defining with a political purpose. And the press, which knows nothing about religion, has seized on the noise and the battle, created this dramatic but simplistic dichotomy between secularism on the one hand and fundamentalism on the other—as if those were the only alternatives. The contemplative tradition, the tradition of meditative practices in Christianity, is one solid alternative to secularism, fundamentalism, and the moralism that makes faith nothing other than a list of dos and don'ts."

Contemplation—quiet sitting in the presence of mystery—*transforms* the sitter/contemplator; and for Jones, that's a key word in understanding Christianity. Christianity is a religion of transformation, at the cosmic and personal levels. "There's a universal process of change going on," he said. "There's a spiritual dimension, a spiritual grounding, to the physical world, and the physical world is becoming more and more open to its spiritual source—and hopefully, that will become more and more apparent to all of us. What you have in Christ is the incarnation, the exemplification of that cosmic process of transformation. To me, that's what the sacraments are about too—another exemplification of this process whereby the physical becomes the bearer of the spiritual—bread, wine, oil, sexual relations, the laying on of hands—all of these very physical things become the bearers of a spiritual presence or a spiritual reality . . . and you see that most clearly in Jesus—a physical person who was the bearer of, the expression of, a spiritual or divine reality.

"What spiritual practice does is facilitate that same process of transformation in each of us individually, so that each of us become more transparently a bearer or expression of a spiritual presence in how we conduct our life."

Be a Spiritual Explorer

Joyce Rupp

I was born in Iowa, and like most Iowans who live elsewhere, I still consider the place home and think of it as a kind of touchstone; returning to the Hawkeye State is a way of measuring myself, of assessing what has changed inside me as I pass through a familiar and slow-to-change rural landscape. I was happy to learn that one of my most likely interviewees lived in Des Moines, a four-hour trip on the interstate.

In an e-mail to me, Joyce Rupp had described herself as "an extreme introvert," and as I approached her house for an interview, I guessed that she had found herself an ideal dwelling place: a small house tucked almost out of sight in a leafy cul-de-sac on a quiet residential street in Iowa's capital. Rupp turned out to be quiet but not shy, a Catholic sister (Servite Order), who peacefully but fearlessly enunciates a spirituality that is grounded in her inherited Catholicism but goes well beyond the perspectives favored by Rome.

She poured me a glass of iced tea and listened patiently as I did my usual fumbling job of explaining what this book is about. One of the first things she wanted to clarify when we began talking was the difference between her religion and her faith. "I look at faith as bigger than religion," she said. "Faith is the core belief that really grounds me in the way I do my life."

The sixty-two-year-old Rupp, whose round face is crowned with gray curls and whose voice is soft but rarely hesitant, has dedicated herself to pushing out the frontiers of her faith with great boldness. She has written many books, spoken at conferences, and led retreats all over the country and abroad—hardly the career of a typical introvert. She's exposed herself to the displeasure of conservative bishops by formulating a spirituality based on Holy Wisdom (Santa Sophia), a spiritual force—well-attested in the Bible—that appears to be feminine.

Rupp blurs the line between the faithful Christian and the spiritual quester open to many faiths. She practices Vipassana meditation daily and treasures the insights of Sufism, the mystical strain in Islam. "And yet," she hastened to add, "I find myself measuring everything by the precepts and the life of Jesus." At the same time, she's convinced that the mantra-like repetition of Jesus's name in Christian churches has put believers into a sort of trance in which it's hard to see and hear the authentic Christ. "We've Jesus-ed everybody to death," she told me.

Growing up Catholic on an Iowa farm, Rupp found that the beauty of the land and the presence of nature had as much impact on her as any other spiritual force. A natural rebel, she often found herself in the bad graces of the elderly sisters who taught in her three-room Catholic school. And then, one day, a change came. "A very young sister replaced one of the older ones," she said. "All I remember of that year was that she talked about Jesus in very personal terms, and she kept emphasizing that this Jesus was our friend. I don't remember her talking about any *rules* at all. I was so thrilled that I took Jesus on as my companion—the way children adopt invisible friends." She would talk to Jesus as she fed the chickens.

"I grew out of that once I was ten or eleven, of course," she recalled. "But something happened to me in terms of my relationship with the divine, and I have to say I've never really lost that. I've had lots of questions about what to name this God, but I've never been to rock bottom where I felt that there wasn't anything to connect to, even if it was just an essence of love. And even later, when I was struggling with the masculine language of the church, patriarchal language like 'Lord' and the rest of it, I still kept a sense of that essence."

Her sense of the divine notwithstanding, Rupp became a sister more or less in spite of herself. In her teens, she was already hearing the call to a religious life—while another part of her fought it tooth and nail. "All the way through high school I remember thinking about the religious life, being drawn to it, but at the same time afraid of it—thinking that it was the worst thing I could ever do! Nothing about it appealed to me." In part to quash the call, Rupp carefully avoided attending a Catholic college, enrolling instead in the University of Iowa. There, however, her destiny caught up with her. A speech professor, a practicing Catholic, took an interest in her. "One day," Rupp told me, "she called me into her office after class. It scared the willies out of me; I was homesick and nervous and sure I was flunking the class—or worse. But she just asked me about myself: my family, where I went to high school. I told her that I had gone to a Catholic one, and there were sisters teaching there.

" 'Is that what you're going to do when you get out of college?' she asked.

"I was just overwhelmed. How did this woman see this in me? I ended the conversation as quickly as I could and never let her get close to me again. I was so scared."

But Rupp found herself turning over the scary proposition in her mind until she decided, as she put it, "to make a bargain with God. I would go and try it. I knew I'd hate it; they'd probably kick me out. But at least I could say I tried." She struggled with the practical demands of her new life at first, but in her second, or novitiate, year, there was much more prayer and contemplation. She found herself falling in love with God and her new vocation.

The death of her brother in a fishing accident when he was twenty-three, and Rupp just two years older, threw her into a tailspin. It wasn't a crisis of faith—it didn't shake her belief in God—but it made her wonder what God wanted of her. "I had tried to be so *good*," she said. "I had entered religious life when I hadn't really wanted to, for crying out loud! I mean, just how good did I have to *be* so that life would go okay and awful things like this wouldn't happen?"

She wrestled with this issue for a full fifteen years, until she had an epiphany on the campus of Notre Dame, where she was doing graduate work. On one of the campus quads there stood a pietà, a sculptural image of the dying Christ in his mother's arms. "But it wasn't a nice, comfortable one like the one by Michelangelo," she recalled. "It was made of rough, welded metal." Rupp understood the message: the way of Christ was not around or above suffering but straight through it. "Looking at the sculpture," said Rupp, "I decided then and there that I had to do something to make sense of my life."

Rupp went on retreat for thirty days, following the Ignatian formula,

in which the retreatant imagines herself present at the various stages of
Christ's life, Passion, and death. When she pictured herself at the Passion, she asked herself, " 'Who am I to think I will never go through
pain?' I began to understand that God was on my side and that what was
happening to me was natural—just part of life itself, like the four sea-
sons. God doesn't cause our misfortunes. Accidents happen because of
circumstances. Illness happens because we have a body that's frail and
prone to them. The Divine is a loving, penetrating presence who is always for us and stays with us through whatever happens."

Soon Rupp would develop a special understanding of that loving presence. In the late eighties, a publisher contacted her to do a book on
women. She had no idea what to write about. She started a letter turning
down the offer while babysitting a friend's three-year-old daughter. The
little girl was playing in a rose garden, watering the flowers, and Rupp
was enchanted. Suddenly she remembered that she knew something
about Wisdom, a force or presence in both the Old and New Testaments
that had traditionally been interpreted as an attribute of God but was always referred to as "she." What about a book that explored this enig-
matic, quite possibly feminine, face of the divine? "What I learned only
later," she said, "was that the Book of Wisdom describes Wisdom as a little child dancing through creation."

Rupp researched Wisdom thoroughly, learning, among other things,
that the early Christians had prayed to her. When she showed the manuscript of what was to become *The Star in My Heart: Experiencing Sophia,
Inner Wisdom* to a friend who taught religious studies at Iowa State University, the professor was impressed, but she had a question: Is Sophia really another word for God?

"I told her I thought so," said Rupp, "but I was scared to say so. She
told me that I ought to come right out and declare what I believed."
Rupp did, and to this day, she prays to Sophia.

Like many unconventional Catholics, Rupp remains connected to the
traditions and rituals of the church even as she explores outside the lines
of its official doctrine. She's careful to point out that her Sophia spirituality isn't for everyone, and she defends her departures from the church's
straight-and-narrow by quoting another devout iconoclast, the New
Mexico–based artist and mystic Meinrad Craighead, who once declared
that she believes in Jesus—and in more than Jesus.

I find myself sympathetic to explorers like Rupp and Richard Rohr because they embody the principle that living religion needs to be an explo-

ration of changing reality, as well as a hallowing of tradition. Their opponents see a New Age contamination of pure doctrine, but the historical truth is that a good number of the saints and heroes of the faith were originally shocking innovators who faced immediate and strenuous resistance from the official church. I'm not referring to forgotten reformers or obscure theologians, but to Saint Francis, Saint John of the Cross, and Saint Thomas Aquinas, to name a few.

I asked Rupp to be my spiritual director for a few minutes. I often find myself struggling with the intellectual side of the Christian faith—things like the divinity of Jesus, which seems bizarre. How would she help me come closer to Christ?

She smiled. "I'd have you read a Gospel straight through," she said. "Probably Luke. I'd have you imagine the life of Jesus, that you were *in* it, very close to him. I'd have you imaginatively experience him. We respond to the divine with our whole selves, not just our minds. I'd have you connect what's in the Gospel with things from your own life. Anything to get you out of your head for a while."

As I drove home through the fragrant Iowa meadows and fields, breathing the bright, cool air, I was (for once) blissfully aware that my body takes in sustenance from all the elements, and my soul and mind take nourishment from a lot more than just ideas, and that Jesus himself is more than Jesus—more than any Jesus we can name, think, or even worship.

EXPECT MIRACLES

Thien-an Dang

Some people read the Bible, and then some people have experiences that seem positively Biblical. Thien-an Dang (known to his native-born American friends and co-workers in Fort Worth, Texas, as "Dan"), escaped from Vietnam in 1975, when he was fifteen. He and his family tried three times to make the eight-hour voyage down the Saigon River to its mouth in the South China Sea; all three times they were stopped by communist authorities, and all three times they claimed to be pro-regime naval irregulars, patrolling the river—a credible claim in the disorganized days right after the fall of Saigon. On one occasion, they lacked the red armbands that identified them as politically acceptable, so as a patrol boat approached them, they frantically tore Dang's younger brother's red T-shirt into seven strips.

Their final release allowed them the dubious privilege of spending twenty-seven days on the open ocean, with absolutely no idea whether they would live or die. "At a time like that, you pray a lot more than when you have freedom and are living your daily routine," he said, with a degree of understatement I could only envy. "I prayed to Jesus and said, 'I believe you are the living God. Please take care of my family. I really don't want to die on the ocean.'" When they reached Guam at around four in the morning, Dang said, "I praised God. And Jon—I meant it."

The forty-seven-year-old Dang is grateful enough to God, and not just for his release from Vietnam, that he gave up a cushy job as a Radio Shack executive—one of the top one hundred Radio Shack managers in the country, in fact—just five years shy of retirement and a stock-split deal that would have made him a multimillionaire. After a lot of prayer and family-consensus seeking, he went to work for the Roever Evangelistic Association (REA), a Fort Worth–based Christian ministry that brings medical teams to Vietnam and gives U.S. veterans of the Vietnam War a chance to visit the country and come to terms with it as a memory and a contemporary reality.

REA is the outgrowth of the personal evangelism of Dave Roever, who first saw Vietnam the hard way, in 1968, as a member of the "brown-water navy," the American sailors who ran patrol boats along Vietnam's rivers. A grisly accident—the explosion of a phosphorus grenade just inches from his face—left Roever frighteningly disfigured but alive; medevaced home, he recovered and returned to Vietnam in 1974, not as a soldier, but as a preacher of the Gospel.

As for Dang, he is not a convert, either to Christianity or Protestantism; he was born into the faith. His father was a pastor in a country that had, when he was growing up, about 65 million people but only 80,000 Protestants. As a preacher's kid, he was expected to take part in church services in the family's house on Sundays, parish activities on Wednesdays, and sit in the front row whenever visiting evangelists came to preach. He considered it all pretty routine. "My heart was empty," he said. That is, until Dave Roever came. "I remember what he said," Dang told me. "He said 'I came to Vietnam with an M-16; I've come back with John 3:16: God so loved the world that he sent his only-begotten son.' I thought that if anyone should be bitter about the Vietnamese, it would be him; but here he was."

Roever also stirred young Dang's conscience by suggesting that belief isn't enough. Even the devil believes in God, said the evangelist. What matters is wholehearted worship. He asked his listeners whether they were sure they had really asked Christ into their hearts, and it's a theme that has stayed with Dang ever since.

After his escape from his homeland, Dang went to college in the United States and passed through a period of religious questioning, wondering if he hadn't been too quick to embrace his father's faith—wondering if even the experience with Roever had been the real thing. After all, his evangelical Protestantism was a minority faith, not only in Vietnam but around the world. What about the ancestor worship at the heart of Vietnamese family religion and, thus, close to the heart of his identity as a Vietnamese? What about Buddhism and Catholic Christianity? With bookish fervor, he looked into them all but couldn't shake his conviction of the Bible's unique weight and authority and his sense that worshipping the God of the Protestant Christian tradition was worshipping a truly divine Divinity. Reverence for ancestors, the Buddha, and the Virgin Mary, all mere humans, seemed to him diversionary at best and idolatry at worst.

But more important than this rather intellectual comparative exercise was the visit that the Holy Spirit paid him late one night. At two in the morning, he suddenly remembered Dave Roever and John 3:16. "And Psalm 95 hit me, too," he said. "It says don't keep your heart so hard." He recalled his family's sea exodus to Guam, and the details of the experience suddenly felt like sacred symbols: "The red armbands seemed like the blood of Christ. Our release came on the third day, just as Jesus's resurrection had. And the flag our boat flew, which said SOS, came back to me as 'save, oh save.' "

Ever since, Dang has found more symbols and many small miracles cropping up in his daily life. At one point, his search for a job after college nearly drove him over the edge. Frustrated to the point of tears by unanswered queries, resumé mailings that led nowhere, and interviews that ended on that unmistakable "thank you for coming in" note, he began telling himself that he had absolutely no hope against the legions of native-born Americans he was up against, with their perfect English and their subtle sense of how things work in this huge, confusing country. Desperate to help his parents financially, he felt like a failure. Driving home from one particularly depressing interview in Omaha, he let himself turn the wheel toward an immense tree and stepped on the gas.

But just at that moment the Holy Spirit paid him a quick return visit. "I remembered John 3:16, and I thought I heard Jesus say to me, 'I died for you—and now you're going to take your life?' I turned the wheel back, scraped against the side of the tree. I'm sure the other drivers thought, 'What's wrong with this guy?' And that day," he said, nodding and smiling, as if he were delivering a punchline I already knew, "I got a letter offering me a job."

The job took him across the Missouri River to Council Bluffs, Iowa, where he was hired, not as a cubicle serf, but as a highly responsible supervisor in a municipal water facility. "Watch out what you pray for," he said with a smile. "I had so much responsibility and so many people to manage that my legs shook. All I could do was ask God to help me."

His next position was with Radio Shack in Omaha. Then came a series of frustrating transfers from store to store inside that corporation, first to Lincoln, Nebraska, and then all the way to Waco, Texas. But, in Waco, it turned out that the job he was supposed to take was no longer available. So the Radio Shack honchos moved him to a store near Fort Worth. He did well there, and when a corporate position opened up in Fort Worth in 1991, Dang made the move up the ladder. His new office was a couple blocks away from the headquarters of none other than Dave Roever, the evangelist who had so powerfully affected him back in 1975. To those who believe that the universe makes no sense and God has no plan for us, Dang makes this simple summation, "God took me from Omaha to Lincoln to Waco to Fort Worth just to show me my calling and help start the Vietnam project."

I used to think that the idea that God leads us through our lives by signs and coincidences, and that we can trust and follow these leads was one of the silliest elements of an essentially childish religion. Then I got sober and experienced miracles like the encounter with a drunken New Yorker who saved my sobriety and the sense of God's presence that flooded me in my apartment (see p. xii). Today the idea that I am being led through life and that I need to be alert and grateful for mysterious promptings from the reality I call God is one of the things of which I am most certain. I listened to Dang's unlikely tale with mounting excitement, nodding at each new twist and turn that brought him closer to his true calling.

Dang's reunion with Roever was the spark that reignited the evangelist's Vietnamese ministry, and when Roever went to Vietnam in 1993, Dang was with him. It was the first time either man had seen the country in eighteen years.

Dang did more and more Vietnam-related volunteer work with Roever—the medical mission, work with orphans and street kids, the veterans' return program, an online Vietnamese translation of the Bible—and he began to hear an uncomfortable but insistent call to the ministry. "I was working, teaching Sunday school, doing a lot as a volunteer for Dave Roever. I had a happy family, and I enjoyed life. Everything was smooth." And then, on a Roever mission to Vietnam, Dang saw something that shook him. A thirteen-year-old girl, blind from birth, was given sight by the mission's medical team.

"She looked at her mother, touched her face, and said 'Mother, you're so beautiful!' I began to weep. I suddenly felt as if *I* were the girl—that for years I had been blind and now I could see—I could see what I needed to do and be. I said to God, if you don't want me to take up this ministry, put an obstacle in my path." But there were no obstacles. Dang vowed that he wouldn't take the economically dire step of becoming a full-fledged evangelist without the full approval of his wife and son, and he soon received it.

Did he make the right decision? It's not a question for him anymore. "You have to listen to your heart," he says. "If it's peaceful, if it's peace of mind and peace of heart you're feeling, well, that feeling comes from God. Like John 15 says, if you are in Christ and Christ is in you, you can *feel* it. The goodness and mercy of God always follows us, but we don't see it. God does huge things for us, but we don't notice. We only notice when something goes wrong and then we blame Him. It may take time, but Jesus Christ wants to train you, to strengthen your faith."

Dang's life, he's sure, has been shaped by God, but he is no champion of a passive response. "When you read the Bible as a storybook," he said, "it's one thing; but when you are searching for the truth, it's different. The Holy Spirit teaches you. If you and I go to a law library looking for a law book because we have a problem related to some issue, we're *careful* when we read. We pay close attention in a special way. That's what it's like to read the Bible when you are really searching.

"Keeping a strong faith is difficult. We have to live everyday life. If we stayed inside every day, just praying and reading the Bible, we could keep up our spirit. But faith isn't about staying in your office and waiting for God to do things. It's going out and doing, while trusting in God. Every time I go to Vietnam, my faith gets a lot stronger. In John, it says: Stay, stay with Jesus Christ; don't be apart from him. And that has stayed with *me,* to build up my faith year by year."

BE GOD'S PARTNER

Peter Gardiner-Harding

When he was a teenager, Peter Gardiner-Harding felt two callings —to the church and to the theater. Tragedy forced him to turn aside from both; then he returned to both, and later he found ways to meld them into a unique life, in which corporate work, acting, and a special kind of spirituality go together. Underpinning it all is a dynamic faith in God that is combined with faith in himself as an active partner with God.

Peter is a friend. My wife, Laurie, and I have spent time with him in his home in Victoria, British Columbia, and he's been our guest in St. Paul, where he has worked with Laurie on public art projects. He's a slim, wiry man just past fifty, although he gives the impression of a youthful thirty-five. A daily runner, he's trim and brimming with energy, an extroverted thespian who loves social occasions and brings a lot of brio with him when he enters a room. Yet, he's thoughtful and deliberate when discussing profound subjects, which he does willingly and skillfully.

Montreal born, Peter has lived in Toronto as well and maintains a *pied-a-terre* there for his business. His company, Focus Management Group/Plays That Work, is invited into hospitals, banks, and other businesses to perform playlets that dramatize workplace problems—boardroom behavior, boss-employee relationships, and other issues of human connectivity in business. Then, using interactive techniques developed by the radical Brazilian playwright and director Augusto Boal, Peter's team helps the audience of co-workers imagine a range of alternatives or solutions—which the actors then dramatize.

It's a successful venture. Peter's client list ranges from major Canadian hospitals and banks to universities and governmental bodies. He recently added a British Columbia–based cast to his stable of Toronto actors. Before launching Plays That Work, Peter had followed family tradition by working for a decade and a half as an accountant, but he's made a great deal more money as a corporate actor-director than he ever did as a bean counter. It was, of course, his experience as a bean counter that gave him the savvy and the bottom-line language to set up this unusual and lucrative theater company, but the deeper impetus was Peter's lifelong love of the stage. And bound up with that love is a spiritual vocation.

That passion for acting was a constant in Peter's life, but he wasn't always able to pursue it. His parents died when he was seventeen, and he was suddenly responsible for his younger sister, Jane. He moved with her from Montreal to Toronto, where the pair lived briefly with an aunt. It didn't work out, and they soon found an apartment on their own. Peter first sought a little inner stability by entertaining the idea of becoming an Anglican priest. A clergyman who was a friend of the family advised him. "He was very kind, and he told me that I had a lot of living to do before I made a decision like that," Peter said. "I think I was looking for a place to escape to, and I saw the seminary as a sanctuary as opposed to a place of learning or struggle. I really had no mental capacity at that stage to stay in school; I was trying to grieve."

One thing was certain; he had to shelve his earlier hopes of becoming an actor in favor of something stable. He studied science for a year, worked in a bank, and then, in his mid-twenties, enrolled in a business course at the University of Toronto. By age thirty, he had a Bachelor of Commerce degree and became an accountant. Only five years later, he knew he had to get out. The theater was still calling him, but his spiritual need was even more urgent. A first marriage had failed, and he was a single dad caring for a young son; he was also getting serious about Irene, the woman who would become his second wife. Most of all, the pain of his parents' death was beginning to surface in a big way. "The energy I was putting into keeping my grief down just went away," he said. "Luckily, the support I was getting from Irene *allowed* me to let everything go. As soon as I let it go just a little bit, it was like an avalanche. And through all of that I emerged with a new interest in the seminary."

He married Irene, moved to Toronto's West End, and became very active in a church, Saint Martin-in-the-Fields. "I was involved with the management of the church, the liturgy, and all kinds of other things," he said. "It was really a good time for me. I had a chance to see myself as being a pastor—in my mind's eye, anyway. And I got a lot of affirmation. People thought I had the right *look*. Some people thought there were too many women going into the Anglican ministry, and here I was, a likely young man. They'd try to put money into my hands to help me with tuition. It was lovely, really. And so I did get to seminary, to Trinity College at the University of Toronto, and I found out that it was no sanctuary at all."

Trinity was troubled during Peter's two years there, full of people with axes to grind, riddled with rumors and rife with gender and social tensions. These factors, along with the pressure of accreditation scrutiny, made the place, in Peter's experience, something of a hell on earth. Peter: "The dean of the school said to me, some months into my first year when I told him how difficult I was finding the place, 'If you were the devil, and you wanted to operate in the world, where would you go to fight your hardest fight? The local bar, where you've already won? Or would you go to a seminary, where you could really wrestle people to the ground?' "

Peter struggled to study in this charged atmosphere while running a financial planning practice (the first incarnation of Focus Management Group) on the side. "It was a prescription for failure," he said. "I didn't end up a priest, but from the standpoint of spiritual formation, that was a really interesting time. One of the things I learned there was that the Anglican church bases itself on three pillars: the Bible, the history of the church, and one's own history. Now, the church doesn't usually advertise all three because it's kind of hard to keep *control* of that third element—the Holy Spirit inside of you that is being called into service. The life you are living, your morality, and the spirit of the time you are living in—the information that comes from that—needs to be factored in, in true Anglicanism.

"That was really liberating for me because, when I understood it, I was able to understand some of these classes I was taking, where they were talking about God as a construct instead of God as a being. I think my current understanding of God draws a lot from John Shelby Spong and his Tillich-influenced understanding of how we probably did construct a God suited to our needs. I need to be clear; if I subscribe to that idea, it doesn't mean that I don't think there is a God. But I think that we as human beings have constructed God around what we need God to be."

Conscious as he is of this human proclivity to shape God to human needs, Peter is hesitant to define or describe God and adamant in refusing a dependent relationship. "It's both scary and challenging for me to start to explore how God could be present in my life if God were not that huge entity outside of me," he said. He prefers a cooperative or co-creative relationship with a God who is not a mighty monarch but an intimate presence living inside of him and in the space between human hearts.

"What I'm being called to do at this stage of the game," he said, "is just to look squarely into the eyes of my fear and understand that there may be realms beyond me, but to focus on them is a waste of my time. When I pray now, I'm very clear that I'm not calling on somebody to deliver something to me—rather, I'm calling up certain qualities in myself. The question is, what do I need to call up in myself to quell that fear and to hear the voice of God in me? And then what do I do with it? That's what matters to me.

"Where is God when a mass murderer strikes? Where was God in the Holocaust? For me, questions like that are not a good use of time. I'd rather ask, where am I in that? Can I call on God-in-me to forgive that killer? Can I find it within myself to be able to accept what happened in Rwanda and find a way to hold people to account for it, while holding both sides in love? It isn't about being soft and mushy, it's about respecting everyone, even the perpetrators of the most heinous things. Respect them, not accept them."

Peter believes that an inherent condition of humanity is separation. "We are isolated from one another. When I try to reach out to others within my community, I am struggling against that. You know that I need to affiliate; I'm probably the quintessential extrovert. I love to be with people, and I love to be seen by people. I think that's where God lives! God is in what we're doing as we do this interview. It's as small as that and as big as that. At this moment in time, my concept of God doesn't have to be any bigger than what is going on between us. It's exactly like theater: if we're doing a scene right now, it's not you and it's not me—it's what's going on between us."

I raised my eyebrows. As someone who puts great stock in the idea of surrender to God's will, a mighty will far beyond my full comprehension, Peter's idea of a God small enough to fit into a conversation between two people, a God who could be the partner—not the lord and master—of a self-aware human being claiming his or her own power, seemed to diminish God.

And yet, after I thought about it, I realized that he had touched on one of the most important truths conveyed by the Christian faith, inherited from Judaism: we *are* God's partners, not God's slaves. We turn toward God of our own free will and to surrender to God's will involves conscious choices on our part. We make daily decisions that maintain or diminish our contact with God—that is, we pray or we don't pray; we love or we don't love; we do justice or we let apathy or anger rule our judgment. And the worlds we build in cooperation with others bears witness to our intimacy or lack of intimacy with God.

And then there is the issue of scale. God is great, but God is also a still, small voice inside. God is the creator and sustainer of the galaxies but also an intimate friend. These amazing paradoxes of scale, which are a problem for the intellect at first, make profound sense when you consider that God is a presence and a force that upsets all our categories and the oppositions that sustain those categories: big/small, transcendent/ intimate, self/other. Of course God can be fully present in a conversation; God is fully present in a daffodil.

I knew that after leaving the seminary, Peter had turned seriously toward his other calling. He'd given himself five years to make it on stage. Six months of auditioning later, he landed his first paying role. Others followed, in a variety of venues including fringe festivals, which abound in Canada. But the idea of melding business and acting was there from the start, and in 1999 he finally jettisoned his financial-planning practice and his accountancy, streaked his hair with blond highlights, and shifted Plays That Work into high gear.

"I remember every character I ever tried to get," he said. "There's that process of going inward to try and find that guy. Getting into the script and getting into ourselves, and being afraid that we're not going to be able to do it. Where does that guy live inside me? We search and search, and it's not going to work—Oh, God!—and all of a sudden, wham! We've got it. There's a kind of breaking out. You're out of yourself and fully aligned with this other person. The character comes out of you and is made manifest. I think that is a religious experience. Did you bring it out? Did God? Who cares? You did the work. However it happened, the spirit is present and the spirit is distinct from you. It's you and it's not you, and it's both together. And I think that's how I conceive of the presence of God: it's me and it's God, and it's both of us together."

ACCEPT THAT GOD CAN
HANDLE ANYTHING

Leonard Griffin

Leonard O. Griffin was a thirtysomething Baptist pastor who had led only one congregation, in inner-city Syracuse, New York, when he was summoned to the helm of Morris Street Baptist Church, the most famous African American church in a legendary American city: Charleston, South Carolina. Morris Street was a source of inspiration, pride, and uplift during the Reconstruction and the Jim Crow decades, and it was a center of the civil rights movement in Charleston. In its one hundred forty-one years of life, the church had only six pastors. The man Griffin was about to follow in the pulpit, the late Reverand Dr. Alphonso R. Blake, served there for no fewer than forty-two years and was a legend himself, a civil rights warrior who was head of the local NAACP, a friend of Martin Luther King, Jr.'s, a leader in civic and state Baptist organizations, and an educator with a campus building named after him. In fact, he was chairman of the board of trustees of the college where Griffin got his bachelor's degree, and his signature is on Griffin's diploma.

"It was quite a challenge to even fathom that this is where the Lord had called me to serve," said Leonard Griffin over breakfast with me at a hotel in Columbia, South Carolina. The Reverand Griffin was attending a huge state Baptist convention, and I was getting an opportunity to learn about this slim, youthful-looking, thoughtful man whose quiet voice and deliberate manner—he speaks in complete sentences and really listens to questions—give no hint of the struggles and changes he's gone through in four decades of life. "One of the blessings in my journey," he went on, "was that, as I got started in ministry, I was embraced by a lot of the older ministers in my region of South Carolina, and they shared with me some of the things that you need to be mindful of in going to a new church.

"One of the major things they told me was that you never want to try and be your predecessor. Be yourself. Preach the way you preach, pastor the way you pastor, and never do or say anything that would denigrate your predecessor. Always do things that will embellish his history or further his legacy. I have tried to do that in coming to Morris Street—feel comfortable in my own skin and do what I feel led by God to do as a pastor."

You can tell a lot about the lives of black people in Edgefield, South Carolina, where Griffin was born and raised, by noting that it was the hometown of the late senator and onetime segregationist poster boy Strom Thurmond. If you were black in Strom's town, you had a hard life and no help from anyone but your own folks. The senior Griffins were relatively well situated—Leonard's father, Glasglow, owned a gas station and his mother worked as a beautician. But there were eight kids in the family, and money was tight enough that family members had to scour the woods and a nearby wood processing plant for branches and scraps to feed their wood-burning stove.

Leonard Griffin graduated from high school in 1985 and began a stint in the Navy that took him far from Edgefield—to Denmark, Niger, Peru, and Spain, among other places. When he came home, he was adrift in his own life. Though he'd felt a call to be a preacher when he was only nine, he'd all but severed his connection with his family's Baptist faith. He used his engineer training in the Navy to do auto-repair work in his father's station and took some evening classes to prepare himself for work in a car dealership; as for the rest of the time, he was, in his words, "pretty much doing what I wanted to do and wrestling with some personal demons."

When you do what you want to do under those conditions, you usually end up doing something you wish you hadn't. Griffin was some forty miles from home when he ran a brand-new Pontiac Grand Am into a ditch and wedged it between two trees. His unsteady efforts to extricate the car resulted in nothing more than a punctured tire. Some high school friends happened by and drove him home to what he was sure would be the sort of family scene every out-of-control twentysomething dreads.

His mother, Alma, did confront him—but what she said didn't beat him down; it lifted him up. "I don't know if he was drinking or under the influence of drugs," she told Charleston *Post and Courier* reporter Michael Gartland in 2006, "but I believe it was one or the other. The first thing I told him was the Lord must have something for him to do."

As confused as Griffin was, his mother's words hit home. He accepted the idea that he had been preserved for a purpose, and he began adding purpose to his life as the old call to the ministry came back.

He enrolled in Morris College, a historically black institution in Sumter, South Carolina, and graduated with a degree in pastoral ministry. A cousin introduced him to a nearby church, and it was there that he got his feet wet as a preacher and learned the ropes from his elders. He practiced their lessons well enough that he was asked to preach at a larger church, in Williston, South Carolina. During four years there, he became more and more certain that he wanted to add intellectual heft to his thinking and preaching by attending seminary. He landed a scholarship to Colgate Rochester Crozer Divinity School in Rochester, New York.

Griffin was looking to expand his intellectual horizons and that's what happened. He steeped himself in the Social Gospel tradition of Walter Rauschenbusch and Howard Thurman and, as he put it to me, "I encountered a variety and diversity of faith systems—Catholic, Protestant, Episcopalian, and so on—and despite all the differences among them, it was the *similarities* that were striking to me. There were certain pieces of the picture of God that we share—that God as creator could create such a wonderful and beautiful world, that our concepts of how God did this are similar. And there are so many parallels in how we wrestle with complexities like death and sickness."

But the most moving and memorable lesson of Leonard Griffin's seminary years took place outside that classroom, when he had to wrestle with one of the most devastating complexities that any human being, or any faith tradition, can confront: the death of a baby. The baby was the first-born child of Griffin and his wife, Wandalyn.

"It really was a challenge to my faith," he said. "I was very angry with God, and I couldn't reconcile that with my faith in God. I believed that my anger at God separated me from God. But a dear, dear friend of mine counseled me through that process. She said it was okay to be angry with God because God could handle whatever anger I had. My anger did nothing to diminish who God was or His closeness to me or His love for me."

Just as Alma Griffin's heartfelt words had changed her son's mind and heart in a heartbeat after his auto accident, these words from a friend made an instant difference. "It was an immediate breakthrough," said Griffin. "I had an emotional outburst at hearing her say those words. Tears flooded my face. I can still remember it so vividly; it was one of the benchmark moments in my life. A complete breakthrough in wrestling with the death of our child and reconciling that with my faith in God. From that point on I felt as if God was right there with me, carrying me through the process."

It's a momentous thing to realize—that, as the great African American gospel song teaches, "my God is able": able to handle all our emotions, able to bring comfort in the worst times, able to transform our suffering into wisdom and even joy. One of the things that makes prayer difficult for me is that I hesitate to bring my whole self to it and, thus, to God: all my angers, manias, confusions, worries, and other darknesses of spirit. But if I am not willing for God to have all of me, and if I don't believe that God can handle whatever I'm sending God's way, I'm condemning myself to a very thin spiritual life.

Griffin has had many occasions to pass these powerful lessons on to troubled parishioners since. "Many parishioners are dealing with grief that doesn't have to do with the loss of a loved one," he said. "In divorce, there's a grieving process much like losing a loved one—and people are wrestling with illnesses like cancer, AIDS, and HIV. And the question can come: why would God allow this to happen? Is this a curse from God? One of the theological ways I wrestle with these facts is to believe that God carries us through valleys as a testimony to the fact that we can get through them and then go up—up to a mountaintop experience. Not every catastrophe is sent from God, but they are all means of testifying to the power of God to bring us through.

"Now, some people come back at me with the 'why me?' question. I don't have the answer for each individual; I try to help people see that the 'why me?' question is really a circular question that gets you nowhere and that it's more pertinent to ask, what can I learn from this or what is the growth process that comes with this crisis?"

Griffin has helped many parishioners at low moments, but he has also been astonished at the resilience of the people he has known. "I'm in awe of how durable people can be in the face of terrible situations," he said. "It's amazing how they are able to come back from devastating circumstances on the strength of their faith in God." Fresh out of Colgate

Rochester, he took the helm of a Syracuse church whose members were feeling the full effect of Rust Belt decline and inner-city poverty. "It was *blight* that I witnessed in Syracuse," he said. "Unemployment, underemployment, educational challenges for many people in the community, and my congregation was suffering. But it was just phenomenal how some people were able to eke out survival in meager circumstances, with the most meager economics."

Not only did his parishioners survive, they gave of themselves. When Wandalyn had complications in her third pregnancy—complications that the Griffins had reason to fear—the doctor's prescription was bed rest and a lot of care. An eighty-year-old member of Griffin's congregation made daily visits to help. "She just refused to allow me to do certain things," he said. "Frail as she was, she just wanted to do them herself."

Griffin has been pastor at Morris Street for more than two years now, working hard in the Rauschenbusch-Thurman-King-Blake tradition of religious activism that means so much to him (and to our country): setting up social and educational programs, proclaiming the Gospel in the pulpit and at revivals, and working on a book to introduce new and returning believers to Christian faith and Baptist practice. A few months after our talk in Columbia, I called him to reconnect and ask a few more questions. I learned that his father had recently passed away and that the breakthrough experience he'd had after his child died was still with him. "That experience allowed me to really grieve in a healthy way," he told me.

I couldn't help asking him if he was still a bit intimidated by the legacy of Morris Street.

"Every day," he said. "Every day. But then I remember that it's not what Griffin says or what Griffin does, but what God wants."

Stay Open to New Revelations

Carie Gross

Carie Gross lives in a spacious, art-filled retreat down a woodsy road in Santa Rosa, near Northern California wine country. She's a free spirit in her forties who does graphic design for print and the Web but is giving more and more of her time to the writing of screenplays—sometimes she stays up until five in the morning, her head and her computer filled with characters and situations, some of them definitely R-rated.

In short, she's not my idea of a Mormon.

She made it clear to me weeks before our interview that she wasn't interested in explaining official Mormon doctrine, only her own experience. I told her that was exactly what I wanted to hear about. I pictured a woman born into a conservative church who was rebelling against it, or at least testing its boundaries in a bid for freedom.

I couldn't have been more off the mark. Although there is Mormonism in her family, Carie Gross is a convert, and she was led toward the Church of Jesus Christ of Latter-day Saints by a male friend who was both a devout Mormon and a brilliantly original and unconventional thinker. Once in the church, she discovered that it could accommodate her restless spirit and her iconoclastic temperament. "Actually, I'm really surprised that I joined any church at all," she said, laughing. "I am not a joiner. When I first felt attracted to the church, I was also determined that I wasn't going to join anything that would debilitate me or shield me from the things I need to experience. There are certain parameters of belief and conduct in the church, and if you accept those, there's lots of room inside."

But at another level, joining the church wasn't a matter of measuring parameters or assessing degrees of intellectual or social freedom at all. A lively woman with a hearty laugh, Carie Gross is also prone to pauses— quiet moments when she searches for the right way to express the state of her soul. She's the sort of person who feels and responds to what she understands as God's promptings, wherever they may lead. And she has felt herself being drawn into a deeper relationship with God for years; the magnetism of Mormonism has been only one part of this subtle process.

Gross's mother was raised Mormon but left the church; while she never disparaged the faith, the family attended Presbyterian services. Eventually, Gross found herself wondering if she ought to officially commit herself to the Presbyterian version of the Christian faith. "Worrying about this, I actually had a vision of Christ," she told me. "He opened his arms to me. At first, I thought he was beckoning to me, gathering me in. But then I realized that, no, he was releasing me into the world. He was saying that I didn't have to join this church. He knew that I had to bang my head, stumble, and fall so that I could become a little smarter."

This wouldn't be the last visionary message that Gross would receive to help her navigate the seas of spirit. Years later, the Santa Rosa native was living in Santa Barbara, very much at loose ends, needing a change. Like many seekers of clarity in similar straits, she decided to move back home. "I didn't quite know what I wanted to do," she said, "but one day the words *be ready* came to me. I didn't exactly hear them; I kind of *saw* them. The words were definite, quiet, and kind—not a warning at all. They were saying, just watch, just be alert."

Soon her youngest brother and his wife invited her to become a nanny for their identical twin girls—"which was a miraculous opportunity," said Gross. "These gorgeous little girls just *got* to me." Coincidentally or providentially, her new calling as what she dubbed a "vicarious mother" coincided with the process of conversion to the Mormon faith. And that conversion began with America Online.

"There was this guy who contacted me via an AOL chat room," she said, smiling. "Now I knew there were a lot of freaks and cads out there online, but this man was smart, well-read, and could write very well. He was a real freethinker, with a lively mind and original opinions. And he said he was a devout Mormon. I was fascinated." Her fascination deepened when her online friend sent her a copy of the Book of Mormon and she began reading.

"When I read the Bible," she said, "I sometimes wonder about specifics. I truly believe that Jesus could have performed the miracles in the Gospels. I believe we can be healed in that way, and I even believe in ministering angels. I have faith in God but not so much faith in man! I wonder if man has recorded the truth faithfully. After all, the history of how the Bible was put together, then manipulated and used as a bludgeon reminds me of what a friend of mine once said: We get our history from the people who *won.* And these are not necessarily the nicest guys, or, really, the most spiritual. The testaments of the Gnostics, for example, were sequestered away, excluded. The Book of Mormon felt to me like one of these exciting, exceptional books.

"We call it 'another testament of Jesus Christ.' How did the prophet Joseph Smith get the text? The church has an explanation, but I don't really know the answer. I only know what I thought and felt as I read it. I can tell you that it feels inspired."

Gross felt even more certain about her conversion when she began meeting Mormons and they began helping her understand the messages she'd been receiving. "I felt a tug toward the church, and I discovered that the people in it were great," she said. "I told them the story of receiving the words 'be ready.' I told them how I felt then: quiet, calm, energetic. They said, 'Carie, do you know what that was? The still, small voice? That was the Holy Spirit.' I feel very grateful that I was given these experiences before I was told about the church. My conversion was experiential; my religion is experiential."

One of the ongoing experiences that is most important to her is her development as a writer. The characters in her screenplays are, she's sure, all aspects of herself. "The nasty ones, the kind ones, the clueless ones—they're all me," she said. "The issues they face are ones that I am dealing with. Like me, they try to be good, but they make huge mistakes, and so my screenplays are not PG-13! And I am getting a great deal of healing from writing—it's way better than paying a shrink a hundred and fifty bucks an hour."

But what about the Mormon church's well-known disapproval of the R-rated life in all its forms? Gross was clear about both the strengths and limitations of the attitude. "There are strict moral codes about sexuality," she said. "The biggest one is a prohibition of sex outside of marriage. I've lived long enough that I don't have a problem with that one. Sex without a promise? No, thanks. Now when it comes to creative expression, sure, there are plenty of people in the church who think that we should spend all of our time on things that are positive and uplifting. We are asked not to go to R-rated movies.

"I don't go along with that. I need the freedom to look at all of life, to consider every idea, to try every possible story line." She pointed out that the versatile novelist Orson Scott Card is a Mormon, and although he has written about Latter-day Saints' church history and is a serious moralist, his best-known books are fantasy and science-fiction tales that plunge deep into the dark side. "There are Mormons who say, 'Brother Card, why don't you write nice stories—warm, happy stories?' And he says 'Nobody will read them because they won't be interesting, they won't hold anyone.'

"My God." She laughed. "Look at the Bible! It's packed with stories of great men and women failing at practically everything. It can be very dark. But beautiful things come out of that."

Despite the social conservatism of many in the church, Gross feels that Mormon belief is powerfully aware of paradoxes like that one and bears within itself an antidote to dogmatism and spiritual narrowness. "I'm drawn to a beautiful phrase in the Book of Mormon: 'There is an opposition in all things,' " she told me. "When I first heard that, I said, Okay! Sign me up! I think it points to the fact that our own judgments can be very limited. It points to the idea that, for example, Adam and Eve *had* to fall; it was necessary for the advancement of human spirits. If you don't know the bad, you can't know the good and truly choose between them. We know this from our own lives, too—my greatest love might have been the one that hurt me the most, the one that forced me to choose, to struggle, and to learn.

"There's another doctrine of our church: the idea that if we are worthy, we will eternally progress. Now, I'm not sure about the 'worthy' part—it seems to me that we will *all* have a chance—but I'm not in charge, thank God! It's the idea that we will always keep learning, always keep growing, that the process is never complete. And that's why it seems so silly to sit here in the chaos and pound your breast and say, I have found the truth—we have eternity to go, and you're banging your chest telling me that you *know*? Give me a break! I mean, the veil is so thick, we can't even see the angels, and you tell me you know what's going on? Holy cow, you goofball!"

Mormonism lays special emphasis on the progressive spiritual development of the individual soul, but I'm convinced that Carie Gross's perspective on it can help all believers. The infinitude of God means that my relationship with God will never reach a stopping point; there will always be "more to be revealed." There's great comfort in that for me; wherever I may be in my relationship with the divine, if I'm willing to maintain and improve the relationship, it will grow and evolve. Listening to Gross, I realized that in a certain sense, even the statement "I believe in God" is provisional; the God I believe in is unchanging, but my view of God will change, and even my understanding of belief will change. If I lapse into spiritual idleness or indifference, the change will be mere drift, but as long as I remain in contact with God to the best of my ability, it will be a real and meaningful evolution.

When it comes to the scenario of Gross's own life, it's clear that a simple, fully experiential relationship with God is still its main theme. "God teaches us whether we fall or not," she said. "He's always there for the lesson. I don't know how much he directs and controls, but he's always there to teach. When I first came into the church, I didn't know how to view myself or what to do with this new group of people. How much was I going to participate? I was in a process of redefining myself, and I felt fear. I got this message from God: *Your fear doesn't come from me.*

"And now, when I don't feel right, or I'm confused or upset, God simply says to me: *What do you know?*

"*I know that you are there,* is my response. And God lets it go at that. He always deals with me where I am, and he is always patient and kind. The truth is, if I know he's there, the rest of the stuff is much less important.

"One of the joys of my life these days is the fact that my oldest brother has come to similar understandings about God—on his own, without a church. He's been sliced and whittled down and roughed up enough, and he's heard what he called this 'quiet, generous voice.' So I said to him, 'You know what that was? That quiet, generous voice? That was the Holy Spirit!' In many ways, we're on parallel paths: he in his way, and me in this strange edifice of the Mormon church. And here's what he says: 'Our purpose is to live daily, to navigate everyday life, and to grow spiritually from that.'"

Go With God's Flow

Cynthia Williams

"**M**y people just don't *do* what I did," Cynthia Williams told me as we ate lunch in a Minneapolis cafe. She was referring to the decision she made five years ago to abandon a high-powered career in financial services management to go to work for a struggling inner-city church on Minneapolis's multi-ethnic south side and to begin seminary studies at the same time.

When white people from comfortable backgrounds jump off the corporate treadmill, we might call it downshifting or voluntary simplicity. When an African American woman does it—a woman who was born into poverty to a teenage mom with a ninth-grade education, and who pulled herself up the economic ladder by dint of sheer brains and drive—what do we call it? Williams called it saving her life.

A short, compact woman whose rapid-fire intelligence animates her eyes and her voice, she told the story of her life and faith with vivacity, often interrupting herself, never hesitating in any of her answers. She combined resonant and traditional religious phrases, the crisp language of the corporate world, and the precise vocabularies of psychology and theology.

"My job had come to be only about the money," she said. "I had never identified with prostitutes, but I was beginning to."

One Monday in 2002, she began work as usual, answering e-mails at her desk in the Minneapolis office of Prudential. She had a meeting scheduled with an employee whom she was coaching to improve his performance, although she knew the company intended to let him go anyway. "I couldn't give him false hope," she said, "so I cancelled the meeting, went to Human Resources, and told them I was going home." She took the rest of the week off.

"I thought it was my hormones," she said with a hearty laugh.

Her endocrine system was fine. But she *was* about to turn her back on the kind of career that represented much of what generations of African-Americans have struggled, suffered, and even died for: a piece of the rock. She had become so imbued with God's love and so alert to God's voice that she realized she had got hold of the wrong rock.

Born in Memphis, Williams was a square peg in a round hole from day one. Although she was an introverted child, she was the peacemaker in a family made chaotic by alcoholism and troubled relationships. She was also bright and motivated, and sure that Memphis didn't have what it took to hold her. When the time came for her to go to college, she would have been happy to fly far away; but family finances were tight, so she enrolled in the University of Tennessee–Knoxville— "as far away as I could get from Memphis and still qualify for in-state tuition," she said with a smile.

Her first serious job—in the insurance industry—took her to Houston for six years and then to Dallas, where she met Bill, a mentor who groomed her for the upper echelons of management. Following him, Williams relocated to Philadelphia, then Chicago. Her positions grew in responsibility, and her paychecks fattened.

Her spiritual horizons were expanding as well. She'd grown up in what she called a "hell-fire and brimstone" Baptist milieu. "I was terrified of God," she said. "I saw Him as a very angry person in a permanent bad mood. Who would want to get close to somebody like that? And I didn't see many happy Christians." But in Houston, she found a different sort of congregation altogether: Brentwood Baptist, a large, cheerful, active African American church in the city's southwest suburbs. "Brentwood was where I learned for the first time about God's *love* and His sense of humor," she said. "After that, wherever I moved, the first thing I would look for was a church. After all, in management, I was usually the only person of color in the room, and church was where I would go on Sundays to see people who looked like me."

After four years in Chicago, Williams was feeling restless. As grateful as she was for Bill's guidance, she realized that, as she put it, "*my* resumé was *his* resumé. Besides, I have pretty good intuition about how long I should stay at a job—when and if my work in a given place is done."

A headhunter approached her about a job in Minnesota. She came to the Twin Cities, interviewed with an insurance company, and got an offer. "My mentor told me to turn it down," she recalled. "He wanted me to come with him to yet another job under his wing, but I figured it was time for me to fly.

"Still, though, Minnesota? I said, 'Lord, I cannot *believe* you are bringing me to Minnesota.' "

As had become her habit, she quickly put spiritual roots down in an African American Baptist church—but the Twin Cities congregation turned out to be as much of a challenge as a comfort. "It was a church under siege," she said. "There were moral issues about the pastor—issues of infidelity. A new pastor arrived; the deacons didn't like him. There were just a whole lot of instances of people behaving badly. I was exposed to the ugly part of church, and I wondered what it said about God, and about me and my relationship with God. I was surprised I didn't leave."

One reason she didn't was that her all-too-human church introduced a new dimension into her spiritual life. "The congregation was doing twelve weeks of study based on a book called *Experiencing God* by Henry Blackaby and Claude King," she said. "The book sets out seven spiritual tenets, and among them are that God seeks a love relationship with you; that God is always speaking to you—through the church, through circumstances, through relationships. God invites you to do God's work, and when God invites you, you *will* have a crisis of belief. Your response to that crisis will tell you what you really believe about God.

"Now, I had been in the church for my entire life, and I had not known that God desired a personal relationship with me. I had never thought about God in that way."

She was excited, unsettled, and changing. She had started studying the art of leadership and what it meant to her and those who worked for her. At the same time, a merger had brought a cadre of cutthroat East Coast executives into her office—"and suddenly you felt that you needed a suit of armor to walk in the office," she said.

The week before she decided to leave her job, she received some work-related criticism that felt mean-spirited and unfair. That weekend, she attended a women's religious conference during which a woman Williams didn't know prayed for her and told her that her time at her job wasn't long. "She told me that God sees my heart, that God is getting ready to restore all the things that the Enemy has stolen from me."

All of which led to that abrupt Monday bailout, an event that, despite all the foreshadowing, genuinely confused Williams. "My doctor asked me if I was depressed," she said. "I said I didn't think I was. I took a week off, met with my employer's HR people. They were very gracious."

Williams decided to quit, and as part of her severance package HR set Williams up with a personal coach and consultant named Cliff Smith. He turned out to be just what she needed. "Cliff *got it*," she said with a smile. "I don't think we did any traditional outplacement work at all. He just had me imagine possibilities. I took six months off. And I read *everything* about purpose I could find."

After half a year of intense self-scrutiny, the get-it-done executive in Williams reasserted herself. "I'd had enough introspection," she told me. Her former boss had gone to work for the state of Minnesota, and she brought Williams aboard on a $50,000 grant to build customer-service strategies for state agencies. She began training as a personal coach, too. "I began to realize that I'm a generalist, that my life is a patchwork quilt," she said, "and that God is sewing the pieces together. I began to have the assurance that my life was taking me somewhere, even if I didn't have or know the master plan."

Like Dan Dang and many others in this book—like nearly everyone, in fact, who really surrenders to God—Williams began to receive messages and experience lucky coincidences that persuaded her that she was indeed on the right track. For one thing, her dream life became vivid and memorable. "I often dreamed I was married, and once, the ceremony was held in a castle in Australia," she said. "I felt certain that the groom was Christ and that he had been wooing me for a long time. Another time I dreamed that I was going up in an elevator, and the elevator broke free of the building and ascended like a flying machine. It zoomed over land— I saw little children jumping rope—and then over very vivid blue water. 'How do I get this thing to land?' I shouted.

"Later I journaled about the dream, and I believe that the Holy Spirit asked me, 'What if you had just sat back and enjoyed the ride?' "

Soon Williams was saying yes to the ride. Her stint with the state was over, and she was now consulting with various nonprofits and struggling to make a living as a fledgling personal coach. Clients were few and far between, and she was not encouraged about her prospects. She was also feeling called to go to seminary. In the classifieds, she found an opening for a director of operations for Park Avenue United Methodist Church, a Minneapolis congregation that was particularly committed to inclusivity—doing everything it could to attract everyone in the rich south Minneapolis ethnic mix. Williams loved the idea of bringing her formidable organizational and administrative skills into this house of God, with its "*Harambee* Wednesdays" social nights (*harambee* is Swahili for *pulling together*), its Spanish Bible study, its Liberian female co-pastor.

After Williams submitted her resumé for the Park Avenue job, Bill, her old mentor, called and dangled a particularly tempting fruit before her: a corporate position in Dallas with a six-figure salary. "I didn't know what to do," said Williams. "You can drive to Memphis from Dallas, and six figures goes a long way in Texas. I told Kevin, a friend who was staying in my house, about my dilemma. And Kevin said, 'Cynthia, why would you divide your attention like that? You know God has called you and has you on this path.' Now, I didn't know if I would even get the Park Avenue job, but I knew I had to say no to Bill. I had to stay true."

But Williams did get the church job and a way into seminary opened up with magical ease. She chanced to open a piece of what she assumed was junk mail that had been sitting around her house for three months. It was a solicitation from Luther Seminary, the distinguished St. Paul–based school of Protestant theology (and home base of theologian Kosuke Koyama—see p. 13). "They were looking for people of color to be nominated for full scholarships—books and everything," she said. "I was shameless. I called everyone I knew who could nominate me. They nominated, I got the scholarship and started school in the fall of 2003."

Though she followed a true call, Williams doesn't exactly have it made. Park Avenue is not a wealthy church, and budget constraints have more than once threatened her position. When we talked, it was uncertain how much longer she would have a job there, despite her success and popularity. She seemed unfazed. "I told them when I first came that I won't stay one day longer than God will have me stay, and I won't leave one day sooner.

"I love Park Avenue. It's a place that really practices community. That can be messy. I've cried more there than I did at the crazy Baptist church. We struggle together, we fall down, we lash out, we laugh. I've learned how to practice forgiveness and how to take all the things that hurt and terrify me and pray about them."

One of the things that has both terrified and delighted Williams has been an emerging vocation as a pastor. Like many of the people in this book, she fought the call at first. "The pastor at Park Avenue saw something in me and asked me to preach. I was frightened, but I did it, and now I preach regularly," she said. "People in the church say, we think you're called to be a pastor. And I'm like, 'I don't *want* to be a pastor!' I want to be an artist and a writer. I want to be an opera diva! I mean, one moment I'm painting, and the next moment I want to start a nonprofit to help young people—and then there's the coaching. I want to learn how to play the piano. I'm forty-eight, so how in the world am I going to get all of this done?

"I believe that anything I put my mind to, I can do and do well, but I have to choose the best. The best is God's best. God knows what's best for me. And a lot of that is actively—not passively—noting the opportunities. You note in circumstances what lines up with what you are starting to sense in your spirit. Then you just open yourself up to walking it out. For a recovering control freak like me, it feels weird to say it, but I am learning to go with the current."

Williams argued that her life changes weren't particularly courageous. "I just didn't have any other choice because this journey has been about choosing life. In the choices I made before, I felt like I was dead; I gave myself away. I lived other people's agendas. I was sleepwalking and I woke up; and to go back is to go back to sleep. The beautiful thing is that the more I continue on this journey, the more me I become. Every time I preach, I feel more and more like myself, as that voice comes out. More and more, I'm whole."

Avoid Both Absolutism
and Relativism

Irving (Yitz) Greenberg

I n any discussion of relations between Jews and Christians, the 800-pound gorilla in the room is the stupefying legacy of Jewish suffering at the hands of people and institutions that were officially, nominally, or culturally Christian. The Holocaust is the nadir and ultimate symbol of this legacy of shame, but the legacy includes much more than the Holocaust: medieval laws that forced Jews into ghettos and forbade them to own land; attacks on communities that ranged from ragtag mob assaults to full-scale pogroms carried out by military units; and a witches' brew of pseudo-ideas and stereotypes, all underwritten by the conviction that Judaism was a vestigial religion superseded by Christianity and that Jews were aberrant beings.

During Lent in 2000, Pope John Paul II gave a homily that was a carefully worded apology for sins committed by Christians against Jews (an apology, be it noted, that stopped short of declaring that the church as an institution bore any guilt for the outrages perpetrated in its name). In response to the Pope's words, and to similar apologies from other Christian authorities, a diverse group of Jewish clergy and scholars issued a statement under the Hebrew title Dabru Emet (Speak Truth)—a declaration of Jewish-Christian solidarity on many points of doctrine and tradition. The Dabru Emet signers declared, among other things, that Jews and

Christians worship the same God, that Nazism was not an inevitable outcome of Christianity, and that Jews can respect Christians' faithfulness to their tradition.

One of the signers of Dabru Emet, and a contributor to a companion book of essays, was Irving Greenberg (universally known as Yitz), a tall, courtly, gentle-voiced Orthodox rabbi who has lived the tensions, pains, joys, and opportunities of Jewish-Christian rapprochement. Greenberg, the founder of the Jewish Center for Learning and Leadership (CLAL), an organization promoting dialogue among the often fractious branches of modern Judaism, has also developed a vision of inter-religious understanding that I find more compelling than any other I have heard. Happy and fulfilled in a rigorous form of Judaism, Greenberg is passionately certain that watering down religious traditions, pretending that differences don't matter, is not the way to help the people of different faiths toward mutual understanding. At the same time, his acknowledgment of the spiritual and moral beauty he has seen in many Christians has led him to a heartfelt appreciation for parts of Christian doctrine that he had once disdained.

In the face of 2,000 years of assault, it's no wonder that Jews have had a hard time being ecumenical about Jesus and his followers. As for Yitz Greenberg, he had to come to terms with the enormity of the Holocaust and its background before he could find a way to appreciate and even love aspects of the Christian faith. He explained this process as we sat in the living room of his house on a peaceful, almost rural-seeming street in the leafy Riverdale section of the Bronx.

"In 1961, I went to Israel for a year," he told me. "I was an American intellectual historian at that time. I had an emotional encounter with the Holocaust. It was a personal crisis and threw a lot of my religious beliefs into doubt. It was hard to believe that a loving, caring God would just stand by, hard to believe in a final Messianic redemption when evil was so totally triumphant. However, one of the side effects of the crisis was a realization about Christianity. I don't believe that any serious Christian wanted the Holocaust, but to an extent, Christianity was an accessory to the crime by having created an environment in which Jews were seen as uncanny, evil, or subhuman, and therefore, subject to isolation and destruction. I also had a very threatened personal feeling that, if this could be done once, it could be done again, to my children or my grandchildren. And so my wife, Blu, and I determined to get involved with Christians. We wanted to tell them to stop spreading hatred. I confess that that's what led me to a serious encounter."

As Greenberg relates in his book *For the Sake of Heaven and Earth: The New Encounter Between Judaism and Christianity* (Jewish Publication Society of America, 2004), Christian liturgy and discourse in 1961 still retained negative images of Jews. He was angrily determined to set things right in lectures and discussions. "I swept down on the dialogue like an avenging angel," he writes, "demanding that Christians cease spreading evil and demeaning images of my faith. Blu and I frequently smote Christian dialogue partners with the rod of our Holocaust anger." The response of many Christians surprised him. "The sixties and the American civil rights movement triggered some of the finest impulses in Christianity," he goes on. "The activists whom we met were passionate idealists who wanted to correct and make up for 2,000 years of mistreatment. Far from resenting our reproof, they validated it and sought to make the church respond. They were eager to connect to the Jewish roots of Christianity, and they drank in our words about Judaism with a purity and intensity that Jewish students would find hard to match. Some of the finest people we encountered became lifetime friends."

Confronted with this degree of Christian openness and with the example of Christians who gave of themselves unstintingly to the poor, the oppressed, and the forgotten, Greenberg's formidable intellectual honesty opened him to the fact that he, and other Jews, also held stereotypes. "The more I appreciated Christianity," he said, "the more I began to ask myself: does the Jewish tradition of defensive apologetics, our self-protective response to Christianity, do justice to it? As a religious Jew, I had to ask myself, how do I account for the power and the scope of Christianity? Christianity has elements that are difficult to believe: God as a man, the virgin birth, and so on. It was easy for us to dismiss these things: Jews are too smart to fall for that kind of stuff, but gentiles don't know any better, and if they did, they'd be Jews! But when you begin to see the power of the Christian faith, you can't go on explaining it that way.

"And so, at some point, I had to stop and ask myself, is Christianity an accident, is it all wrong, is it to be dismissed because Christians mistreated Jews? Or should a religious Jew entertain the idea that maybe this is a serious vehicle of divine communication with people? And that moved me to this whole idea of trying to see Christianity as an outgrowth of Judaism that was intended by God to become independent because God does, I think, speak in multiple ways to humanity."

This realization became the keynote of Greenberg's understanding of religious pluralism. "For much of human history, it was easy to believe that one's own religion was absolute and exclusive because there was no serious encounter with the reality of the other," he said. "In modern culture, when people discovered that their absolute truth wasn't the only one, and, in fact, there were truths that contradicted it that were also powerful, there was a kind of a collapse of all authority. That's what relativism is about. Basically, it says, all faiths are equally credible, which means they're all incredible. There's no principle by which to choose one over the other, it doesn't really matter. Don't take them seriously. Whatever you were born into, whatever appeals to you, that is as good as anything else.

"I think the logic of relativism has two very deadly consequences. One is, in the end, it says that nothing is important, nothing really has an authority claim. I think we have seen, in the last 200 years particularly, that when all other authority claims are overridden, the result is not freedom. The human becomes all powerful. And because there's no check, no higher authority, the political system makes itself into the new god, making total claims and prepared to back them with violence. Then what began as relativism turns, as in the case of Communism, into a new absolute that denies the right of any other absolute to exist.

"So, relativism, I feel, is the unhealthy or skewed response to the discovery of multiple truths. What pluralism says is that there's another option: I take my religion or some other religion very seriously; my religion is a true religion, has a connection to God, has absolute commandments from God, yet I believe it is not intended by God to cover every human being. I have no right to claim that God's love is exhausted by loving me or my people. God's communication with us is not exhausted by the Hebrew scriptures, by the New Testament, or by anything else. God is a creative, diversified Creator and not a monolithic, tyrannical one who runs one club and if you don't join the club, you're finished. That would make God cruel, arbitrary, whimsical."

Greenberg suggests that pluralism, or something like it, is the only path for the world's future—given that relativism has failed and fundamentalism is not only flawed but also flies in the face of religious reality in the twenty-first century. "Some people think that their own absolute claims are undermined by the alternative religion. For some, the only way to resolve the tension is to get rid of the other. And since you can't do it the old way, which is to withdraw to a ghetto or put the others in a ghetto, you resort to ever more radical or violent ways of trying to suppress the others. Or you become indifferent. The contemporary push seems to be toward either relativism or fundamentalism, which I think are the mirror images of each other. In both cases, you deal with the others by removing their absolute claims—either by being indifferent to them or attacking them.

"The alternative, as I see it—and I think this is what God wants of us—is to reevaluate our own tradition and others, removing the negative justification of our own traditions. This removal drives us from the dark side to the positive side. What does Judaism teach me that makes me a better person and worthy and willing to live a good life? What does Christianity stand for that would make me want to be a Christian? God asks us to serve God out of love and understanding of the richness of our own tradition, and not out of the belief that all the others are benighted and will go to hell. Pluralism can encourage all religious groups to improve, deepen, enrich."

One of the less frequently noted consequences of attacking, demeaning, or discounting another faith is that it tends to blind believers to abuses and problems within their own religious circle. As Greenberg put it: "You say to yourself, well, what we're doing may be bad, but they're worse. We shouldn't give aid and comfort to them by admitting our own weaknesses. But if you lose that demonization of the other, suddenly you're free, emotionally and theologically, to try to improve what is meant to be improved in your faith. In my own case, the Christian-Jewish dialogue opened my eyes; I came back to my own community and looked around and said, why is there no serious relationship between Orthodox Jews and liberal Jews? Religious groups need real dialogue with the other for their own best purposes, not just because of the other."

I admired Greenberg's insistence on a religious openness that respected the absolute claims of other faiths, but I wondered how it might work in practice. How does an observant Jew understand the most paradoxical Christian mysteries, affirm them, yet maintain the vital Jewish difference? Greenberg's answers were exploratory, far from final, and yet full of conviction. Vital to them was his certainty that God possesses the freedom to communicate with humans in many ways. Just as important is his conviction that God allows genuine divergence of views about God—an ongoing dialogue among groups with different traditions and, thus, differing perspectives. As he talked, it seemed to me that this dialogue he referred to represented a permanent plurality of views—no final consensus or resolution, no universal triumphal image. A permanent diversity would, thus, seem to be evidence of God's power to create multiplicity rather than a refutation of God's existence.

"It's entirely possible that things like the Resurrection and the Incarnation really did occur in the context of Christianity—and not just as illusions or human tricks. God may well speak to this community literally in those kinds of gestures and symbols. I, as a Jew, don't have to disprove that in order to prove my own tradition. Christians say that God became flesh in Christianity; the traditional claim went on to say that this fact made Judaism second class. Now, obviously I believe Judaism is first class, but that doesn't mean I have to deny or undermine the claim that God became flesh in Christianity. Given that so many Christians now understand that Judaism goes on being a valid religious covenant independent of Christianity and Christ then I think Jews can afford to allow for that claim in Christianity."

Pluralism is a balancing act between enunciating real differences and eliminating false or unnecessary ones—a back-and-forth dance of respectful disagreement and willing embrace. "Jews may think that the Incarnation is a wrong application of a religious idea, but at least they can recognize, say, that the idea of the Trinity is trying to serve the real, monotheistic God. The Trinity is not three Gods, as many Jews have traditionally believed; it's three-in-one. Now, you can argue that that's not credible logically or rationally, but of course, God can act beyond reason. It's not necessarily acceptable in Jewish theological terms. We do not believe that there are intermediaries between God and man. But we have a long tradition of speaking about God anthropomorphically, both in the Bible and later. So at least we can admit that Christianity is not off the wall. It's an *extension* of ideas, ideas that we accept. I'm probably going to say it's an extension that goes too far; but then again, my argument is that we should agree to disagree.

"Any critique I might make of the claim of Jesus as God Incarnate does not mean that I want to abolish or demolish Christianity. After all, in modern Christian theology, there have been tendencies emphasizing Jesus as the vehicle bringing humans to God and de-emphasizing the literalness of his claim to *be* God. There's room for a wide range of affirmations."

As Greenberg and I concluded our talk, I couldn't help thinking of the diversity of understandings of Jesus, of the Incarnation, and of other mysteries among my Christian interviewees in these pages. It's true that Christ is central to their lives in a way he is not for Greenberg, and yet "a wide range of [Christian] affirmations" is exactly what this book represents. What if that range, and the range of religions beyond it, were evidence of the grandeur of God, not of the failure of humans to "get" God in the right and only way? That would be what I want: a fervid pluralism not an angry fundamentalism or a tepid relativism. That would be an acknowledgment of God's power, complexity, and finesse. And I believe that it would only threaten entrenched, fear-fueled dogmatism, not living tradition.

Greenberg maintains a tension that appeals powerfully to me. He's an Orthodox Jew who honors the depth and resonance of an ancient tradition, and lives within its values and the texture of experience it creates. He's an inheritor as well as an innovator, and a mere modernization of religion isn't what he's about. He reaches into the tradition for ancient but living values that can support his very twenty-first century take on the challenges of religious pluralism.

This dynamic relationship between the old and the new seems to me to be the essence, not just of religion, but of healthy culture and probably even a healthy personal life. It's very much the way I want to practice my religion: neither running backward into the safety of changelessness nor rehabbing my faith according to every change in the psychic or intellectual weather.

UNITE WITH ALL LIFE

William Bryant Logan

I nterviewing Bill Logan was a reunion for me, maybe even a home-coming. We had first met in 1976, at Stanford, as first-year graduate students in comparative literature. Our friendship blossomed fast, and we were soon sharing an apartment, where we drank local wine, made pasta sauce from mussels Bill picked off the rocks at a nearby beach, and read poems aloud. Bill's main literary passions were Spanish: Federico Garcia Lorca's poetry and the work of other great Generation of 1927 poets. I had studied Japanese poems for years, but Bill's voice, modulating from a rich baritone to a whisper as he read the lines he loved most from Lorca or Luis Cernuda or his teacher Kenneth Koch, was my real introduction to poetry.

Neither of us liked Stanford much, but Bill's eventual withdrawal from the university was orderly, while mine was alcohol-fueled and chaotic. We reunited a few years later in New York. Bill and his first wife, Susan Ochshorn, not only provided me with a temporary couch to sleep on but with a career start; I worked under Bill at a book publishing company, and Susan got me my first jobs in the magazine business. They also had the courage to make an issue of my drinking. Their compassionate but firm words pushed me hard toward getting help.

During our New York years, I knew that Bill had done something that none of our academic or ex-academic friends had come near doing: he'd made a commitment to a Christian church. That the church was the rather fabulously eclectic, New Age–tinged Cathedral of Saint John the Divine in upper Manhattan didn't really mitigate the oddness of it, given our background as secular intellectuals. And Bill was much more than a parishioner; he was Writer-in-Residence at the great cathedral, with an office high over the sanctuary, an eyrie you could only reach by clambering, Quasimodo-like, up a very disorienting spiral staircase.

His workaday writing for the cathedral was part of a career that was shifting from the purely literary to an engagement with the spirit and with the natural world. Although he still did masterly translations from Spanish in the years we both lived in New York (including Lorca's play *Once Five Years Pass*, brought out by Station Hill in 1989), he was turning into an accomplished horticulture and garden writer—*House and Garden, New York Times*—who also liked to explore topics such as the form and meaning of the Gothic cathedral and the evolution of the American landscape. (His 1996 book, *Dirt: The Ecstatic Skin of the Earth*, established him as a naturalist with a poet's feel for language and a narrative historian's sense of significant detail, and *Oak: The Frame of Civilization*, released in 2006, continued in the same vein of lightly-worn erudition in both nature and culture.)

In our years in New York, Bill also became a member of a group of students of esoteric spirituality influenced by the writings of Gurdjieff. By the time I was ready to interview him for this book, I had no idea what that group meant to him and where or what his Christianity was. I'd been out of touch during the period when his first marriage ended. I knew he was remarried—to artist-designer Norah Humphrey, whom I'd known too, in my New York days—and that he had become a professional arborist in Brooklyn.

So when I joined Bill and Norah inside their comfortable, cluttered, cheerfully bohemian house on State Street, I felt like a time traveler looping back to California 1976 via Manhattan 1986. Rangy, bearded, given to both explosive laughter and sudden moments of very serious and focused introspection, Bill was unchanged: the same mix of Pacific Coast poet, Upper West Side intellectual, and alert outdoor guy that I remembered. We ate a dizzying variety of informal hors d'oeuvres proffered by Norah, played with Orion, a mammoth white dog, and I asked Bill about the state of his soul.

He took me back to his first adult encounter with the Christian faith, which came about by a combination of accident and a sense of responsibility. Norah—who was one of Bill's co-workers then—asked him, out of the blue, to sponsor her baptism at Saint Thomas's Episcopal church in Manhattan.

Bill laughed. "I said, that's the stupidest thing I ever heard. I haven't been in a church in twenty years, and I'm not going now. But she persuaded me. And it did seem as if something actually *happened* to me there—I don't know what. Outside of texts, which I loved to read, my actual experience of church had been: dull! Dull! But this experience—including the music—was very pleasant, and I was kind of intrigued. So I decided it was my duty as Norah's sponsor to take her to church. And my favorite church was the Cathedral of Saint John the Divine."

Bill met with Saint John's legendary Dean, James Parks Morton, whose eclectic approach to Christian spirituality included a strong social-justice and interfaith focus, an openness to environmental concerns and to earth-centered spirituality, a love for theater, music, and the other arts, and a generous dash of New York media savvy. Morton knew Bill's work and invited him to contribute to the cathedral's newspaper.

"I told him flat out that it was the kiss of death for anyone who wants to be a writer to write for a church paper. It didn't faze him. 'We're going to have this thing where all these animals come to church,' he said, 'and we're going to bless them! And I want you to write about it.'

"I looked at him as if he were out of his mind. 'Just come,' he said. 'If you don't like it, you don't have to write about it.' "

It was the first of the animal-blessings that have come to be a signature of the cathedral and one of the most beloved yearly events in the city. "It was one of the most beautiful things that I had ever seen," said Bill. "It made me see—no, it made me *feel* that there was an entirely different possibility for a Christian life. You could do things that had never been done. You could bring people together in ways they had never been brought together before. And you could have a great deal of fun! There were 1,500 people in this church, half with their animals beside them. There were people with birds on their shoulders. There was a guy who had brought his pet tuatara lizard. There were people with snakes. There was a man with his *beehive*! It made me feel the whole thing was alive and not dead—and I loved the fact that it was taking place in this massive monument to rich Episcopalians of the nineteenth century.

"At first, I had thought the whole thing was a sort of crazy liberal fiesta of everything-is-everything. But soon I realized that it wasn't that everything was everything—everything was *what it was,* and there was the possibility of it all existing together. Jim Morton would preach that that's what religion is: bringing everything back together again."

At the same time that Bill was falling in love with the cathedral, agreeing to be its Writer-in-Residence and then its director of communications, he was joining the Gurdjieffian group. For quite a while, the two commitments supported each other. Under the group's tutelage, Bill developed a daily spiritual practice and learned, as he put it, "to change my way of seeing, to put the rational and the emotional together." He also appreciated belonging to a circle of devotees who took spirituality seriously. "I had desperate troubles with people on the Upper West Side who said: 'Bill's a very smart guy, but he has this little quirk. We tolerate it. Someday he'll outgrow it. Probably has something to do with his childhood.' It was great to be in a place where nobody said that. It was this thing that was my secret, which was disciplining me and forming me."

The group required its members to form study groups, and Bill and his colleagues plunged into the study of the Gothic: cathedrals, art, and the medieval psyche. "It was some of the most fun I've ever had," said Bill. Close study of medieval art and architecture revealed a world of symbolic beauty, mathematical intricacy, and complex faith that, as he said, "the modern world has simply forgotten."

But his doubts about the group as a whole were mounting. "In retrospect, I think it probably could be described as a cult," he said. "We were supposedly helping people but, in fact, letting higher-ups know what people were doing in order that the leaders could claim to have esoteric knowledge of them. And after a few years, I was going broke. I couldn't hold a job because I was doing so much work on behalf of the group, everything from building houses to recruiting members. And like other religious groups, we felt that everything we did 'proved' we were better than other people. More holy, more on-the-path, more this, more that. The idea was that the spiritual life really isn't open to everyone—only to those who *chose* it in the way we did.

"Soon I came to hate that idea because it seemed to be the contrary of a lot of what the cathedral was about—that spirit of trying anything and welcoming all kinds of people, all kinds of different ideas."

Bill's turning point came when he and Norah, newly married, took off for a two-week cabin vacation. "The group really frowned on the idea of any of us being away from it for any length of time," he said. "But we went away anyhow and, sure enough, in the cabin I found this book by C. S. Lewis. I picked it up, thumbed through it, read it, and thought 'Hmm . . . do you mean that anybody sitting next to you at church—the butcher or the used-car guy—could be a servant and a great warrior for God?' It was so liberating. The whole impulse of Christianity is to offer the treasures of spirituality, of God, to anybody—not just to the greatest, the best, the brightest."

At this point in our talk, I nodded. For decades I had been a victim of best-and-brightest thinking, trying feverishly to prepare myself to become a member of an academic-intellectual elite whose values represented the only things I respected: agile intellect, bookish knowingness, a way with words. It was a kind of torture because it cut me off from full membership in the body of humanity.

"In a way, the cult was just a spiritual continuation of the same stuff that's everywhere in the culture, from sports to academia," said Bill. "All the time, rewards for the best and the brightest! Well, that seems exactly what Christianity is an antidote to. People complain about Christianity's authoritarianism or hierarchy, but to my mind, Christianity is the foundation of what true democracy would be. It's the body of Christ, for heaven's sake—everybody, every part, has a role in helping the body live. We don't all have to become the best hand, the best brain, the best eye."

He ditched the cult and began attending church—trying different churches, glad to be anonymous and free of any group attachment. Eventually, he found a quirky Catholic congregation, run by priests of the Oratorian order who appear to have much the same open attitude and generous theology as James Morton. "I remember Jim saying, 'The whole damn problem is organized religion!' " said Bill. "But you're the dean of the Cathedral of Saint John the Divine, I wanted to say. These Oratorian guys say the same thing—if it weren't for this damn organized religion! But I was *saved* by organized religion. I was saved by the fact that there is such a thing as plain old everyday Christianity. So I couldn't understand what they were saying at first. But now I'm not sure I'll get any closer to living as I'd like to live by simply going to church every week.

"It's more that I've developed certain habits that I can't shake. One of them is reading the psalms every morning, or another part of the Bible. There's this anthropologist, Keith Basso, who interviewed Apache children living in urban areas. Every kid he talked to said that their parents or grandparents had told them stories—and the kids said, 'the stories hunt me.' The stories don't let the kids go. I feel that way about stories in the Bible, and especially about the psalms. They hunt me. They're tough. Especially the ones that are depressing—the 'I can count all my bones' psalms. They make contact with something in me that is more real than what's going on around me or in the newspaper. They touch feelings about myself and who I am. They probe into a part of me that I'm not familiar with looking at. They confront my feelings, and they don't ask me to do anything about the feelings. The psalm just goes in there and stirs stuff up, and that stuff sometimes remains stirred up for a day or a week."

If for now Bill's spiritual search is more about the soul than the pew and pulpit, it's also clear that he lives and works in a cathedral that's even bigger than Saint John the Divine—the world of nature, where trees are the architecture and sculpture. "When I'm working with trees," he said, "feeling a certain kind of involvement, I'm not really thinking about what the client thinks of me or whether I'm going to get the job. There's a lot of liveliness in the process when I'm immersed in trying to figure out the truth of this tree now. The tree's been sick probably twenty-five years, and you're looking around, racking your brains. You're becoming a part of the process of everything living, and living together, and it's really vivifying, not only to me, but to the person I'm talking to, whether or not they ever become my client—and it's also vivifying to the tree!

"If you've touched, felt a certain kind of tree again and again, you can almost feel when there's something wrong. There are physiological reasons for this. When a tree's circulatory system is not working properly, the relationship between the bark and the circulation system will change, so you can actually feel differences in that tree. I want to be a part of that whole intimate living of life and not this creature set apart from it, trying to be above or below it. The recognition that *there is a God*—as Jim Morton would say when he found a parking place—makes you feel this connection and this freedom."

BE HONEST ABOUT WHAT YOU DON'T UNDERSTAND

Leo Lefebure

One of the saddest results of the current battles between the partisans of conservative and liberal religion in America, it seems to me, is the loss of a sense of religion as the exploration of mystery—probing a truth so compelling that it must be explored but so vast that it will never be comprehended. Traditionalists seem frightened of the exploration and would rather boil religion down to a set of carefully bounded doctrinal or moral dos and don'ts, pegged to Biblical tags or papal utterances but oddly lacking in the freedom and joy of real contact with God. Liberals, for all their willingness to experiment with forms of religious thought and expression, often distrust the mystery and are more comfortable, say, with Christ-as-Gandhi, a very saintly man and a noble social reformer but hardly the sort of searing, transfiguring presence who could bring an ecstatic smile to the face of a dying martyr.

How could we overcome these polarities and become willing to explore the mysteries? Where might we find a traditionalism that's radically exploratory, an openness steeped in two millennia of faith, a fusion, or at least a dance, between knowing and not knowing? According to Father Leo Lefebure, who was professor of systematic theology at Fordham University when we talked, and now holds the Matteo Ricci Chair in theology at Georgetown, we can find it right in the mainstream of Christian theology. A scholar and teacher who has spent his career demonstrating the breadth of the orthodox Christian tradition and its resonance with other faiths, he opened my eyes to an aspect of that tradition that I had not exactly missed but had severely undervalued—its openness to paradox and permanent tension; its exploratory courage and brio; its willingness to not know.

These are easy qualities to miss in an era when orthodox belief is usually equated with a sullen, defensive certainty, and the secular disciplines, chiefly science, claim a monopoly on questioning and the careful testing of premises and results. But as we spoke in his office at Fordham, Lefebure reminded me that, as he put it, "there's this wonderful sense in the Christian tradition that God is always *greater*. A movement between intelligibility and incomprehensibility that is always going on. If we understand God within the limits of our understanding, how little we understand! And the flip side of that is the mystery of *human* existence. If we're created in the image and likeness of God, that means there's something incomprehensible about ourselves. We're never done understanding God or ourselves, but there's always this movement: knowing and loving but acknowledging the limits of our knowing and loving—back and forth."

Lefebure has also been studying the dynamics of this tradition in the context of other religions. He's written comparative studies of Buddhism and Christianity, explored the Jewish consciousness of Jesus, and lectured extensively—especially after 9/11—on Christian-Muslim relations. And he's examined one of the thorniest issues in those relations, which also happens to be one of the greatest blocks to embracing religion, especially the Christian religion: the grim record of violence that seems to accompany human claims to holiness.

Born in Chicago and raised in a devout family, he opted for the priesthood early, attending a high school seminary as well as a collegiate one. He spent nine years as a parish priest and enjoyed it. "In some of the helping professions, like counseling, you're dealing with problematic cases pretty much nonstop," he said. "Whereas the joy of parish life is you deal with the other side of life too. I had people with horrendous problems coming in. At one point, I was doing part-time work for the Marriage Tribunal in Chicago, so I would interview people who had been divorced and were applying for annulments. I heard the whole list of horror stories, from attempted murder on down. But I also had the chance to celebrate new life: baptisms, graduation, the whole array of joyous celebrations, as well."

Despite these satisfactions, his calling was to scholarship, and an early goal was to become a general Biblical specialist. But in his studies for a licentiate in sacred theology at Mundelein Seminary near Chicago, a particular portion of the Bible had attracted his attention: the wisdom books of Job, Psalms, Proverbs, Ecclesiastes, Wisdom, Sirach, and the Song of Songs. "In ancient Israel," he said, "there was a cosmopolitan dialogue going on. The writers of the wisdom books borrowed from Mesopotamia and from Egypt. One part of the book of Proverbs is an adaptation of an Egyptian source. In a sense, they are acknowledging that wisdom is everywhere and at least the wise of other nations are in touch with it, so it's not a monopoly of Israelite religion. Just about every culture has proverbs, wise sayings that parents tell children when they're little. How do you grow up to be both virtuous and successful, how do you navigate through the difficulties of life? And this flows into the later mystical tradition in various ways."

The wisdom tradition is by no means confined to the "official" wisdom books of the Hebrew Bible. Lefebure sees important similarities in form and content between the "official" wisdom books and much of the teaching of Christ in the Gospels—including the Sermon on the Mount. There is, he claims, "wisdom language" in the complex Gospel of John and in Saint Paul's letter to the Colossians as well.

For Lefebure, this golden vein of wisdom discourse running through the scriptures and, thus through the teachings of Christ represents a unique form of openness and non-exclusivity at the heart of the tradition. For his dissertation at the University of Chicago, he chose to examine the impact of wisdom discourse on modern liberal theology, focusing on the great Catholic thinker Karl Rahner and the innovative Anglican theologian Norman Pittenger. He mainly analyzed their Christology— their understanding of the nature and meaning of Jesus. But before embarking on the actual writing of the dissertation, Lefebure went on an epic cosmopolitan journey that was to change his life.

"A couple at whose wedding I'd presided in my first parish in Des Plaines, Illinois, moved to Bangkok, and the woman invited me to come to visit them," he told me. "I thought: this is too good an offer to pass up! I was cramming for my comprehensive exams, and so I said, this will be my reward. If I pass the comps, I'll go to Bangkok. And then a good friend told me he was interested in going with me. So I had a traveling companion, and I stretched the trip."

Lefebure and his friend spent a week in Kyoto, visiting gardens, Buddhist temples, and Shinto shrines, then Bangkok and five days in a Buddhist monastery in Chiang Mai. "They weren't a bit interested in dialogue; they just assumed I was there to learn to meditate," he said with a smile. In Burma, they toured the magnificent 800-year-old temple complex at Pagan; and then came Bali, for five days, in the company of a missionary priest who had lived on the island for forty years. He introduced the travelers to Hindu leaders. "I saw this very vibrant Hindu faith," said Lefebure, "combined with the earlier traditions in Bali. It piqued my interest. As I was writing my dissertation on wisdom Christology, I concluded it with some reflections on how the biblical wisdom trajectory can open out to dialogue with other religions."

Soon this dialogue was to become Lefebure's main preoccupation. In 1989, he published *Life Transformed,* a book of meditations on the scriptures that compares Christian and Buddhist views of life and holiness. On a fellowship from the Association of Theological Schools in the United States, he returned to Kyoto and studied with Masao Abe, a philosopher whose work has centered on interpreting Zen Buddhism in a philosophical language that spans East and West. Abe, whom Lefebure had originally met in the United States, introduced him to leading lights in Japanese academic philosophy and the Japanese Christian world as well as Buddhist thinkers of various schools. The fruit of these studies was *The Buddha and the Christ* (1993).

The books caught the eye of members of Monastic Interreligious Dialogue (MID), a group of Benedictine and Trappist nuns and monks who promote contact among monastics of different religious traditions and sponsor forums where they exchange and share perspectives. Lefebure became an adviser to MID's board and attended the first Gethsemani Encounter, an MID-organized interfaith confab at the monastery where Thomas Merton lived and wrote. There, Lefebure met the Dalai Lama and other eminent Buddhists from around the world. He would go on to become a major force in Catholic-Buddhist dialogue, to meditate with, interview, or share podiums with Buddhist teachers like Norman Fischer of the San Francisco Zen Center, Hawaii-based American Zen pioneer Robert Aitken, and Vietnamese meditation teacher and peace activist Thich Nhat Hanh.

Above and beyond his scholarship, Buddhism came to have a powerful effect on his mind and heart. "I made a beginning at Buddhist meditation when I was in Chiang Mai," he said, "but it was a couple years later when I made a vipassana retreat that I had a very powerful positive experience that was purifying. I wasn't consciously thinking; I was just doing walking meditation. I felt myself letting go of things from the past, and at one point, I had an overwhelming sense of peace. My spontaneous interpretation was Christian. It was like my normal ego was out of the way and I felt that no matter what happens in my life, the Holy Spirit will handle it. It wasn't that everything would go well in an outward sense. It was that, even with the worst catastrophes, what's to worry? The Holy Spirit will be there."

His unwavering commitment to Catholic Christianity, his scholarly and private experiences with Buddhism, and the overall intent of the movement toward Catholic-Buddhist dialogue strongly affirmed both faiths, but soon Lefebure's mind grew restless. "I was kind of stepping back," he told me, "and asking myself, okay, what have I not looked at sufficiently yet? And it struck me that, in a lot of the dialogue, we've been focusing on what's positive in both religions, which is perfectly appropriate. But that's not all there is. And then I began to look at the shadow side—the ways in which religious perspectives have so often justified violence toward other groups, however the other is defined, the other tribe, the other religion, whatever."

Lefebure was attracted to the theories of literary-critic-turned-religious-anthropologist René Girard, who sees the origin of human violence in what he calls mimetic rivalry: humans' need to imitate others in order to define themselves. Imitation—mimesis—is a necessary process that builds up culture by creating common needs and goals. But it also means that many people come to want the very same things and begin to compete for what they have learned to desire. The threat of generalized violence that this competition poses is defused by the surrogate victim, or scapegoat, mechanism: an innocent symbolic victim is chosen and sacrificed, purging the community's violent urges by enacting them ritualistically—and human culture goes on.

For Girard, this process is exemplified in the Bible—but with a tremendous twist. The Hebrew scriptures begin with mimetic rivalry and scapegoating firmly in place—the story of Joseph and his brothers is a prime example—but as the Biblical narrative proceeds, the savage practice of scapegoating comes into question. The Hebrew prophets question it; and ultimately, in the New Testament, Christ collapses the whole system by being simultaneously the sacrificed scapegoat and God himself.

According to Girard, the paradigm-shattering Christian idea is that God is forever on the side of the outcast, the outsider, the surrogate victim. In the new dispensation, the scapegoat mechanism implodes.

Lefebure found much to admire and much to criticize in Girard's thesis. He doubted, for example, that the Christian tradition was the only one to resist or transform the mimetic desire-scapegoat pattern and said so in a paper at a meeting of the Colloquium on Religion and Violence, an association of scholars of religion that explores Girard's ideas. "Girard's critique really does not adequately address the Buddhist tradition," he told me. "There are very strong practices for overcoming mimetic rivalry in Buddhism. If you're really doing the *Brahmaviharas*—Buddhist attitudes of love and compassion for all beings—you're practicing sympathetic joy directed toward your worst rival. Meditating on that rival, someone you hope falls on his face, you say: may your success be unending. May your success be unending. In that form of meditation, you don't even have to be able to will this benevolence; you simply try to be *able* to will it. You're basically offering lovingkindness, compassion, and appreciative joy to all beings, to yourself, to your family and friends, to people whom you're neutral toward, but also to people who are 'enemies,' who are in conflict with you, or people you just don't like."

And yet, not even Buddhism has escaped the lure of violence. At a later Colloquium on Religion and Violence gathering, Lefebure was a respondent to a paper by Buddhist scholar (and practitioner) Christopher Ives, who often writes on the deep complicity between the Japanese military and the Buddhist clergy, from the middle ages through World War II. "He did the bloodiest history of Buddhism that you could imagine," said Lefebure. "He was deliberately out to debunk the naïve Western idea that all Buddhists are like the Dalai Lama or Thich Nhat Hanh. He had one harrowing story after another.

"Both sides—Christian and Buddhist—have an ambiguous history. Both sides have resources to critique violence. But both have often gone down horrendous paths as well. After the attacks of September 11th, I was asked to do a whole variety of talks all over, often on religion and violence. I looked at all three Abrahamic religions: Judaism, Christianity, and Islam—in terms of the model that there are principles that critique violence but there are also ways in which each of these traditions has justified violence on religious grounds. I tried to cut through the generalizations and acknowledge that there is one strand of Islam that justifies violence in the name of Islamic principles, but other Muslims are completely horrified."

In another talk, Lefebure detailed the sordid history of Christian violence, and then recalled Pope John Paul II's call for a "purification of memory," fully acknowledging the horrors perpetrated in the name of Christ. "Dr. Ahmed Khan, a Muslim originally from India, said he thought Muslims needed to do a similar purification of memory," said Lefebure, "or even a purification of *message,* because sometimes what certain people think the Qur'an says isn't really what it says. Islam is an ambiguous tradition, like all human traditions. I don't know of any nation or any religion that is completely innocent."

As a scholar who has confronted the worst elements of his own tradition, studied other traditions in depth, and still finds Christianity to be a magnificent mediator between God and human beings, Lefebure has a fearless formula for dealing with doubt and increasing one's faith. It struck me as a powerful and simple way for anyone in the modern world to journey toward faith.

"Be honest," he said. "Saint Augustine ends the *Confessions* with the theme of 'seek and you will find.' In a sense, that's what saves his life, the fact that he keeps seeking, he doesn't rest content at any of the different points along the way toward God. The point is to be honest to your own experience, to your own questions and doubts—the real doubts, not the merely cynical ones—and to attend to the movement of your mind and heart together. I think if we're really honest and listening, we can hear something beyond the doubts. Karl Rahner asked: How do we get in touch with the primordial experience of God as the horizon of our lives, the all-enveloping *presence* of God? It's basically nonverbal. It's brought on, not by a long series of questions to God, but by facing the questions of human existence, of doubt, of suffering, of human evil, and listening. Listen. Don't try to push the problems or pains away. This also resonates deeply with the Buddhist tradition; it's like a Buddhist meditation practice. Listen. Attend. Acknowledge."

"If we listen, we will hear the most important questions. Where do we find the strength to take the next step in times of great difficulty and suffering? Where do we find the courage to be faithful, even when it's not automatically rewarding and pleasant? The great Protestant theologian Paul Tillich called that the courage to be in the face of the universal challenges to being: sin, meaninglessness, and death. Tillich understood that, in the modern world, people aren't afraid of being condemned to hell, they are frightened of meaninglessness. Acknowledging that traditional images of God had lost their power to grant our lives meaning, he used the image of the God beyond God. He saw that the God of conventional theism can be a projection. Culturally constructed images of God are all limited. At times, they can serve oppressive ends, racism, sexism, violence—you name it. There's a strong line of atheistic thought that says religion is basically a series of projections. And, in large measure, that can be true. There are any number of Christian writers who have taken up the same theme: The God we project often is the God tailored to meet our needs. God to make me feel good.

"In a sense, that image of God has to die. Let it. We haven't gotten rid of *the* God, who transcends all our definitions. At the end of the day, in one way or another, that God will still be there down the road."

ACCEPT WHERE YOU ARE

Anna Bradshaw

In the spring of 2004 when my mother was dying, she was cared for, not only by the dedicated, overworked, underpaid staff of her assisted-living facility, but also by visiting nurses and a chaplain from Iowa City Hospice in Iowa City, Iowa. It was my first experience with hospice care, and I was amazed by the knowledge and skill of the nurses—and perhaps even more amazed by their courage. Day after day, they arrived on time to carefully hold, clean, and comfort the emaciated, almost inconceivably fragile, and—to me—somewhat frightening body of Gladys Spayde, as life ebbed and flowed through it.

The hospice chaplain was not a clerical-type male with a booming baritone voice, but a trim, attractive young woman with a short, rather Parisian haircut and a manner that made you want to confide in her. Anna Bradshaw went well beyond professional protocol to really make friends with my mother, and my mother's immediate and obvious love for her seemed to light a light inside her in her last days. Anna didn't come selling God or the afterlife or any specific comfort; she came to listen to my mother's life. Together, they went through some of the photo albums and scrapbooks that told the story of that life: childhood on the Saskatchewan and South Dakota prairies, orphanhood at thirteen, early theatrical ambitions, a European USO acting tour in 1945, marriage to my director father and roles in his summer stock and civic theater productions, and then a turn to teaching speech in junior high school, which she loved far more than the smell of greasepaint. Throughout, Bradshaw displayed a vivid, charmed, and charming receptivity that is as rare in clerical people as it is in the rest of the population.

I wanted to know what accounted for Bradshaw's powerful and unfeigned ability to be present to and for others at the end of their lives. So as soon as I could after my mother's funeral, I returned to Iowa City to talk with her. We sat at a table in the hospice office, and before I knew it—before I could do much about it—Bradshaw was asking me about me: my world, this book, my feelings in the wake of Gladys's passing. I love to talk about myself, so it took me a while to steer the conversation to Bradshaw and her life and faith.

Once I did, it wasn't long before I grasped one of the most important spiritual principles that guides her life and has been guiding it for years: complete acceptance of who and what we are, and *where* we are in life, in the struggle toward God, in the inevitable long walk toward death.

Born in Idaho, Bradshaw was raised in a strict evangelical denomination with roots in Pentecostalism—a no-dancing, no-drinking, no-card-playing faith. Her family had been prominent in that denomination for three generations. It was almost a matter of course that she would work for the church, and she did, earning a ministry certificate that was a prelude to ordination. But instead of attending one of her own church's seminaries, she went off to what she called the "scarily intellectual" divinity school of the University of Chicago. Studying outside the sheltering arms of her ancestral church community, she began to wonder if it really was for her. She struggled to understand her role in a faith that, as she put it, "was wrapped around rules and was there to save you from yourself."

"Eventually," she said, "I had to tell my church that it just wasn't working for me. I returned my license in 2001 and expected a big explosion. But nothing came from the church leadership. You'd think they might have been interested in why one of their own was leaving, a good candidate for their ministry, but they just weren't. And that made me feel more justified in going."

She may have felt justified, but she didn't feel particularly happy. In fact, her leaving the family faith—right in the middle of her divinity studies at Chicago—pushed her into a sort of spiritual free-fall that she didn't hesitate to call a dark night of the soul. In some important ways, that negativity was exactly what she wanted. "I was like a trapeze artist who lets go of the bar," she said. "I had no idea what was out there to catch me or if anything *would* catch me. For a while I had no friends, no construct around me that made sense, and I was depressed. For a year I didn't go to any church; I felt that joining a new group and pretending to be happy ever after would be false. I needed to feel the discomfort of falling. I needed to feel the darkest dark—ground zero."

This need for a particular kind of spiritual discomfort, the need to know what it's like to let go absolutely of certain institutions, objects, memories, and details of identity that orient us and keep us safe, seemed so important to her that I wasn't surprised when she related it to her work as a hospice chaplain. "Oh yes," she said. "I think that that period of free-fall is what helps me do the work I do now because the people I'm with are actually feeling like that. They're letting go totally. And I'm able to sit with that because I've been there."

What Bradshaw eventually found was Quakerism and, within Quakerism, a quality of absolute acceptance of her flawed humanity that was missing from the experience of her childhood faith. "As I learned about the Quakers," she told me, "I said to myself, This doesn't step on who I am. In the church I left, I always had to cut some corner or other off myself—the so-called bad parts. I felt like I was wearing a very tight coat, but that if I sucked in my stomach and cinched the belt tight enough, nobody would notice that it was too small and the buttons were about to pop." She laughed and told a story of one early Quaker worship meeting she attended in which a man, probably suffering back pain, began to stretch out on the floor. "That's weird, I thought, and then I noticed that everybody else was okay with it. Wow, I told myself. You can be yourself here. You can be flesh. You can be embodied."

She also found an orientation toward the individual and the individual's interior life that refreshed and released her. "Some spiritual groups," she said, "will tell you that the answer lies outside yourself; look to an exterior God, look to the guru. The Quakers say that 'there is that of God' in every person. I believe that, I believe that the answer lies within us. If we can stop saying 'Mother told me this, Father told me that,' and quiet our minds for once, well, 'that of God' within us can come forth. George Fox, one of the founders of Quakerism, once said: 'I know that Paul said this, and Jesus said that—but what do *you* say?' When I first heard that, I was amazed. Do you mean that my life matters and history isn't totally *over*?

"What this kind of spirituality calls for is trust—trust that God is going to reveal God's self to you eventually. Maybe not in the resounding way we see in the Bible stories, but in a way that will be yours."

I asked her if there weren't some tensions and frustrations for her on a spiritual path that provided so few explicit guidelines. "Well, sure," she said. "For me, the security that I had everything right left me when I left my family's denomination. I'm glad I left, and yet in some ways I feel I left the Garden, that I left a blissful place, you know? Today, I live the questions rather than the answers, and the questions beget questions, and that can be uncomfortable. I notice longings in myself that I have felt all my life—perhaps these are longings to know for sure, longings for answers. Or maybe this is the longing of the soul for God, and since you can never grasp God, you will always feel that longing.

"I guess that because the answers I once lived with fell flat for me—felt tinny—the freedom I now have to say, that wasn't quite right, feels so good that I'm not really obsessed with answers. And as a Quaker, I'm a newborn: It's been about five years. Ask me again when I'm eighty!"

And then she paused—as if looking inward. "A lot of the truth for me lives in ambiguity," she said, "in the tension of opposites. Somehow an *answer* just doesn't hold the same compelling tension. And yet, I realize that we humans have a natural desire to resolve tension. Sometimes I wonder if my tolerance for ambiguity, my love of the tension, isn't a little smug. See? I can live in uncertainty and you can't! *Develop* a little, for God's sake, and you'll get where I am! I'd like to believe I'm beyond that attitude, but no, it's there in me. Any position you take, no matter how enlightened or freeing or realistic, can get brittle and fall in on itself."

She waved away the conundrums and smiled. "What I do is, I go and hang out with dying people to cheer myself up."

My eyebrows shot up and I barked a strange little laugh, but she nodded earnestly.

"Really, I do. People somehow wake up in the dying process in a way that's very special and rare. In that awakeness, that aliveness at the end of life, I learn so much about God. I mean, I have the privilege of watching people explore the meaning of their lives. They ask themselves: when I sift through what I have done, what rises to the top? What was my greater purpose, and what is greater than I am? Being reminded of these things every day puts me right in my spiritual center."

But surely some people feel deep regret and sadness, and "rage against the dying of the light"?

"Sure they do. I had a patient once who thought that the physical pain she was in was a sign that she had let God down, that the pain was due to some shortcoming in her. And some people are disappointed in how it all turned out—'Gosh, I thought I'd end up as more of a person than I have.' But I think God is as present at death as he is in life, telling us that he is working with us just as we are, that we don't need fixing, that we don't have to be somebody else to be okay."

This was an electrifying thought for me; for most of my life, I have stubbornly hung on to the idea that I really do need to be someone else to be okay: a better, brighter, more honorable human being—and certainly someone with a better understanding of God and of his place in God's world.

The interviewees in this book had been chipping away at these ideas of mine: first, by letting me know that the will (the will to do good, to honor God, to love and help others) is more important than mere intellectual understanding when one is on a spiritual path. After all, a path is something you walk, and the map is only an aid on the journey. Secondly, nearly everyone to whom I had talked had emphasized *relationship* with God—that purely personal, absolutely unique give-and-take between me and the Creator. And thirdly, there was this matter of worthiness. The message I was hearing was: forget it. You will never be worthy of God's love. Worth doesn't come into it. A good parent doesn't love a worthy child more than her less worthy brother, and God cannot love me more when I do the right thing than when I fall short. So achievement doesn't come into it either, and at the end of what may seem to us a "failed" life, we are no less loved than at the end of a life packed with Pulitzers, Nobels, and addresses to the UN General Assembly. The thousand-dollar question is: have we opened ourselves to that love?

"In death, people are traveling through their lives again and saying, well, this is what my life was," said Anna. "Part of my job is to be there as they go on that journey. Some are able to say that their life was enough. But I'm there to reassure them that, even if they can't get to that acceptance, well, that's perfectly okay too, that maybe perfect acceptance and serenity are not for them. There's freedom in that, and for me God *is* that freedom."

Honor Other Paths

Joan Kirby

"I don't think of truth as out there, separate, universal, and stable. I think the truth is showing itself at all times, and so as I see other people going to God on a different plan than mine, well, I recognize that we each have our own perspective—nobody sees the whole thing. The claim that we do see the whole thing doesn't fit with my worldview anymore. We shouldn't be claiming that we see the whole thing because everything human is fabricated according to somebody's perception."

A Catholic sister, not a postmodern philosopher, is speaking. Joan Kirby is a member of the Sacred Heart order and Representative to the United Nations of the Temple of Understanding, a New York–based organization that promotes interfaith understanding and dialogue through educational programs, a yearly award, and work with the UN. She's a quietly passionate woman who's lived in many different worlds—she's been the headmistress of posh Catholic prep schools, a street-level advocate for the poor on Manhattan's West Side, and now, an advocate of a wide-ranging vision of faith. Her commitment to interfaith dialogue and relationship places her, I feel, on the cutting edge of religion today. She, and other interfaith explorers in these pages, such as Joyce Rupp, James Jones, Leo Lefebure, and Yitz Greenberg, are pushing us all toward something beyond ecumenical dialogue: a vision of the real greatness of God, which can show forth in many ways and in many idioms.

Kirby and I met in the midtown Manhattan office of the Temple, a busy, book-and-paper-crammed set of small rooms under a ceiling so low that I was reminded of the cramped half-office in Spike Jonze's *Being John Malkovich*. To avoid the late-afternoon bustle, we pulled a couple of chairs together beside a potted plant in a nearby hallway. Every so often, someone from the Temple peeked in to see if Sister Joan was available. But Kirby was unfazed; patient and gracious, she told me the story of her life and faith as if she had all the time in the world.

She described a rather traditional beginning to her religious life—an early vocation to be a sister, strengthened by the devout atmosphere of her boarding school; a struggle in college at Manhattanville to, as she said, "ditch it" via a lively social life and some love affairs; and a final decision to enter the order. "I had a very strong calling," she told me. "Over the years I've seen a lot of people come and go in religious life—in the sixties and seventies in particular—but I've always said I think my vocation is very deep. I've never regretted joining a religious order, and I love the order I joined."

After five years, Kirby was required to make a final commitment to the Order of the Sacred Heart in Rome. She spent a short time in Paris improving her French, and then went on to theological study at the great Catholic university at Louvain, Belgium. It's a center for training orthodox theologians, but it's also a fully modern university, and it opened Kirby's eyes. "In Louvain, I had a foundational breakup," she said. "My whole mental perspective changed—not my faith so much as the philosophical basis of my faith. I'd always been interested in philosophy—that is, in Thomism, the medieval scholastic philosophy based on the writings of Thomas Aquinas, and I was sent to Louvain to learn Thomism. But I came away as a real phenomenologist with a great attraction to Heidegger. From a very static, absolute-truth, universal-truth perspective, I came to what was a very profound realization for me—that I see the world through my perspective, that the truth is not absolute, and that people see things differently. It was a real intellectual paradigm shift."

Kirby became a teacher and then an administrator in Sacred Heart schools, including Stuart Country Day School in Princeton, New Jersey, and the Convent of the Sacred Heart on 91st Street in Manhattan. "I loved teaching," she told me, "and didn't like administration at all. I guess my tendency is probably more intellectual than it is practical."

In the sixties, Kirby's life was going through massive changes. The Sacred Heart order in Rome adopted what the church calls a preferential option for the poor—a special concern with issues of poverty and special care for its victims. The sisters were asked to choose whether to remain semi-cloistered or to engage fully with the outside world. They chose the world, and they gave up the habit as well. "It was a profound, radical change in our lives," said Kirby. It was also a change she welcomed. "Our schools largely attracted upper-middle-class students, very smart, very attractive, very polished people. I felt I had committed most of my life to that group, and in the sixties, I had a very strong inner sense that I was not contributing anything to bettering the situation of the poor."

Kirby the intellectual mentor of wealthy young ladies metamorphosed into Kirby the fighter for decent housing for the powerless. She moved to Hell's Kitchen on the west side of Midtown—a very rough district in those days—and went to work in a storefront tenants' agency on 10th Avenue. "It was a real dump. People would come into our agency and say that the landlord was putting them out or their housing was threatened some other way. We would send them back to try to organize their building, and if they couldn't do it, we would go and knock on doors and organize the place ourselves, bring all the tenants together so they knew their rights. And then, if necessary, we took the landlord to court."

The streetwise veterans at the agency knew that Kirby wasn't suited for day-to-day duke-it-out advocacy in the bowels of the justice system. "They said I didn't have a strong enough killer instinct," she told me. So she was put to work on another project. Eight residential buildings on 50th Street were for sale by their owner. If Kirby could get the buildings' tenants to pony up $2,000 apiece, they could buy the buildings, turn them into cooperatives, and have a little security in Manhattan's always volatile housing market. She traveled to Washington to negotiate low-interest Federal loans for the residents who couldn't come up with the cash. "The idea was that this would anchor the neighborhood and act as resistance to gentrification. It worked," said Kirby with obvious pride. "And the work of that housing organization has kept the neighborhood very mixed since then. There are hundreds and hundreds of poor people left in that neighborhood."

She went on to administer a micro-loan fund—a $100,000 kitty from which she made $2,000 loans to low-income folks for plumbing and heating repairs and other upgrades. "It was a beautiful experience. They always paid us back on time," she recalled. She found herself traveling to City Hall, to Albany, and to Washington, D.C., to advocate for legislative relief for low-income tenants.

But it was the poorest of the poor who increasingly came to dominate her thoughts—New York's homeless. "It was getting so I couldn't step over their bodies on the street anymore without trying to do something." Her chance came when a philanthropist donated money to create Housing for the Homeless, a program that bought and revamped buildings, such as hospitals and hotels, into residences. James Parks Morton, the social-activist Dean of the Cathedral of Saint John the Divine in upper Manhattan, asked Kirby to be Executive Director. "I'm not that good with money or numbers," she said. "So they kicked me upstairs to be president and got a director who could manage a twenty million dollar budget more easily than I could."

The Kirby-Morton connection proved crucial in shaping the latest phase of her life: her deep commitment to interfaith work and the Temple of Understanding.

Founded in 1960, the Temple is a remarkable example of just how rapidly a simple idea can grow. Julia Hollister, the wife of a well-to-do New York attorney, wanted to create a space in which the many religions of the world could meet in friendly dialogue. What turned the idea into reality was a chance meeting at a cocktail party three days later between Hollister and a cousin of Eleanor Roosevelt. Impressed by Hollister's vision, the cousin put her in touch with Roosevelt. Armed with letters of recommendation from the well-connected former First Lady, Hollister enlisted the support of a gallery of world spiritual and temporal leaders, from Gamal Abdel Nasser and Jawaharlal Nehru to Pope John XXIII and Albert Schweitzer (his reply: "Come at once and I will send a canoe.").

By 1968, the Temple was up and running, organizing the first of several Spiritual Summit Meetings in Calcutta. One prominent attendee was Thomas Merton and another was the sister of the Dalai Lama, who urged Hollister to visit the exiled Tibetan leader in Dharamsala, India. Hollister's warm relationship with him presaged the other alliances she would forge during succeeding Summits with the likes of Joseph Campbell, Sufi teacher Pir Vilayat Khan, Buddhist adept Chogyam Trungpa Rinpoche, and eventually U Thant, Secretary General of the United Nations.

In 1993, Dean Morton, who had been involved in the Temple almost since its inception, asked Joan Kirby to join its board, and in short order, she became its Executive Director. During her six years in that position, she also developed an interfaith curriculum for Auburn Seminary, a Presbyterian school that shares the Manhattan campus of Union Theological Seminary. It was no stretch for Kirby, who had been practicing Buddhist meditation for several years. "I think that Christian traditions, and the Roman Catholic tradition in particular, have overemphasized the word and the I-Thou separation from God," she told me. "The ideal is always union with God, and I think Zen teaches you that—that there isn't any separation. I was very attracted to prayer in the beginning, but I came to a dead end because I wasn't getting any nourishment—so I turned to Zen. It hasn't made me a Buddhist; it's deepened my faith in my own tradition. Union with God, that's what our Eucharist is all about—and we ought to be emphasizing that more. And if we could only share the silence instead of all those *words,* it would be much better."

Kirby's emphasis on seeking union with God, the mystical strain in Christianity, puts her in communion with many other Christians (and I'll include myself among them) who want a dynamic faith based on a living relationship with God, not merely a religious club to join and a set of rules to obey. Many of us also want a faith that learns from and finds the maximum amount of common ground with other religions or, at the very least, with the more mystical, union-seeking expressions of faith within those religions.

In several books, the scholar of comparative religion Frithjof Schuon has argued that while the diversity of religious practices and doctrines can't, and shouldn't, be reduced or diminished, the mystical approach to God, which seeks unity with God and moves beyond belief in dogmas or doctrines to a powerful certainty stemming from a living knowledge (gnosis) of God, is remarkably similar from religion to religion. In this sense, unity with God and unity across religious boundaries are two sides of the same coin.

As the Temple of Understanding's UN liaison now, Kirby carries on Julia Hollister's vision of the Temple and the UN as partners (Hollister once called the Temple "a spiritual United Nations") by promoting the interests of religious non-governmental organizations in the world body and by making sure that UN proposals and programs embody religious values and goals. The work has taken her around the world and exposed her to most of the world's faiths on their home ground. She's not afraid to declare a deep love for other faiths—"I think I have a Hindu soul," she told me—but she also insisted that going wider into the interfaith dimension has deepened her Christian faith.

"I keep saying: to be truly interfaith each religion has to give something up," she said. "Judaism has to give up that sense of chosenness. Christians have to give up the drive to go out and convert everybody. There's a profound enrichment from recognizing that there are many different paths to God—I'm on one path, and it's where my roots are, and it doesn't appeal to me to think of changing—but that doesn't constrict me from being open and learning and being enriched by the other fabulous traditions. I think it strengthens my faith. Jesus is my path to the Father. He has shown me the most profoundly human way to live. For many, many years, I would study the gospel in order to pattern my affections and my choices on what he chose. Seeing compassion in Jesus and trying to let that grow in me. And the Samaritan woman, that alien whom Jesus blessed, well, she taught me to respect the Other, so I go for the Other too."

As she spoke, this very accomplished woman of social-justice and interfaith affairs grew less and less businesslike, quieter and quieter, yet also more intense; even the Temple office grew still around us. I asked her how her image of Christ has been affected by her contact with other faiths.

"I don't look outside for Jesus anymore," she replied. "The whole goal is to be transformed into Christ, and I think that's what the Eucharist is all about—you stick with the Eucharist, and you're transformed. I think that's what Christianity is all about too: transformation. And I don't mean transformation into anything but someone more human.

"Somebody said to me recently that our religious traditions will be changed as we become more interfaith—and that's good, that's one way to help religion to be more human. I see it happening in myself and others. But I don't think you have to be part of interfaith to get rid of rigidity— you only have to look at Jesus to become much less sure of your righteousness. And I think just trying to be more Christ-like makes you much more open toward other people, no matter who they are and what they believe."

Focus on the Good

Chuck Robison

The interview for this chapter took place live, on the air and in cyberspace at the same time, as a fifty-five-minute segment of an Internet radio show called "What If It Really Works?" on the Contact Talk Radio website (www.contactradio.info), which highlights New Age and "new paradigm" thinkers and writers. The founders and hosts of "What If It Really Works?" are Chuck Robison and his wife, Karen.

I'd met Chuck Robison when he was pastor of Christ Presbyterian Church in Telluride, Colorado, and was impressed by the energy of his presence and personality—he's a large sixtyish man who seems to fill any room he's in—and the breadth of his experience. Aside from preaching and pastoring, he had been a professional photographer and a high-octane businessman, among other things. He's an unconventional Christian—a thinker who worships God and Christ in the light of a spirituality that encompasses other faiths, advanced science, and what many see as a spiritual revolution under way planetwide.

I was intrigued by what he told a Telluride journalist at Christmastime in 2004: "The discovery of infinitesimal particles, such as photons for example, the particles composing light and forms of electromagnetic radiation, confirms for me that our world is all about light. My God does not have a long white beard, nor does He sit up there in heaven on a throne as William Blake pictured Him. I believe God exists in these particles without charge or mass. He is also in those charged particles that collide with photons. He occupies the spaces in between the smallest particles of nature. He is omnipotent, omnipresent, and omniscient. Therefore, all allusions to the 'universal light of God' are apt. So the celebration of the birth of Christ is all about light coming to the earth, God's gift to mankind. This holiday is about accepting that gift and coming to understand that light is also love. Where there is light, darkness disappears. Where there is love, fear cannot exist."

Robison, who now lives in Texas, told me he'd be happy to be interviewed, and he wondered if I'd like to do it on his show, as a sort of turning of the tables. Normally, Chuck and Karen interview spiritual teachers and authors; this time, I'd be both the guest and the interviewer, by phone, and Chuck would answer the most probing questions I had about his spiritual life.

Now, I have a very modest background in broadcasting: three years (1967–1969) part-time on a 250-watt AM station in rural Iowa while I was a high school kid. I spun easy-listening vinyl, read the news off an AP teletype machine, and recorded ads for local businesses such as Leck's Dairy Creme and Flamingo Bowling Lanes. This was only about two rungs above ham radio, but I flatter myself that I can sound pretty smooth on the air—or on Wi-Fi, for that matter.

So I agreed to do the interview on July 27, 2006, at 5 P.M., Pacific Standard Time, under the deterritorialized conditions of the digital age. The engineer was at the Contact studio in Bellevue, Washington; the Robisons were broadcasting from the Unity Church of the Hills in Austin, Texas; and I was at home in St. Paul, with our cat sleeping on my laptop keyboard. I was better prepared than usual but still plenty self-conscious as I tried for pear-shaped vocal tones.

I led off with a question about Robison's childhood openings to the spirit, and in his rich West Virginia–Texas-bred baritone, he told me about the altar call in a Dallas Presbyterian church to which he responded at fifteen.

"I don't know what happened," he said. "I came down to the altar when the minister asked people to let Jesus be their leader, or whatever the magic words were at the time. I didn't know I was doing it; it just happened before I understood what was going on. From that point forward, I simply *knew.* Of course, I didn't know all the twists and turns my life would take—nobody does—but I certainly knew that I was supposed to be part of something big. And it seemed natural for me to become a minister; there were plenty of good role models for that in Dallas.

"But my first priority was to get out of high school! As my friends could have told you, that wasn't necessarily an easy thing to do. I was way better known as a hell-raiser than as a scholar."

By leaving hell where it was for a while, Robison managed to obtain a diploma and then go on to undergrad work at Austin College, the leading Presbyterian liberal arts school in Texas. He was serious enough about his studies and his faith to decide to apply to Union Seminary in Richmond, Virginia, then the number-one Presbyterian seminary in the South. But as it turned out, he was headed to an even more prestigious academic perch. On a visit to Austin College, the late Dr. James I. McCord, president of Princeton Theological Seminary, met the young clergyman-to-be and was impressed. "He said, 'I want you to come to Princeton, and I'll make it possible," Robison told me.

At Princeton, he threw himself into the civil-rights and antiwar ferment of the sixties, taking part in demonstrations and protests and developing a social conscience that is still an important facet of his personality and calling. Robison's first post-seminary church posting, back in his native West Virginia, coincided with the birth of another passion: photography. With his very first pastoral paycheck, he bought his first camera, and right away he found himself relating photography and faith. "Once I had taken a few pictures, I knew I was *supposed* to be doing this," he said. "I believe that, when I take a picture of somebody, I can connect with their soul. When I can hand them a piece of paper that reveals that soul in a positive way, I'm doing healing and ministry."

Robison was then posted to a church in Philadelphia, and he eventually found himself on another track as well: working part-time doing marketing for the Presbyterian Ministers' Fund (now Covenant Life Insurance), the oldest insurance company in the country. Whether he knew it or not, he was taking his first steps out of organ-and-altar ministry and into something else.

"I never, ever doubted that God exists and is present to us," he said. "But what started eating me up was that I didn't seem to fit anyplace in the church as it was structured then. I spent a lot of time going to afternoon coffees with charming elderly ladies. I could be very nice to them, but it just wasn't *me*. I was looking for something that was simply beyond the church of that time."

Eventually, he left Philly for Manhattan and a job with Metropolitan

Life. He also divorced his first wife. It was a difficult time but full of promise too. Perhaps the most dramatic pivot point in this unsettled period came in a hospital room in Dallas at the moment his father died. "He died in 1975, at the age of seventy-one," said Robison. "I had fed him his last meal the night before. I asked him to be a guardian angel and protect my son. I watched him and my mother exchange their last words—and then he died.

"As he died, this strong wind rattled the venetian blinds and swept through the room. I felt it and had no idea what it was. But it was so powerful as it rushed through me that I knew right there my life was going to change forever."

Experiences like this made him alert to the free-floating, many-faceted, and more or less countercultural spirituality that was flourishing in the seventies, and he wondered why its energy and questing spirit hadn't penetrated the stained-glass windows of the church. "In the seminary," he said, "we talked all the time about what went on in the Bible, but never once did we talk about things such as the experiences that living people were having with angels. I had learned all this ministerial stuff, and I knew how to do it, but there was something else going on out there, and I wanted to know what it was. So I started asking questions, questions the church wasn't asking, and things started to open up for me."

His insurance career was taking off too. At MetLife, he was an agent-recruitment whiz. Then, at New York Life, he designed the company's mass marketing plan and became the youngest officer in its history. At the age of forty, he went solo as a consultant on training, outplacement, and other human resource issues.

"Forgive me if this is an impertinent question," I said at this point in the interview, "but the insurance industry wouldn't be the first place I would go to widen my spiritual horizons. What did it mean to you?"

Robison was ready for that one. The corporate office suite may not have been a meditation room at Esalen, but it allowed him to regain a sense of vocation—a sense that he was ministering to people under the battle conditions of our business culture.

"Say there's a guy who makes two hundred and fifty grand a year at the age of thirty-one, and he has a deal sheet that's three pages long," he said. "He comes to me ten minutes after he's been fired, and he's hit the wall. All he can think about is, 'Hey, I can't do deals anymore. What am I going to do with my life?' I could help somebody through that. I could give him a chance to take a breath and ask, 'Is this really about deal making, or is it about something else?' As a minister, I had something very concrete to do, something measurable. And I didn't have to be in a church with an organ playing behind me to do it."

Robison was so good at this real-world ministry that he was asked to give seminars to senior officers in the New York Police Department. "I stood up in front of three hundred of these tough guys and said, 'Life is about having a vision of where you are going, and I can help you find one,' " he told me. "After panicking for about five minutes, they realized that they were getting a day off and they might as well sit back in their chairs and enjoy it. I talked, and they learned some things. And I learned that they were good guys, good officers. The cream really does rise to the top in an organization like that."

Meanwhile, he was commanding good money as a formal portrait photographer and studying *A Course in Miracles,* a text very influential in the New Age movement that has been described by one scholar as a Christianized version of India's Vedanta. And he was having powerful psychic experiences—seeing visions of departed family members and hearing phrases and sentences from passersby in the street that felt like spiritual truths. One epiphany in particular has remained with him.

"I saw a woman approaching me on crutches," he said. "She had a beautiful face, but you could tell that she had never had the feeling that she possessed real beauty. As I looked at her I thought, 'This is a whole life right in front of me. I am going to make the conscious decision to see her as beautiful as she is. I am going to see her as healthy and whole.'

"I began to realize that I'm not really a Jesusian; I'm a Christian. Jesus was the man and the teacher, the sainted one. But the Christ is the Son of God. The Christ will not come back because the Christ never left and is here always, in all of us, whether we recognize it or not. The trick, of course, is that lots of us don't recognize it or see it only fleetingly. So I see it as my responsibility—and I'm not very good at this—to look for it in each person I meet, on the off-chance that they have forgotten it and my seeing it will help them remember.

"I once sat down and counted the places in the New Testament where Jesus used the words *sin, sinning, sinner,*" he went on. "And I found fewer than twenty instances. I don't believe it was a big concept for him. And I don't believe it's about Jesus dying for our sins. I think it's all about us realizing that Christ *lives* in us!"

Robison's spirituality was re-energized to the point that he began preaching again, as a volunteer, in various churches around the New York area, and his message was profoundly positive. "These were not Fifth Avenue churches," he said. "They were in the Bronx and Brooklyn and Queens. I preached about 'Ask and ye shall receive,' 'seek and ye shall find,' 'knock and it shall be opened.' I preached about God's presence. About the fact that we are all one, and I mean all six billion of us; that's not an easy concept to get, but it's real." He was experiencing global reality regularly too, as an adjunct chaplain at the United Nations Church Center.

In 2000, after living in Manhattan for a period of twenty-three years (which he called "the adult dose"), Robison followed the suggestion of a friend, the *echt*-sixties folksinger Peter Yarrow, to move to Telluride, Colorado, the picture-perfect mining-town-turned-ski-mecca. There he returned to something like old-time ministering, running the historic Christ Church along traditional Presbyterian lines while extending the church into the community by hosting AA and the local choral society, and operating a food bank.

In 2002 he met Karen, another lifelong spiritual seeker, via the Internet, and they were married two months later. Three years after that, the Robisons decamped for the White Bluff Resort in Whitney, Texas, about eighty-five miles southwest of Dallas. From this comfortable base, they lead seminars on spiritual growth and carry on their broadcast work.

I didn't want the interview to end without asking Robison about sin and evil, which, to me, seem ubiquitous in our world and which his optimistic and generous Christianity, with its New Age feel, seems to discount. Again, he didn't hesitate to respond and to remind me of his moral convictions. "Questions like the war in Iraq are seen solely as political issues, but they are really moral issues," he said. "Is it moral for a country to believe that because it might be threatened, it is okay to go and destroy another country?

"I do know this: as an individual, I have a choice. On a minute-by-minute basis, I can choose to look at the bad stuff or the good stuff. If I choose to look at the bad stuff, I am not going to simply bemoan it or become depressed by it. My only realistic option is to try and make it better. It is not easy, and I don't claim to be good at it, but I am getting better at it."

It was something for me to chew on. When I look at evil, I like to think I am realistic about it, but often this "realism" is little more than a sort of frisson of negativity, a boost to my feeling of superiority over the Pollyannas and my political opponents, followed by paralysis, during which I do nothing against the evil. Chuck and Karen Robison believe, as he told me, that "if enough of us decide to look to the good stuff, there isn't going to be room for the bad stuff." That sounds a little childlike to me, but then Robison has been doing the good stuff his whole life. Do I believe in the good stuff strongly enough to try to do it, by my own lights? Can I remember that the Christian faith is a path to walk and work to do, not just a set of ideas to ponder?

And what if it really works?

FIND THE TRUTH FOR YOURSELF

George Bassilios

"If this were Egypt a couple of hundred years ago," said George Bassilios as I sat at his dinner table, "we would wash your feet, just like in the Bible—because you would have come on foot, of course—and we would feed you, and we would give you a new robe. Tonight, I'm sorry, all we can do is feed you!"

We were about as far from the Egyptian desert and the other Bible lands as you can get—in a spacious house in a hillside development in San Ramon, California, northeast of Hayward and across the bay from the San Francisco peninsula. Bassilios, his wife, Miranda, and I were about to enjoy the rice and shrimp that Miranda was cooking. Bassilios is a slim, handsome man with an open face and an easy and frequent smile; his idiomatic American English is touched just slightly with the rhythm of Arabic. He emigrated with his family from Egypt when he was in his teens and now works in the marketing department of AAA. American-born Miranda, a nurse practitioner, is half Texas Baptist, on her dad's side. These young Bay Area professionals belong to an ancient, noble, and (to most Americans) practically unknown church: Coptic Orthodoxy, the Christianity of Egypt.

While we may be unfamiliar with the Copts (from *Hikaptah*, the Egyptian name for the ancient Egyptian capital, Memphis; it passed into

Greek as *Aigyptos* and gave us *Egypt*), Christian history and doctrine are unthinkable without them. Tradition says that Saint Mark, the evangelist, brought Christianity to Egypt in the first century C.E. The brilliant theological school at Alexandria, founded in 190 C.E., became the most important seat of Christian learning in the ancient world. The home base of many of the fathers of the church, including Clement of Alexandria and Origen, it attracted distinguished visitors too, including Saint Jerome, translator of the Bible into Latin; Saint Athanasius, author of the Nicene Creed and the Coptic Pope of Alexandria in the late fourth century; and Saint Antony, born in Upper Egypt and the first of the Desert Fathers, the solitude-seekers who abandoned the city for desert caves, and thus gave birth to Christian monasticism.

Egypt was so determinedly Christian that it was nearly five hundred years after the Muslim conquest in 641 before the country had a Muslim majority—and as late as the sixteenth century, the majority of Egyptians still spoke the Coptic language rather than Arabic. Descended from ancient Egyptian, Coptic is still the liturgical language of the church.

Today the Copts are a minority but a widespread one, living in every province of Egypt and contributing in important ways to the modern state. The contemporary Coptic Christian best known outside Egypt is probably Boutros Boutros Ghali, the former UN Secretary-General, but there are communities of Coptic immigrants as far afield as Holland, Brazil, and Australia. Most East Bay Copts worship at Saint Antonius's Church (named for the pioneer desert father) in Hayward, where George Bassilios is a volunteer religious educator.

It's a role that fits him. The son of a priest, he "practically grew up in church," as he told me. Unlike many preachers' kids, he was no rebel. His ancestral church, with its colorful vestments and icons, its incense clouds, and its solemn and dramatic liturgy, fascinated him even when he was little. "I liked how the liturgy was tangible, how it appealed to my senses," he said. "I could see a lot of things going on, smell the incense, hear beautiful hymns. It was very dynamic and entertaining for a kid."

The Orthodox, whether they belong to the Greek, Russian, Armenian, Syrian, Coptic, or any of the other Eastern churches, think of their liturgy as a teaching tool, a living demonstration of theology, and that's how Bassilios experienced it as he grew up. "I became more and more able to translate that incense and that behavior I saw into doctrine," he said. "I had this autodidactic kind of desire to learn—why are we doing this? What's the reason behind that? It's something I try to convey to the youth in our church today. It's not a bunch of people performing a play, and we're not just spectators. Every single movement means something, and if you know it, you will be more and more engaged."

Bassilios himself got more and more engaged in Orthodox theology and particularly in the writings of the Fathers of the Church: Augustine, Cyril of Jerusalem, Clement, Gregory Nazianzen—writers who are the common resource for all Christians, whatever the denomination. "The deeper I get into their theology, the more love I have toward it," he said. "There's so much richness there that, even after several years of study, I realized that I was only scratching the surface."

College—at De Anza in Cupertino, California, and Cal-State Hayward—exposed him to many other Christian denominations and to world faiths. (He was, of course, familiar with Islam; Egyptian schools required minute study of the Qur'an.) "I was grateful for this because it led me to study my own faith further," he told me. "I wanted to see which of the various Christian worships could tie me back to the original church, so I went back into history, to the age of the church fathers, and I realized that, outside of a few changes over the years, the Orthodox liturgy of today isn't much different from how it was then. Our service is four and a half hours long, as it was then! I felt the antiquity and beauty of our church.

"But I try to distinguish between the mental knowledge—just understanding something mentally and intellectually—and practical knowledge. I can simply study and study, and it makes little difference. The Bible says that even the devil knows about God. But I need to ask myself if I use my knowledge to become a true Christian, not just a Christian who knows a lot about Christianity. There's a quote we repeat in the church: Make your theology your biography. And there is another one: When people see you, do they see you or the Christ in you?"

We took a break to eat the delicious meal whose aroma had perfumed our conversation, and when we were done, he talked about one of the central paradoxes of the faith: weakness as strength. "Now, consider what I call the Constitution of Christianity, the Sermon on the Mount," he said. "Christ says that the old commandment was an eye for an eye; the new commandment is, if I am slapped on one cheek, I'm to turn the other toward the one who slapped me. Now this is really a deep mystery, isn't it? Carnally speaking, it makes sense to me that, if you hit me, I'll hit you back. This is logical. But I feel that Christ's new commandment takes me beyond that carnal level, that earthly level. And at that new level, I find strength. Saint Paul says, 'Christ has shown in his weakness what is greater than power.' This power that's greater than power is magnified love."

The biggest challenge that Bassilios presented to my own spirituality was his insistence that the differences among religions are foundational and that, because truth is singular, the various faiths cannot all be true. In his religion classes at Saint Antonius, he encourages his young listeners to see the religious quest as a search, not for inner peace, but for truth. Interestingly, he does not insist that the kids choose Christianity; but he suggests forcefully that deciding not to choose is a cop-out. "The biggest challenge I have in my service to youth—particularly the college-age youth—is what they experience of the New Age movement," he said. " 'All is good, all is God'; we're all climbing the same mountain, just taking different paths; you can't say Christianity is better than Islam or Hinduism—they call this spiritual racism.

"I tell them there is one truth, and it is your duty to search for it. I say that, from a logical standpoint, two contradictory statements can't be true at the same time—that's what Socrates said. Now, it's more likely that both of them are false—but they cannot both be *true*. Because they contradict one another, Islam and Christianity cannot both be expressing reality. Christ cannot be, at the same time, a mere prophet among many prophets and the living God. Our society tries to sugarcoat this and say, 'Let's not look at the differences, let's look at the commonalities.' But I think that is disrespecting the intelligence of these kids. You're basically saying, 'Don't look at the substance of these religions, look at the surface.'

"I don't tell them that Christianity is the truth or Islam is. But I tell them there *is* just one way home, and it's their duty to research and be educated on the question of which way is that way. Now, I think Christianity is the one way, but how can I support that—historically, archaeologically, scientifically, logically? I try to stay away from the spiritual because that could be just for you, that could be a matter of feeling only. I tell them that they must make an informed decision because it is a decision that will impact their entire lives.

"I believe that what we know is far more important than what we feel. The goal is to make sure our thoughts are based on truth—reality. The person who takes primary care of his thinking will not have to worry about the validity of his emotions—but the person who judges the validity of his thoughts on the basis of how they make him feel is in for big trouble."

I asked Bassilios where he looks for the strictly historical, archaeological, and logical proofs of Christianity, and he referred me to the books of Lee Strobel, especially *The Case for Christ* (Zondervan, 1998) and *The Case for Faith* (Zondervan, 2000). These popular books, written by a professional journalist who is a former atheist, are collections of interviews with mostly evangelical Christian scholars, clergy, scientists, and other authorities. Strobel puts to them challenging and perennial questions such as "Was Jesus's death a sham and the resurrection a hoax?" and "How can a loving God torture people in Hell?" The responses of the interviewees emphasize testable propositions, evidence, and reason over experience, feeling, and faith-as-a-leap.

It's difficult to call Strobel's books rigorous in their testing of the issues they take up; the only authorities consulted are conservative Christians, albeit thoughtful and intelligent ones. No liberal Christian opinion of comparable force and subtlety, let alone detailed atheist or agnostic critique, is admitted. And many of the arguments advanced establish a degree of likelihood but nothing that would pass scholarly muster as conclusive proof.

In any event, I'd suggest that fully rational, evidentiary proof of whether or not a Jewish man in late-antique Palestine was also God is more a modern preoccupation than a spiritual necessity. At the end of *The Case for Faith,* Strobel himself draws a limit-line around the strictly objective. "Ultimately," he writes, "faith isn't about having perfect and complete answers to every single one of 'The Big Eight' objections. After all, we don't demand that level of conclusive proof in any other area of life. The point is, we certainly do have sufficient evidence about God upon which to act. And in the end, *that's* the issue. Faith is about a choice, a step of the will, a decision to want to know God personally. . . . Or as [evangelist] Lynn Anderson had told me, 'When you scratch below the surface, there's either a will to believe or there's a will not to believe. *That's* the core of it.' "

For me, and for many of the people in this book, "sufficient evidence about God upon which to act" was *experience* of God, not scripture, archaeological evidence, or the internal coherence of theological propositions. Yet I couldn't, and can't, shake George Bassilios's challenge: Ask myself if this experience is the foundation of my belief and, if it is, is this experience now anything other than a good feeling and a happy memory, liable to fade on cloudy days and return when it's sunny? Do I believe that truth is single or multiple? In believing as I do that all faiths point to a single God in different ways, am I perhaps defining God in far too abstract and general a way? Is my attraction to Jesus Christ, which I've tried to deny many times over the years, the choice of a spiritual ideal that suits me, in the Hindu fashion, or a surrender to a compelling truth outside myself?

As much for myself as for the readers of this book, I asked Bassilios what advice he might give to someone who was trembling on the brink of Christian faith but scared or reticent to make the act of will that would put her or him over.

"To look deep within, to search," he said. "Search within and realize that you are longing for something that the world can't give you: perfect happiness, perfect peace. As a human being, you are part of this world; but notice how hard it is for you to reconcile yourself with much of what happens in it. The world is full of war, hate, violence, disaster. As C. S. Lewis points out in *Mere Christianity*, if I were really reconciled to this world, when I see a crime I ought to be okay with it. If I am really of this world, it ought to be all right for me to see people being murdered or raped or whatever. And it's not.

"All of us want to be happy, all of us want to be secure and fulfilled. We want those things that the world sort of gives with one hand and takes away with the other. Everybody wants to be young, but before you know it, you're old. Everybody wants to enjoy the sunshine, but before you know it, here comes the darkness.

"The fact that the world as we know it does not fulfill us is an indication that we were meant for a different world called the Kingdom of Heaven, where, the Bible tells us, there is no sadness, no tears. But in our world, there will always be suffering, always be crime, always be pain, and if you try to run away from it, it will follow you. It's all around. So you might want to search for this other world."

UNDERSTAND TRADITIONAL TRUTH
IN FRESH WAYS

Aiden Enns

T humbing through the inaugural issue of *Geez* magazine, out of
Winnipeg, Manitoba, is a somewhat disorienting experience for a
magazine-industry fossil like me. The cheeky title, the subtitle—"Holy
mischief in an age of fast faith"—and the retro cover graphic (fifties' families dressed up and lined up in church pews) all suggest an irreverent
take on religion. The magazine's statement of faith opens in a vein both
Gandhian and prankish: "*Geez* is your story of experiments with truth.
Because it's time we untangle the narrative of faith from the fundamentalists, pious self-helpers, and religio-profiteers. And let's do it with holy
mischief rather than ideological firepower. We'll explore the point at
which word, action, and image intersect, and then ignite. So let's blas-
pheme the gods of super-powerdom, instigate spiritual action cam-
paigns, and revamp that old Picture Bible."

There's no perky "front-of-the-book" section of tidbits, news notes, or
other short takes interspersed with ads (there are, in fact, no ads). There's
no "well," the center section of long pieces, and no "back-of-the-book"
collage of book or film or record reviews.

The issue is organized as chapters in a parodic "Altar Counselor's
Guide." Within the chapters are first-person accounts of struggles with,
and escapes from, conventional Christianity, an altered ad that tweaks

the Billy Graham empire as a multinational corporation like Coca-Cola, quote collages, a shortie on the ethics of Dumpster diving, another shortie on "planet walker" John Francis, a pilgrim who crisscrossed the United States on foot under a self-imposed vow of silence. The unpredictability of the mix, rollicking along from parody to testimony to prank to prayer, and the sense of an underlying preoccupation with the process of communication as well as the process of faith formation make *Geez* one of a kind. The messages are multiple, but the loudest one is that it is possible, and actually increasingly necessary, to develop an improvisatory, genuinely personal relationship with God and Jesus Christ outside of churches that have become all too comfortable living within capitalist culture.

When I talked with founder/publisher Aiden Enns in his home in Winnipeg, I wasn't surprised to learn that Enns, born in Vancouver, once worked as an editor at *Adbusters*. That Vancouver-based magazine, founded by reformed market researcher Kalle Lasn, turns the visual virtuosity of consumer culture against that culture with slick ad parodies and articles that advocate and chronicle resistance to consumerism, militarism, and the global status quo—while ironically copying the look and language that supports all of that business-as-usual. After going to seminary, working for eight years at a Mennonite publication, earning a second MA, in journalism, and spending some highly unfulfilling time at the Vancouver *Sun* (owned by the gigantic and unabashedly conservative CanWest conglomerate), Enns shucked his expensive suit and his office overlooking the cruise-ship docks in downtown Vancouver. At age forty, he took an *Adbusters'* internship. He became managing editor in about two years.

"*Adbusters* challenges the powerful, the corporate elite, the military, and the economic and social structures that allow the powerful to stay in place," he told me. "The criticism is leveled at them from both a structural and a communications-theory level—Kalle Lasn talks about memes and meme warfare. But the end in view is empowering the populace. That really fit with my agenda; I wanted to help those at the bottom and the fringes to regain some composure as humans—individual identity or autonomy. Fundamentally, to be human is to be free and alive.

"The problem with *Adbusters* is two-fold. It's so emotional that it ends up as primarily a rant, and it doesn't directly address spiritual concerns. I wanted to take the *Adbusters* agenda and my background in the church press and bring the two together in a magazine that had the same critical assumptions about empowering the grassroots—a subversive presence—but that would be spiritually oriented and also nurturing. I left *Adbusters* on good terms: I even asked them to help me imagine a magazine for disaffected Christians—that 'demographic'—and they gave me some good suggestions."

I asked Enns if he considered himself a disaffected Christian. He's thoughtful and articulate, and he takes his time to answer. When the answers come, they tend to have the lucidity of the written word. On this one he paused for a long time.

"If you sat next to me on the bus," he finally said, "and I'm not flying these days; there's something about the cult of speed that takes us away from our humanity—if you sat beside me, and we didn't know each other, and you asked me if I were a Christian, I would have trouble saying yes. Even though I'm a proud member of a Mennonite church. I'm disaffected with the *representation* of mainstream Christianity, but I'm in love with a community-oriented group of people who are spiritually minded, seeking to make a political difference through lifestyles that are counter to consumer capitalist culture. If I wanted to look at it pragmatically, which I don't, I'd say that if you want to effect change for the long haul, spiritual resources are essential. Even if you're not a churchgoer, a religious person per se, you do need strength of character, the ability to envision a brighter, better, bigger, more sustainable future—that's a type of spiritual vision. Taking part in something that is not complete—the creation of that future—is a spiritual venture.

"But that's so utilitarian. There's something irrational in it too, something that is profound in that it is incalculably large and very small as well—how significant something small can be! This is a spiritual dimension, and I would call it the window to joy. It's a manner of perceiving that enables us to see, in the face of all the struggle and the danger and the evil, glimpses of hope. You are enabled to move forward toward something bigger, better, more beautiful, which I would call—this sounds tacky, but spirituality always sounds tacky—the triumph of love."

He made a comparison with the return of spring, something that Manitobans, Minnesotans like me, and other northerners long for in ways that are hard to fathom south of the 40th parallel. "After the snow begins melting, the mud in my garden is literally muck—black and sticky," said Enns. "And out of the muck comes the beauty of the tulip: first leaf, then stem, then flower. That, for me, is a metaphor of the inexhaustible resource called love, the spirit, beauty. Beauty to me is eternal. It's found in the flower, sure, but in you and me too if we have the eyes to see it. And there is beauty when people get along, when reconciliation happens, when the eyes of the powerful are opened. That's why spirituality is important to me in my thirst and hunger for social justice because I'm driven toward the beautiful, which is peaceful but also just. It's why I can't be content to rant. I'm not angry at the system; I'm moving toward a better system. I am not motivated by anger. I'm motivated by love. I ask, 'can't we get along?' and when we can't, I weep. But I have this vision."

I asked Enns how his vision fit with the Christian story, and he smiled and used a term from literary theory. "I've thought a lot about the Christian metanarrative," he said. "The myth, the legend. And I see the figure of Jesus Christ as an inspiration on several levels. At one level, as an incredible human being. How could he do what he did with so much grace and compassion? He was at the periphery, challenging the exploiters in the Temple and in Rome with his vision of love, compassion, and forgiveness. I marvel at his ability to walk around penniless, bringing this good news of liberation and justice, bringing down the mighty, and eventually facing a brutal death. That is motivating. It's like the presence a mentor has.

"I did my first master's in seminary on sin and atonement, and I learned that, in Paul Tillich's terms, original sin is estrangement. We are estranged from God, but also from ourselves, from all that we can be. We are not fully human. It's sort of Platonic: we are aware of the ideal, but we know we're not it. I should do better with my diet, my friendships, my work habits, but I fall so short! This is Tillich's idea of the human condition. This missing the mark creates anxiety, and out of that anxiety, we can act in a helpful way or a destructive way. What do we do? The pattern for humans, as Tillich sees it, is destructive for ourselves as individuals and collectively. The collective destructive path leads to what we call structural sin—the sin built into the system.

"The figure of Jesus is able—because he is fully human—to share this estranged condition but to overcome the estrangement and unite with the divine. He could bridge the gap between the existential, where we live, and the ideal. He invites us to participate in the magic of that blending. As I follow in his footsteps, become a disciple, and pursue those values of love for neighbor and so on, I am participating in that union that Jesus had with God. Jesus overcame the estranged human condition, and we can participate in that reality now, here on earth. In other words, you can have glimpses of the beautiful, even in this black muck of creation."

As for the resurrection, Enns called upon his experience with postmodern knowledge-theory in a surprising and illuminating way. "Of course, I started out wanting to know 'did it really happen?' " he said. "Well, it was troubling to me at first, but I have to accept the social construction of reality. How do we know what we know? How do we know what's real is real? We agree—that's how. Jesus rose from the dead. How do you know? We're agreeing that we saw it. This is a post-Enlightenment understanding of truth, an understanding that does not posit literal truth, if it could be found, as the only truth. I'm not hung up on the rational question here, the question 'did it happen literally?' I'm more hung up on getting the eyes to see it because it is a wonderful thing that cannot be denied. Where reconciliation happens, like in South Africa, that's the resurrection. Where I've done something seemingly unforgivable—if there's a breach of trust between me and my partner, Karen, and the trust is restored—I feel the presence of the resurrection even in that little microcosm."

For all his political sophistication and passionate opposition to the "religio-profiteers," he made it clear to me that the evangelical Christianity of his Mennonite youth is a heritage that he values and a connection he keeps. And that heritage and connection are personified in his relationship with his identical twin brother, Aaron, who, as Enns put it, "stayed in the faith of our biological father, who was conservative, a Biblical literalist. Aaron is an elder at a church of the Mennonite Brethren—a conservative branch within the denomination. He's my soul mate. What do I do with the manifestation of his faith, which is something I say I 'grew out of'?

"Well, the first thing I have to say is that I have not ceased being the person I was. I grew out of that tradition, but I still claim it as mine. People who go to the church of my youth are still my brothers and sisters in the faith. I hold President Bush, a Methodist whose faith-expression seems to be more theologically conservative than mine, a brother in the faith. I have this default kinship with Christians of all persuasions. But I also have this kinship with"—and he broke into laughter—"all of humanity! Part of my coming to have eyes to see has been developing the capacity to love both the good and the bad—out there and within myself. I see unhelpful things in conservative religious communities—very rigid binary thinking, for example—a lack of a class awareness, of how middle-class lifestyles seem to ratify a status quo that is oppressive. Many of them accept what I would call a corporate-style Christianity and celebrate an individualized, atomized idea of salvation. At the same time, I maintain kinship with conservative evangelicals because, well, they're me. I *am* middle class, and I have to live with that fact. And I don't believe I'm very far along on the spiritual journey or that I am living an exemplary life, the life I want to be living.

"And there are seeds within conservative evangelicalism, seeds of compassion, that defy the consumer mentality—sharing and love of neighbor. Evangelicals have seeds of an alternative value system, where material goods are not all that there is. Love of neighbor and something transcendent, those are subversive ideas that I would like to fan into flame for the sake of Gospel and peace and equity and, well, joy! Because material things don't satisfy, they create a longing; and love of neighbor is intensely gratifying.

"I sort of take a family approach; you can't pick your family, you have to get along with its members. In the same way—and this is going to sound a little strange—you can't pick your earth. This is our Earth, we have good and bad, and I have to live in it and on it with both friends and enemies, and with the things within myself I love and the things I don't like."

My talk with Enns reminded me of Leo Lefebure's insistence on the value of honesty and particularly honesty about one's doubts. For Enns, doubt and faith nurture each other in a way that I found exhilarating and very contemporary. Postmodern thought, which many religious people equate with a flat-out secularism and faithlessness, has actually provided Enns with a stimulating way to look at religious narratives and doctrines: as neither false nor literally true but as bringing together the power of truth and the power of imagination in order to transform us—to give us, as he said, "eyes to see" the transcendent dimension of human existence.

I'm hungry for this transcendent dimension. I believe I have glimpsed this wider and deeper reality beyond the regular, observable, measurable world that science and technology have defined, and the language of literal truth will not give me access to it. With that language and way of thinking, I begin with two options: Christ really rose from the dead and sailed off into the sky or his resurrection and ascension are meaningless. Fundamentalists embrace the former, their atheist enemies assert the latter, and the fight goes on. A third option, the New Age perspective, suggests that all of this happened on a spiritual plane, the "real" reality beyond the material realm.

But following Enns and the other Christian thinkers in this book, I want to maintain the paradox at maximum tension: Jesus was real, a man of flesh and blood; he bore God within him in a mysterious way, and he testified to God's eternal presence in this very real world. His resurrection and ascension, like his two natures as God and man, are profound truths that cannot be verified, are not literal, but can and must be contemplated—contemplated until we are transformed.

Enns's perspective on his personal struggles with faith has the same combination of theoretical astuteness and hunger for the eternal with which he approaches the resurrection. He's straightforward about his doubts, and he struggles to find a place for them in his faith, rather than exiling them to the margins of his consciousness. "I have cycles of negativity about the church and the faith: there's too much violence in the Bible, patriarchy isn't questioned enough in the Bible, Christianity got it wrong, look at the damage it did, and so on. And sometimes I am simply troubled by the fact that I can't know anything for sure. I teach communications at Canadian Mennonite University, and I read the cultural studies literature—my God, there are a lot of constructions of truth out there! I was brought up to believe in absolute truth. What am I supposed to do? But those things are the plagues of my rational mind. My heart doesn't go through these cycles of agony. Does it make sense? Of course it makes sense."

Enns's leap to heart from mind doesn't mean he wants to crush doubt or his own nature as a doubter. "I just see my doubts as participating in the archetype Doubting Thomas," he said. "I'll doubt, but I'll still join the party. Some people are prone to doubting, because . . . well, some people are prone to doubting. There are people *not* prone to doubting, like my twin brother, whose struggles are elsewhere.

"I love the questions. When I find answers, guess what? Way more complicated questions come along. So I'm perpetually troubled—the rational plague. But I almost delight in that struggle. Saint Paul says there are many gifts but the same spirit. As the contemporary Mennonite theologian John Howard Yoder interprets Paul, some of us are given to do theological inquisitions, others have the gift of hospitality, or of soul caring, or of feeding the poor. You can go around the circle of people who are engaged with each other, and they each bring their own gifts. One of the gifts I hope I can bring is the ability to question. If it's done in a circle of mutuality and accountability, you can question, but you don't privilege the questioner over the one who comforts the sick or hands out the bread. They all belong."

Cultivate Readiness and Willingness

Helen Hansen

"The Holy Spirit is going to present itself to you some way, and you can't know how. You can't prepare yourself for it. You can only empty yourself, lay aside your particular obsessions and addictions, lay aside how you think life needs to be."

The words are those of Helen Hansen, a woman who, on first acquaintance, seems mainly a model of the sort of self-directed, goal-oriented upward career progress that our secular culture expects of us and rewards us for. Born in the college town of Ripon, Wisconsin, she chose nursing as a career, moved into nursing administration, progressed all the way to a PhD, and today is an associate professor in the University of Minnesota's highly regarded school of nursing. But Hansen's life of achievement has also been a life of self-emptying, self-opening, painful, and joyous spiritual revelation, and ever-deepening faith in a God who keeps surprising her.

Her poise and her articulate, careful approach to my questions—she spoke slowly and mostly without hesitating or correcting herself—suggested both the well-prepared professional, used to dealing with large issues, and the woman of faith who has found substantial spiritual home ground. Yet, as she told her story, I learned that there were times when

Hansen didn't think she would make it, and the Spirit carried her—often to unforeseeable new places.

Hansen is active in the Episcopal House of Prayer, a retreat center in the otherwise very Catholic community of Collegeville, Minnesota—home of the world's largest Benedictine abbey, Saint John's. As we talked in her St. Paul home, she was also preparing to lead a convocation at the U of M nursing school honoring the great pioneer nurse Florence Nightingale. "For me," she said, "it will be inviting the Holy Spirit to become active within us, to heal us as healers, to strengthen us, and make us more of a community." She spoke often of the third member of the Trinity, and when I called her attention to that, she smiled. "Oh yes," she said. "That's where it all comes together for me, in the Holy Spirit's flow—a flow within my own body or in relationship with others, in my experience, of a worship service or in meditation. It's the *movement* of the Spirit that I feel. I feel it when I get a massage or take part in any kind of healing."

And yet she understands her faith in terms of the full Trinity, too. "I think of God the Father as Creator; he put it all in motion, and it's God's divine order that continues to work today," she said. "But I don't have *any* trouble understanding why we suffer and are at odds with each other, why we go to war and ruin the planet. God gave us a holy order, and if we choose not to be in communion with it, it's going to fall apart and poison us. We simply are going to suffer and be at odds. Of course God *allows* it; it's not his doing, it's ours.

"It's just not that complicated. We reap what we sow. If I drive too fast, I get ticketed or have an accident. If I'm not attentive, passionate, and compassionate in my relationships, they wither. If we don't do our part, the order will not work as God intended."

And as for the remaining member of the Trinity, Jesus Christ, well, Hansen's encounter with him is a very good story indeed, and it begins with her only-somewhat-religious childhood.

Hansen was the child of a mother who'd grown up in the Congregational church, later the United Church of Christ, and a very lapsed Catholic father. "The church had been painful for him, and he put it way behind him," she explained. A colorful, expressive, theatrical figure—he headed the speech department at Ripon College—Hansen's father had what she described as "not a love-hate, but a sort of push-pull relationship" with the Congregational churches the family attended while she was growing up. "He directed the Sunday school for a while, he would guest preach occasionally, and he even directed a workshop for Baptist preachers sponsored by the American Baptist Convention. He believed preachers ought to know how to speak!" The senior Hansen was also a frustrated and troubled man. He could be abusive to Helen's mother and brother, and sometimes retreated to the basement for days of solitary drinking.

Despite such rocky times, Hansen remembers her mother and father as conscientious parents and models of social compassion and commitment to others. "We lived in Oklahoma briefly," she recalled, "and do you know what we did on Sundays? We drove through the black neighborhood of town, so my father could point out to my brother and me just how wrong it was that a community should be divided because of race. My parents had grown up in the Depression, and both of them cared deeply about these things." And in explaining sex honestly and clearly to their kids, the Hansens made it clear that they saw the gift of sexuality as sacred and precious.

Hansen, the older child in what today we would call an alcoholic family, quickly took on an outsize sense of responsibility. At home, she did her best to calm the waters—"I always felt guilty that I couldn't protect my brother from my dad's rages," she said—and, at church, she sang in the choir, gave talks on Youth Sunday, and, as she put it, "could always be counted on to read the scripture—and read it correctly!" She lived at home while she attended Ripon, majoring in German and acquiring a lifelong love of German poetry. And like many other young people in the sixties, she found her ties to the church of her childhood weakening as she discovered new faiths: civil rights, feminism, and opposition to the growing American involvement in Vietnam.

Then, when she was a sophomore, her father died. "Oh, it had been hard to live with him, but it was terribly hard to be without him, too," she said. "I just didn't get it. I didn't see why he had to die so suddenly— it was cancer—and in such a conflicted, unhappy, bedeviled state of mind. Kids naturally assume guilt when a parent dies, and, of course, I had been living at home all the time, so I hadn't really made the break with the family that happens when you 'go away to college.' And in those days, there was very little counseling or other help with grief; you were expected to deal with it on your own."

Still, there was some help for Hansen in her pain. Her mother suggested that her father had at last been released from the demons that had tormented him all his life, and that made some sense to Hansen. A friend gave her a rosary, and she tried praying with it. Most of all, though, she depended on her love of nature and of physical exertion—hiking, skiing, sailing—to steady her nerves and calm her spirit.

She was also discovering her calling. "Nursing was completely off the track of anything I'd wanted before," she told me. But having helped her mother care for her father in his last illness, she realized that she had a gift for it. Soon, she volunteered as a nursing assistant at a hospital near Chicago, and then, in 1967, she set off with her new husband, Bruce, to Seattle—she to enroll in a bachelor's nursing program at the University of Washington, Bruce to attend grad school. Still devoted to the antiwar movement and immersed in their studies, the couple made no move to affiliate with a church. But they also had a child in Seattle—"a truly out-of-body experience," as Hansen described it.

"I suppose every woman thinks she's the first person in the world to have a baby," she said with a smile, "but it was *so* profound. On the one hand, I wondered how in the world I thought I was qualified to have a kid and what kind of person could volunteer to raise a child in the midst of the Vietnam war and the turbulence over it; the campus was up in arms, buildings were being evacuated. On the other hand, I just loved the experience of mothering May, nursing her, bonding with her. Though we had no intention of affiliating with a church, we had her baptized. Classic, isn't it?"

When the couple moved to Kansas City for Helen's first job as a nursing administrator, she was, without realizing it, turning up the spiritual heat in her life. They moved into a rented house next to a Presbyterian minister, his wife, and their two daughters. Soon the two couples were close friends, and Bruce and Helen were even sending daughter May to church with their neighbors—without attending themselves.

Then came a bombshell: Bruce left. With no warning, he simply walked out of the marriage, and Helen had to fight the blue devils of abandonment for the second time. One way she coped was by starting to attend church with May and neighbors Bill and Joyce. The inner-city congregation, Covenant, was a revelation to her: not a stiff, formal house of worship but a vibrant and exciting community, alive with concern for both social justice and personal spirituality. "There was nothing in-your-face evangelical about it," she recalls. "Just this powerful sense of the presence of the spirit. In this community, it didn't matter if you were gay, straight, black, white, old, young, divorced, or married—you were an important part. It wasn't a huge congregation, but every pew in the place was full every Sunday. It was such an alive place—it was there I started to learn what prayer was about." Hansen plunged into the life of the congregation, joining the choir and never missing a Sunday service. When she met and married her second husband, Bob, the ceremony was at Covenant.

But lasting happiness still eluded Hansen. She was injured in an auto accident. Tensions in her marriage required attention. Anxiety and depression assailed her as she began to come to grips with the traumas she'd undergone but never really recovered from. It was a painful time of real change and, as a result, real hope. The Catholic hospital where she was employed was both a place of work and a place of faith. Two skillful psychotherapists helped her face her tormenting feelings of abandonment. "I doubt if it was their intention," she says, "but they built up in me a spiritual center." She felt the Spirit helping her heal physically and emotionally through the hands of masseurs and Rolfers. She enrolled in the PhD program in nursing at the University of Kansas Medical Center in Kansas City. With Bob's financial support, she could devote all her time to studies she loved.

And then came the turning point. Studying for her prelim exams, she realized that she was feeling a peculiar, very family-centered anxiety. In her progress toward the doctorate, she was about to go further than her father. "My mother was aware that I was doing something that was taking us past a point in our family life—past the point where my father's illness and alcoholism had arrested him. 'He couldn't have done it,' she said. 'He didn't have the discipline.' There were patterns in my own life that could have arrested me too—but here I was, developing the spiritual strength to move beyond a boundary that, I think, had been set up inside me in my childhood."

Hansen had left the Covenant congregation after the departure of her friends Bill and Joyce, who had taken the helm of a church in New York. But she returned to ask the new pastor for some help. "I asked him to help me ask Jesus to come into this process I was going through," she said. The pastor gave her passages of scripture to read, and she prayed for the presence of Christ in her life.

"I was sitting in my study one morning, with my note cards and study materials in front of me. I had started the day by reading some scripture and praying—centering myself. Suddenly, I was aware of a presence in the room, behind my left shoulder: I didn't turn around and look, but I knew it was my father, whole, healthy, and confident in me. All this time, I had thought of him as a sort of Marley's ghost, rattling his chains, but in this visitation, he was in a suit and tie, as he might have appeared before his classes. His presence told me I could do this exam, that I could get this degree.

"It was at this point, too, that I knew there was an afterlife, and I realized that one of the things I had to do was become a spiritually formed person, so that if anyone needed me later, I would be there. I truly believe that my father reached through to me. I made my appeal to Jesus Christ, and he gave me my father to help reconcile me to him and to Jesus. To let me know that there was this kind hand there, a presence that would never abandon me. I also learned that it was my readiness, my request, that mattered. A readiness not just of the moment; over a period of time, I had been making myself ready to say 'Lord Jesus, be present to me now.' And then, not knowing what form it would take—or that anything at all would happen—I had waited."

Ask: What *Did* Jesus Do?

Jim Rigby

I know that people who practice the Christian faith are supposed to turn the other cheek, but it's still hard to believe that anyone—even a clergyman—would actually help the people suing him.

Yet, that's just what Jim Rigby, pastor of Saint Andrew's Presbyterian church on the north side of Austin, Texas, did a couple of years ago. Rigby had presided at a ceremony, blessing some fifty same-sex couples on the campus of the University of Texas, part of a "Marriage Equality Day" rally in April of 2004. UT student Robert Brown and his pastor, the Reverend William Parr of Nor'kirk Presbyterian Church in the Dallas suburb of Carrollton, brought charges against Rigby for violating his ordination vows and the constitution of the Presbyterian Church-USA, which defines marriage as a male-female union.

Rather than denouncing his accusers, Rigby met with Robert Brown in an Austin restaurant and helped him plan his case. He even recommended that he and Parr engage a high-powered Washington lawyer, Paul Rolf Jensen, who had filed complaints against a number of Presbyterian ministers and groups for what he sees as left-leaning heterodoxy.

It wasn't entirely a love-your-enemies matter; Rigby, a serious advocate of gay rights, wanted the national church to declare itself on the gay-marriage question. He hoped for a result favorable to his own convictions, of course, but he chiefly wanted a clear yes or no. He hoped that the church wouldn't waffle on the issue, and his advice to Brown was aimed at closing any loophole that would lead to the dismissal of the charges. He was prepared to accept any unambiguous result, even if it meant that he had to part company with his church. "If your conscience tells you that I am guilty and this is wrong," he reportedly told the investigating commission from Mission Presbytery, a governing body of South Texas congregations, "I'm asking you to kick me out of the church."

The panel found no grounds to try Rigby; an appeal by Jensen and his clients was also dismissed. The loophole? A clause in the denomination's by-laws that allows clergy to be present at same-sex "ceremonies," which are, by definition, not marriages. His day in court voided, Rigby goes on working for what he sees as simple justice for gays.

Rigby is a rather unlikely activist: slight, youthful (in his mid-fifties, he looks thirty-five), bookish, and self-deprecatingly witty, he originally planned to be a professor of comparative religion—or perhaps the sort of scholarly pastor who brings subtle theological points to bear on the private spiritual dilemmas of his parishioners. As we sat in a community room at Saint Andrew's and drank coffee ("We're lucky today; we've got Starbucks instead of fair-trade," he said with politically incorrect gusto), he told me the story of his progressive, often painful abandonment of that image of himself and his evolution into someone who takes big risks in public for what he believes Christ stands for. "I get mad when I hear the phrase 'What would Jesus do?'," he said. "It's not like he didn't come. The question is: what *did* he do?"

Born in Dallas, Rigby was the sort of kid who worried when he saw animals mistreated or heard people cry, who felt that humans ought to help each other. Growing up in an era when Texas public buildings had restrooms marked "men," "women," and "colored," Rigby knew there was something wrong. "I had the sense of being imprisoned by something," he said, "even if I couldn't see the bars. And I knew I needed to get outside."

One way out was to learn about other cultures and other faiths, which he did as a student at the University of Texas. He explored Eastern religion and the writings of Gandhi, Albert Schweitzer, and Saint Francis. "I was looking for whatever tradition had the most God in it," he said. "And I wanted to learn about the people whose lives I admired. In the process, I discovered something about the theology of people such as Saint Francis, Gandhi, and Schweitzer. They started with what Jesus taught—love your enemies, don't judge others, take the last place. Then they did their theology around that. Now, I'd always been taught that you put the stuff the church says about Jesus in the center and work the sayings and the parables in around that somehow. Schweitzer once said that people have turned the religion *of* Jesus into a religion *about* Jesus. Once you do that, you can memorize Bible verses and use them like Legos to build any sort of edifice you want.

"But if you start with what Jesus said and did, it's another matter. How did he treat people? It's no mystery. We just don't *like* what he did. We don't like taking the lowest place. We don't like not judging each other. We don't like giving up our priestly status by being a servant."

Rigby "backed into" seminary. Despite a load of skepticism about the church's claims and about religion in general, he was very much a seeker—an immature one, he reflected, "since my spirituality was all about wanting to feel a certain way—spiritual." For many of the seminarians, close study of the Hebrew and Greek of the Bible was a shock because it revealed the patchwork nature of a scripture that has usually been presented as a seamless whole. "If you take it literally, you simply don't know what the Bible is," said Rigby, "a quilt woven together by various people, everybody with a different sense of what pieces go in there and where they fit. There are so many differences in the thousands and thousands of manuscripts that exist. That's very disturbing for most people.

"As for me, I sort of went the other way. I had done my soul-searching before seminary, and I was looking for reasons why you needed religion in the first place. As I studied scripture, I realized that some of the revelations I'd had in daily life had their counterparts in the Bible. For the first time, I was able to connect my experiences to an ancient, living tradition, a lifeline going back thousands of years. And everything I'd found in other religions—Taoism, Hinduism—was there, in the Bible. I'd just been taught a narrow interpretation of it."

He also discovered the cosmopolitanism and universality of the Bible's world. "When I visited Israel," he said, "I saw ancient mosaics and objects from India and Greece. I realized that the Biblical world had been a melting pot, not a set of airtight containers. In scripture, I found a lot of stories that you find in other traditions earlier. I found a universal horizon, people very cognizant of other traditions."

Taking the Jewishness of the New Testament seriously, he discovered a breadth of vision that was, not literal, but traditional and deeply spiritual. "In rabbinic storytelling," he said, "the purpose is not to record history but reveal the sacred. When the impossible occurs—like someone walking on water or flying up to heaven—the rabbis don't demand that we accept a miracle on faith. They're signaling that a transcendent truth is being told through the miracle story. Not the story of a one-time wonder, but a larger truth that is *always* true, always happening. When you hear it as an oral story, you see the twinkle in the rabbi's eye at that moment. Written in a book and taken as literally true, it can be deadly; it doesn't come from the same loving place.

"Taking in these parables is supposed to work on you. It's like inviting a baby elephant in the house. That's great at first, but as it grows, you suddenly realize it's going to tear the house down. You invite this little parable into your worldview, and it keeps growing and growing, and all of a sudden you realize your worldview's going to crack. But then everybody begins the spiritual journey selfish, and it winds up being a bigger lesson than anybody signed on for."

Rigby smiled as he recalled these powerful moments of learning. "Then," he went on, "I got out into the real world. In the real world, you realize that you have all these tokens you've been given, but there's no machine that takes them."

His first foray into the real world was a year of counseling/chaplain training that took him to San Antonio and Odessa, Texas, and to Oklahoma City. "What I learned as a chaplain," he said, "is that your theology needs to be pretty fluid, and at first, I was offended by that. But theology is a bridge between what Christ taught and what people actually need in the moment—and that can be a pretty long, thin bridge. A Navajo Catholic wants me to take his deathbed confession; I can't understand what he's saying, but I know that I just need to sit there and nod and pat him on the shoulder. If someone thinks they have a demon in them, and that's not my theology—well, it doesn't really matter what I think. That's the language they need me to speak if I'm going to have any impact on their life.

"That year was painful but wonderful, life-giving. There's no greater gift than when somebody trusts you to be with them in their last moments. It's late at night, you're tired, there's a hundred other things you should be doing. But the sense of the sacred is just so strong. It's difficult for an introvert and an egghead to sit and listen to people dying. But it cracked my shell."

I asked him what forms the shell-cracking took.

"You have to change a lot," he said. "For one thing, you have to realize that they don't need any answers that you have. Mostly it's a matter of you honoring what *they* are doing. The training I got was basically how to be real, how to take your mask off. How to shut up so you can listen and be there. And that's really hard."

Learning to be quiet like this taught Rigby a powerful lesson about God. "When I was a philosopher, the silence of God meant God's absence, like in a Bergman movie," he said. "Now it means presence to me, pure presence. The silence *is* God. There's a Jewish story about a prophet who hears the thunder and the storm in the heavens, but only comes out in the silence that follows because he knows *that* is when God is present. When you associate too closely with any of the particular expressions of God—the earthquake, the fire, the ice, the water, even the baptism—you're going to lose God. But adhere to the silence and realize that everything is an expression of that—the unrung bell, as they say in Zen—then you simply *can't* lose God."

Rigby interned in a church in San Antonio—a community that was loving, totally accepting, and quite elderly. "I told them once that our youth group was anybody who still had their prostate." He laughed. His next church was full of retired military people, but Rigby felt no less loved and accepted there. Yet, an uncomfortable truth was dawning on him. "What I began to realize," he said, "is that you can say what Jesus said, and everything's fine, you upset no one, as long as you don't act on it. About this time somebody asked me where I saw myself in five years. I saw books all around me and me as a sort of self-help guru with a Christian flavor. A wonderful, wise, kind of Bishop Sheen.

"Then, one year, two women in my congregation were raped, and I was sitting there talking to them, using my little pastoral skills, and I could feel I was making it *worse* for them. I didn't know why because I was being, you know, very helpful. Filling in the silences. But I felt like I was kicking somebody with a broken leg. It was like when I was a kid in Dallas— I didn't know what my prison was, but I was in one."

He volunteered for training at a rape crisis center, and a whole new education began. He learned about the concept of a "rape culture" rooted in attitudes about male control of the female, and he saw stunning statistics about the frequency of rape in the United States. He began to look at some of his own attitudes, too. "I realized that I believed, as a male, that I ought to control things because that's what I had been taught," he said. "In a relationship with a woman, I'm supposed to set the pace. I learned that you don't have to personally hurt someone. If you just take up your role in a power system, you can crush other people without realizing it. The system will oppress people for you. Realizing this, I got very sad. I thought I was sad for the women, but what I was doing was grieving over my role as a male in the culture."

These realizations pushed Rigby into action and into an understanding of gay issues as intimately related to these very questions of (heterosexual) male power and threats to it. He worked on hate-crime legislation, spoke at gay-rights rallies, ordained a gay deacon, blessed same-sex unions—including those at the UT extravaganza. He's been threatened, vilified, and sued, and has had scripture quoted against him. Rigby is quick to point out that scripture does not put forward the best argument for conventional sexual mores. "In the Bible, you've got people with multiple wives, people impregnating their slaves, and they'd like you to believe that 'Biblical' marriage is the American nuclear family!" Both allies and opponents have assumed he himself is gay. A turning point came for him when he realized that he no longer cared if anyone made that particular error. "A gay colleague said to me, 'Jim, you know that by now you really are *queer*'—by which he meant that I had placed myself outside the heterosexual power system on this issue.

"I've been tattooed with the gay and lesbian issues, but I don't have any more interest in them than if someone were Jewish and being discriminated against. Everybody has a right to life, liberty, and the pursuit of happiness. That used not to be a radical leftist premise. It's about universal human rights and living in the whole world."

But isn't that a political, as opposed to spiritual, position? Rigby shook his head. "Politics is how we treat each other. There can be no true spirituality without politics, without love and care for others in the real world. And there's no politics without a spiritual dimension. I picture Jesus as taking the political seriously but not being reduced to it. He's not *fighting* the Pharisees as their political opponent; it's deeper than that. He's calling everybody to a universalism, to a place where we treat one another with absolute equality before God.

"I try to embrace that universalism. I don't accept the premise that there's a struggle between the left and the right that I'm a part of. I don't think the environment or human rights are partisan issues. I think Martin Luther King, Jr., and Gandhi were coming from a whole different place than left and right. There's nothing that people like better than to reduce what we're doing to just being liberal. But the thing is, you *will* be misunderstood; the press used to run articles about Martin Luther King protesting about something. They never let him speak for himself. They quoted the powerful people and showed pictures of angry minorities, and you wondered, why are they so angry again? I mean, you have to be willing to be put on a donkey, wearing a stupid hat. And you have to be willing to realize that, in pushing for certain changes, you will trigger someone's fear and that it's only human for them to lash out at what frightens them."

We finished the Starbucks, and Rigby stretched and smiled. "I don't consider myself to be against anybody; what I do is amazingly invigorating and life-giving. You can't have real friendships when you're stuck inside the power system, trying to get power over one another. Today, I have the first real friendships I have ever had—and I almost never get tired. What's tiring is to turn your head from oppression. What's tiring is not to be able to look someone in the eye who is being oppressed. What's tiring is not being able to look at *yourself* in the mirror."

· · ·

I was initially interested in Rigby because of my deep agreement with him on issues like feminism and homosexuality, but as we spoke, what impressed me about him was the spiritually centered and profoundly generous way he enunciates his position. It's clear that he's not interested in annexing liberal politics to Christianity, a course that constantly tempts me. Instead, he is acting out of a profound personal transformation that happened to him when he took a central message of the Gospel into his heart: be a servant, take the lowest place, and then act decisively on that conviction.

When Rigby tried to do that, he saw that he could not serve others and still hold on to the social power and privilege represented by his maleness and his heterosexuality—a power and privilege that has long defined the male and the straight as the norm of the human and established the male and the straight as the position from which "deviance" may be judged, with the Bible always handy to provide short, pithy "proof texts." He had to become the servant of women and gays, and that meant to take them at their word about who they were and what they needed.

I firmly believe that if people who consider homosexuality a sin would take the time to listen to gay people and identify with the ways they experience and understand love, they would change their views. I firmly believe that love is love, and gender is a side issue that has mysteriously become a central issue in many conservative churches.

But I want to be challenged by Rigby too, and his challenge to me is to hold my convictions compassionately, in Jesus's way, and to ask myself where I am claiming power and superiority, refusing the servant role. Do I feel superior to conservative evangelicals or traditionalist Catholics or Orthodox believers because I consider myself more enlightened than they are? Do I discount the fervor of their convictions because I disagree with them? When was the last time I took the time to listen to them and identify with the ways they experience and understand love, God, or truth? What might I discover if I entered their world more fully than I have been willing to in this book?

TRUST THAT GOD LOVES YOU
FOR WHO YOU ARE

Gerald Gafford

I n the 1997 film *In and Out,* Kevin Kline plays Howard Brackett, a small-town teacher whose former student, now a film actor, "outs" him as gay in public—in an Academy Award acceptance speech, no less. The deeply closeted Brackett is appalled, as are his fiancé and friends. But in the course of the film, Brackett comes to realize that he really is uncomfortable in a straight straitjacket. At one point, he uses a videotape to help him practice macho hetero moves: how to stand, how to stuff his hands in his pockets, how, in short, to portray a "real man" according to the rules.

Gerald Gafford loves that scene. The Austin, Texas, Realtor and church elder can relate because, before 1986, he often found himself making the same assiduous study of "normal" guyhood. "I remember going to football games, watching my son play," he said, "looking to see how guys sit. You had to try to not move your hands too much. Never have a limp wrist! And *try* to be up on sports."

He was trying hard; after all, he was a former campus minister in the Church of Christ, a strict evangelical denomination. He had become a prominent Realtor. He had a wife and kids, and a reputation as the sort of guy who could be depended upon to do his job, help others selflessly, and not make waves. But he was coming to realize that he was playing a losing game.

"One morning I woke up," he said, "and I felt terrified. I felt that everything was slipping away. There had been a downturn in the real estate business, and I knew that unless things turned around, the company I had built was going to fail. I would be faced with bankruptcy— something that, if you had my background, just didn't happen to you. I felt so beat down that my spirit let something else come up and out.

"My wife was lying beside me, I was staring at the ceiling, and I said to myself, 'I can't do this anymore.' I couldn't hide any longer. I had lost control of my façade."

A minister friend gave him the address of a psychologist in Austin, and Gafford went to him. After a battery of tests that determined that he was sexually and emotionally attracted to men ("I knew that," said Gafford with a smile), the psychologist asked him a life-changing question.

"What he asked," said Gafford, "was 'If I could give you a pill that would cause this gay thing to go away, would you take it?' And after all the years of struggle and anger and falsehood, I just broke down in tears and said, 'No.'

"For the first time in my life, I realized that if that element of me disappeared, there would be no me there. The only me I really, really knew was this, and everything else I'd just been able to get away with. I loved my kids and I loved my wife, but I had been a liar. I needed to approach God as the person I really was."

And so, at forty-seven, Gafford's new life began. The university church he had served in in Austin sent two elders, Bibles in hand, to "save" him, to challenge him to justify his "lifestyle choice" scripturally. "What I told them is part of my basic faith message," he said to me. "I knew that there was another way, even if I wasn't sure what it was. So I was like an electrician. I *wired around* those Bible passages they quoted and wired in direct to God through Jesus Christ. I have an Advocate in Jesus, and I approach God with him. I am glad that people wrote the words called scripture, but I had to have a different approach and that was believing that God loves all God's children. I said this then to save myself, but today I believe it."

He had been a mainstay of his extended family, caring for his relatives' kids and doing other family chores without complaint. But when he came out, most of his relatives shunned him and still do. His wife, Carol, understood, and helped his children to understand as well. "She told them, 'Your dad is the same person he was before you knew this about him—it's just that you know him better now,' " he told me. Gafford and his wife divorced, but he remains on good terms with her and has been an active and involved father.

Today, he's two decades older, a large and quietly affable man with a minister's resonant voice, a purebred Texas accent, and classic southern good manners. His career is on track; he's been with a partner, Jeff, for more than twenty years; and he's an elder at Saint Andrew's Presbyterian Church in North Austin, whose pastor is Jim Rigby (see p. 178). Besides helping with church governance, the traditional role of the Presbyterian elder, Gafford has been filling in, along with other volunteers with pastoral experience, to help lighten Rigby's load since the resignation of the church's associate pastor. He takes calls, visits the sick, and does other ministerial jobs.

It's territory he knows well. A pious country kid from central Texas, he grew up in the Church of Christ, a Presbyterian-descended sect so scrupulous about basing itself on the Bible that it refuses to give itself an official name—since Jesus's followers did not name their movement anywhere in scripture. When referring to the denomination, many members even prefer to keep the *c* in *church* lowercase. Every local church is completely autonomous, and every believer is encouraged and expected to interpret the Bible for him or herself, under the guidance of God; there is no creed and no official theological authority.

Gafford attended Abilene Christian University, a Church of Christ institution. He taught school for a few years and did graduate work at Stephen F. Austin State University in Nacogdoches in east Texas and further work in several theological schools, picking up courses that he needed to round out his religious education. Then, he embarked on a career in campus ministry.

It was the Vietnam War–era, and campuses everywhere were alight with idealism, political passion, and new ideas of varying degrees of practicability. Gafford loved it. Despite his conservative, deep-in-the-heart-of-Texas background, he identified almost by instinct with the civil rights movement, and his exposure to campus ministers from other traditions widened his faith. But even in this atmosphere of experiment, Gafford was far from ready to accept his sexual leanings and needs. "I thought I could cure myself of my orientation if I majored in psychology," he said. "In a psychology book, I read about homosexuality as 'aberrant behavior,' and I knew I had a disease. I did many things to get 'right.' I tried a second baptism as an adult. I tried the ministry. I think I went into ministry partly with the thought that, if I worked enough, studied enough, prayed enough, helped enough people, then God would somehow have to cure me. I was going to *buy* God and do it through servitude."

Gafford's sense of unworthiness turned him into a classic people-pleaser. "I didn't have a lot of opinions," he said, "and I was easy to get along with. I was drawn to people, and they were drawn to me because I wasn't judgmental. I couldn't afford to be judgmental! I took on racial issues but never gay and lesbian issues. That would have been a giveaway, and I was afraid of it."

Gafford's experience of his faith at this point will surprise those of us who think conservative Christianity could be nothing but a roadblock to a gay man's self-acceptance. "There were many negative things about the little church I grew up in," he told me, "but there were positive things, too. One was that we were taught to study the Bible for ourselves. No one could interpret it for us—we would be given insight into what the scriptures mean. Though they weren't big on the Holy Spirit, they believed that God would direct us to an understanding of what God wanted us to know. What I knew by the scriptures was that God loves us, that there is grace, that there is nothing that can separate us from that love we have from God through Christ. I learned those scriptures and hung on to them. And I had an ultimate faith in the grace of God that probably saved my life."

Still, coming out, when Gafford finally did it, was a step into a frightening unknown. "I knew what truth-telling was about," he said. "And I knew that the scriptures said that if a man is going to go out and build a temple, he needs to count the cost, so that he doesn't get halfway into the building without being able to finish it. I went into this thinking I could lose my children—and their love. I could lose my wife and her respect. I could lose my church. But I had to know who I was, and who people would think I was if I stopped deceiving them."

His questioning went even deeper. He wanted to know why God had allowed Gerald Gafford to have sexual feelings for men. "I figured that one of three things had to be true," he said. "God might be a terrible practical joker. I didn't want anything to do with a God like that. Or maybe gay people were some kind of genetic mutants, which I couldn't accept either. On nights alone, wrestling with this, I decided that the only answer I could accept was that somehow I was intended to be the way I was. That somehow I had something to do—that I was sent with a message and a ministry."

In the same year that he came out, he met Jeff. The couple began attending Austin's Metropolitan Community Church (MCC), one of a network of gay, lesbian, bi, transgender (GLBT)-oriented churches around the world. But his new relationship turned out to be as important for his spiritual growth as any religious affiliation. "Jeff had parents who were Catholic and were faithful," Gafford said, "but they never placed the church above their family. We never knew, and still don't know, what their true thoughts are on the matter of our sexuality and our relationship—but their actions are that they love us. Nothing was going to stand in the way of their relationship with their child. They evaluated me on whether I was good to Jeff, whether I cared about him, and whether I was a decent guy. That really increased my faith because my picture of the average rural Catholic family was not that at all."

The only thing missing at MCC was children. In the late eighties, gay couples were only beginning to bear and adopt kids, and Gafford, the veteran dad, and his partner both missed the patter of little feet at church. So they tried to find a more mainstream congregation that was openly gay-friendly. They spent several years searching and, as Gafford put it, "unchurched." Then they bought a house in North Austin and noticed that a church right down the block was displaying hundreds of crosses on its large lawn. "The crosses were white, blue, and pink, and there was a big sign near them that said, 'in memory of men, women, and children who've died of AIDS.' At the time, to talk about AIDS was not very . . . churchy," he said, smiling a little. "So we contacted the church—Saint Andrew's—and Jim Rigby came out to visit us. We asked him if we would be welcome. He said, 'You would not only be welcome, your help would be solicited.' And from the first day we walked into that church, people were asking us to teach Bible school. We had never seen a church that said to us, 'We want you to teach our children, and we know that you are two gay men.' "

For almost two years, Gafford waited, as he put it, "for the other shoe to drop." But the Saint Andrew's congregation went on treating him and Jeff as if they were human beings first and foremost. "Eventually," said Gafford, "I got it that these people were for real. They weren't afraid of us, and they weren't afraid of what people would think. We never left."

Today, Gafford helps Rigby, not only with regular pastoral chores, but with the minister's wide-ranging work on behalf of GLBT people. The centerpiece of this work has been Rigby's effort to force the Presbyterian church to declare itself on the issue of whether gay people can be full participants in church life. "Jim believes that, if we really talk about scripture on this issue, people with open hearts and minds will listen," said Gafford. "Although Saint Paul has harsh things to say about same-sex acts, as he understood them, Jesus never says a word about them. So Jim basically said to his investigative committee, 'If you will bring me the scriptures where Jesus condemns homosexuality, I will go with you.' We believe that we approach God through Christ, and if that's true, then let's go with Christ rather than with Paul."

Gafford continues to carry the message that he and others like him are the beloved children of God by a simple (but not necessarily easy) process he calls "personing the issue." "I understand homophobia," he says, "because I don't think I'm totally free of it myself. I understand that people might have fear of homosexuals. They might fear for their children. They might be uncomfortable with sexual feelings they have themselves. They might think of us as evidence that the country is going to pot. But the more we 'person the issue,' the more we are out and people know that their Realtor is gay or their banker is gay—the more people see us and see that we seem to be okay, that we're honest, that we do a good day's work, the better for everybody.

"I'd been in the realty business twelve years when I came out, and the people who stuck by me were Realtors! A few years after I came out, I was elected president of the county association of Realtors, with everybody knowing that 'Gerald is a gay guy.' I think a life well lived is the best witness I can bear. If someone who was not exactly 'on my side' were to say to me, 'Gerald, I don't know what to do with the scriptures about homosexuality, and I don't understand why you are the way you are, but I like and respect you,' that would be, for me, success."

LET YOURSELF BE CRUCIFIED

Gangaji

"I knew these people thirty and forty years ago who went to India to find a guru and came back with Indian names, and they seemed absolutely absurd to me," said Gangaji, a striking, silver-haired woman who was born Antoinette (Toni) Roberson in Clarksdale, Mississippi, in 1942. In the sixties and seventies, she was a serious, if somewhat jaded, spiritual seeker who saw gurus come and go, dominating, cheating, and molesting their dewy-eyed American disciples. She wanted none of that, and she had no interest in mystic India whatsoever. "I didn't like the incense, and I didn't like the food," she said. "I was *not* a vegetarian."

Today, she is an Oregon-based spiritual teacher in a noble Indian tradition. Her name, derived from the holy river Ganges, was given to her by the late Sri H. W. L. Poonja, a guru known affectionately as Papaji, whom she met at his home in Lucknow, India.

So what happened?

In the early 1990s, Toni Roberson was a case study in baby boomer spiritual burnout. She had dropped acid, swallowed hallucinogenic mushrooms, struggled to find the right man, the right job, and the right attitude toward patriarchy and politics. She had read the classics of Taoism and Confucianism. She had done Zen meditation and Tibetan tantra in Berkeley and Bolinas, California, and she hadn't found what felt like peace or truth.

The husband she met and married in Berkeley, Eli Jaxon-Bear, had been on an even wider and wilder trip that included a stint as a federal fugitive and initiation in Zen, Tibetan Buddhist, and Sufi spiritual traditions. But when Jaxon-Bear met Papaji in 1990, his search was over. Sri H. W. L. Poonja was a guru without an ashram or permanent disciples, a retired businessman (he had once worked for Allis-Chalmers) and an ex-army officer. He was also a spiritual teacher who didn't ask for money, reverence, or service. He simply told Eli to stop, to call off the quest, to cancel all attempts to find anything or do anything, including meditation. Most of all, he told Eli to stop being anything or anyone his mind could dictate in order to discover what and who he had been all along: identical with Being itself, which may also be called God.

This awareness of our permanent, immutable, ineffable connectedness with the Oneness that underlies the apparent variety of being, an awareness whose philosophical name in the Indian tradition is *advaita*, non-duality, had been the message of Papaji's own teacher, the South Indian spiritual giant Sri Ramana Maharshi (1879–1950), who ranks with Gandhi, Rabindranath Tagore, and Sri Aurobindo among the spiritual fathers of modern India. Papaji passed the message to Eli with simplicity and directness, without Sanskrit arcana or philosophical mystification. And he passed it to Toni, whom Eli persuaded to visit Lucknow.

"What I got from him right away," said Gangaji during our conversation in her large, peaceful, earth-toned home on a sidestreet near downtown Ashland, Oregon, "was this enormous love and welcome. I hadn't ever really seen that in someone who didn't know me or want something from me. He basically said, come on in, and take all the riches I have to offer you; take it all.

" 'What are you interested in?' he asked me, and I said: 'Freedom.'

" 'You're in the right place,' he replied. 'Now don't do anything. Just stop.' I came to understand that he meant stop searching. Be still. Stop thinking of yourself as a searcher, as a woman, as a person. At first I tried to *do* that. I tried to meditate, and he said to stop meditating, too. He was saying, in this moment, die. Surrender. And in that moment—which is really *this* moment, too, right now—the silence was and is the divine presence of God. The divine presence of Christ."

Gangaji teaches non-dual awareness in the Ramana-Papaji tradition via the Gangaji Foundation in Ashland. On her own and in collaboration with Eli, she meets with groups of seekers in the United States, Europe, and Australia.

Non-duality is not Christianity, and no one would call Gangaji a doctrinal Christian, but she is a lover of Christ, and her understanding of him and his message differs from the purely spiritualized and overly metaphysical Jesus espoused by many New Agers. While such writers and teachers usually prefer to view Jesus from the standpoint of Easter (resurrection, new life, overflowing love, the Christ-principle alive in our hearts), Gangaji has a lot to say about Good Friday as well: the human, suffering Christ, the Agony in the Garden, absolute loss and pain preceding rebirth and freedom. Her Christ is a mystical, but not an ethereal, Christ. And while he is not the single way to salvation for her—she sees him as one of many God-men who have appeared on earth to embody the divine—her love for him, rooted in a southern American childhood, is foundational.

Gangaji's voice is hypnotic: a soft, low, unmistakably southern alto that conveys the peace and clarity she has evidently found. As she told her story, I felt the power of Jesus Christ as man, divinity, and symbol reaching from one culture to another and from one way of seeing the world to another. Gangaji made it clear why he is a universal figure of light, love, and sacred suffering.

"I didn't grow up Baptist, though everyone around me did," she said. "We were Episcopalians. When I was six, I was a very sickly and skinny child, and my parents sent me to something called a preventatorium, a place where they fattened kids up so they wouldn't get TB. This was 1948, and it was the latest thing. My parents meant well, but it was a horrific experience for me; I felt totally abandoned. In the sort of criblike iron bed I slept in, I prayed to guardian angels. I somehow took solace in the idea that there was something outside myself that was protecting me, something I could fall back into that wasn't either mother or father."

Because she had missed a lot of school while she was in the preventatorium, her parents enrolled her in a Catholic school, where they hoped she would get more individual attention and could catch up with her schoolwork. "They blasted the catechism at us, and I didn't resist," she told me. "I took it in! I fell in love with Jesus, the Virgin Mary, and the saints. The nuns were mean; they really did whack our hands with rulers. But going to church there was a profound experience because the mass was so *alive.*

"This totally flipped my parents out, and they took me out of Catholic school. But I believe I was feeling love and the promise of love, an ecstatic, passionate kind of love, an all-giving love. I had never been to an evangelical church or a black church then, but I was feeling what I would later feel in those churches: a sense of giving myself. Our Episcopal church was quite different. There I had to learn not to be too over the top. I had to learn to be reserved. It made me neurotic to suppress this beautiful opening to love."

It was a suppression that, she believes, cost her a great deal emotionally, and her sense of loss and her rather confused desire to re-experience early spiritual joys turned her into a spiritual seeker. "That sense of aliveness never really left me," she said, "and that is what Christ means to me to this day: the aliveness of the divine."

Gangaji's encounter with Papaji rekindled her spiritual fire as nothing else had, yet she was visited by some doubts, too. "Papaji was raised a Hindu, but he didn't teach Hinduism at all," she said. "He gave me permission to be myself, and I reconnected with the gratitude and joy I felt at having allowed Christ into my life as a girl. But there was a crucial moment during the time I spent with him when my early Christian conditioning kicked in. I was walking behind him, and this thought arose: What are you doing? You're going to the devil! This man isn't God; he isn't even a Christian! And at that moment I really had to make a choice. I said to myself, 'This feels pure and true. If it's wrong, I will just have to find that out.' At that moment, I believe I broke out of some conditioning about what hell is, what right is, and where God is. It was my moment of freedom."

Paradoxically, by breaking out of her Christian conditioning, Gangaji felt herself able to receive the truth of her Christian background in a new way. "I was able to see the love I was experiencing in that moment as the same love, the same promise, as Christ's love. After that, whenever I read the scriptures, I read them from a different point of view. I could feel the living truth in them. And it wasn't a binding kind of truth; it was an inclusive kind of truth that understood heaven on earth and heaven within. As Jesus said in the Gospel of John, 'I and the Father are one.'"

The experience allowed her to reconcile herself with the church as an institution. "I could see the place that a church had, that it served a need, and that there were better and worse churches, just as there were different sorts of people," she said. And the shakeup of her previous prejudices—the more or less unquestioned left-liberal prejudices of a baby boomer with alternative-culture credentials—extended out into the political sphere. "It was a revelation to me that I actually loved George W. Bush," she told me with one of her wide smiles. "I deeply oppose his policies, but I love him, and that is wonderful because I didn't *try* to love him. It's fun to love him because it really shakes people up in the anti-Bush subculture I move in.

"But part of my job as a teacher is to challenge institutionalized beliefs, whatever they are. And it is simply true that even someone who has done evil—someone like Hitler or Stalin or Mao—has that within him or her, that which is not evil. It seems to me that this is Christ's message."

Gangaji's understanding of some of the central tenets of the Christian faith isn't "churchy," but it is suggestive and stimulating. She sees the virgin birth, for example, not as a one-time event, but as a permanent condition within the human soul. "It's very interesting for me, as a woman, to think about the virgin birth because I have been with men and I have given birth," she said. "But if I look inside myself, I see that there is still virginity there. It is not a physical thing. It's deep in, so deep in that it is not even a *female* thing. Virginity is there as our essential self, virginal consciousness, untouched. Mary is a symbol of what is inside all of us. When we recover our essential self, it is a virgin birth. Something that was always alive and hidden deep inside us comes out at last; the birth is a rebirth for us."

Unlike many seekers who understand certain Christian truths in this way—as esoteric, inner, and symbolic of eternal mental and spiritual states—Gangaji does not shy away from the suffering that Christ had to undergo and that we all must face if we follow him. "There is no rebirth without crucifixion," she said. "We all have to experience it if we want greater knowledge. We have to be humbled totally: to feel forsaken by God and totally alone.

"I'm so moved by the story of Christ: this young man, so full of promise, teaching with passion, and it's working! And then he's struck down. His disciples flee and not even God is there to say, 'I'm with you.' This was the darkest night. We have to go through that night because all of our concepts, especially the concept of what success is, have to fail. They have to fail, so we can see what is untouched by concepts.

"Now, most of us are just striving to be normal, to have a good life and then we die. But what if there is Something Else that won't let you alone? Some imperfection that makes you seek? Well, that something, that imperfection, is good luck; it's a grace. And if you follow it through all the way on the spiritual path, it will lead to absolute humbling, to crucifixion. The time will come when you say 'I can't do it. I've failed, I'm lost, I'm separate from God, I'm totally alone.' That's hard! That's exactly what everybody wants to avoid."

The moment she was talking about came to me when I realized—not with blinding clarity but with a subtle shift of perspective—that I could no longer sustain my life on the basis of ego and alcohol. I had come to an almost literal dead stop. I couldn't go on, couldn't live life for another moment without a massive infusion of help from some other or higher power. I had no idea if any such power really existed, but I made an unconditional surrender to Something I hoped was out there. The surrender did not move me away from my alcoholism and despair—it was a profound, almost cellular-level acceptance of my alcoholism and despair. I really was lost, and I knew it, and I was tapping out a ragged Morse code signal to some notional rescue party out there somewhere. It was the mustard-seed-sized beginning of faith for me.

Papaji's message to Gangaji—to simply stop seeking, doing, and being anything or anyone in particular—defined such a surrender. It was a call to humility, she said—and it brought with it an emptying of the self that was, at first, anything but joyous. "This came home to me—literally—after I returned from India," she explained. "I was just thrown into misery one night. I was thinking that it had been a mistake to go to India. What was I thinking, what was I doing? I wanted to back up time to before I had met Papaji; my earlier mild misery had been a lot better than this! I was separated from my guru—he didn't want me to 'follow' him—and I felt separated from grace, still this miserable person with these miserable attributes, and *nothing had changed*!

"It was 4 A.M. I felt I was being bounced off the walls like a rubber ball. Then came a remembrance: Stop. Stop here. Now. Stop in this. Not 'stop this,' but 'stop in this.' Stop trying to fight this, to get away from this, to be 'saved' from this. And at that actual moment of surrendering and being forsaken, it was over. My suffering was over. The night went on for hours, but after that moment of surrender, I was free.

"This is not a gentle death in your sleep. This is a conscious death, and it's what the church celebrates. Easter comes, this redemption, this recognition of No! No death! Death and eternal life are together and always will be. That's what makes the story of Christ such a true story for all of us. It's the story of a soul in a body. A soul that, through surrender and 'thy will be done,' meets itself as eternal life."

DON'T THINK ABOUT GOD

Pier Giorgio di Cicco

Pier Giorgio di Cicco lives a life that seems rich in contradictions. Born in Italy, he grew up in Montreal, Baltimore, and Toronto. By the late seventies, he was one of Canada's most important poets, a pioneer anthologist, and a promoter of poetry by Italian-Canadians. In verse that explored the meaning of Italy in his own life and through tireless organizing of readings, gatherings, and groupings, di Cicco not only gave shape to the Italo-Canadian literary community, he helped all Italo-Canadians find a sense of belonging in a country that was, at the time, bilingual but hardly multicultural.

In 1986, he stopped writing and entered an Ontario monastery, emerging as a priest of the Catholic archdiocese of Toronto. In 2000, he returned to poetry but refused to pigeonhole himself as a devotional, or even a conventionally Catholic, poet. One of his more recent books, *Dead Men of the Fifties,* reverberates with nostalgia for vanished American popular culture: Jack Benny, Jack Paar, Kim Novak, movie matinees, venerable bars in Baltimore.

Di Cicco was declared Poet Laureate of Toronto in 2004, and essays he has written on the role of aesthetics, ethics, and civic spirit in contemporary urban culture have made him one of the most significant voices in the worldwide discussion of urban revitalization. Against the grain of this discussion, which has mostly centered on how the "creative class"— artists, designers, digital innovators, musicians, marketers, and the like— can transform rusty, once-industrial cities into enclaves for the digital elite, di Cicco has emphasized the importance of the entire urban fabric and of every citizen as a creator of urban vitality.

He is a private and deeply tradition-minded man who lives in a spartan, somewhat down-at-heel house in rural Ontario, treasures beauty as both an artistic and a spiritual ideal, and considers everything he does as ministry. "A lot of what I do has become city-building and consultation about urban matters of all kinds," he said as we sat over coffee in his kitchen. "I'm kind of out of breath about it. But I'm a priest, and I look for God, see God, and listen for God in everything. I'm obsessed with God."

For all his participation in urban design forums, civic roundtables, and academic life, di Cicco has little patience with the ideologies of contemporary urban intellectual culture, from ecology to feminism to alternative spirituality. "Between you and me," he told me, "Pope John Paul didn't see the real problems of the church. What enfeebled the church was not communism; it was all kinds of other ideologies and diversions. All these isms—West Coast ecologism, socialism, liberation theology, transcendental this and that, Fritjof Capra, Matthew Fox—came together as tributaries into one big river of—what should we call it? *Worldspeak?* This was an ocean of ideological searching for God. Eventually, these spiritual strip malls took business away from the downtown stores— that is, the church."

For di Cicco, what all these currents have in common is a disdain for what he calls the vertical paradigm. "That's where the battle has been," he said. "Between vertical thinking, vertical theology—thought that values hierarchy—and the horizontal dimension. The vertical is *the* object of antipathy for the contemporary intellectual, so religion, even if it is not fundamentalist, is being discredited just *because* of its verticality."

If di Cicco were simply a spokesperson for the vertical paradigm— a conventional Catholic traditionalist—I am sure I would find him less interesting than I do. But like most of the interviewees in this book, he is struggling to bring paradoxical opposites together: tradition and modernity, faith and doubt, the Christian message and the truth of other faiths, the profane and the sacred. He's not about replacing the worldly horizon-

tal paradigm with the holy vertical one—in fact, as his poetry and urban-
ism show, he is every bit as much in love with the world as he is with the
Spirit.

The point of the holy mystery of Christian faith is, for him, the fusion
of the two dimensions in the Incarnation, God's assuming flesh in Jesus
Christ. Though no friend of the political, religious, and spiritual left, he's
less hostile to it than he is to the habit of left-right thinking, and every
other form of dualistic thinking, the habit of mind that splits the great
unities, such as faith, Christ, God, worship, poetry, love, into pairs of opposites and often bids us choose one over the other.

"Wherever we look in society, we see things in twos: male or female,
left or right. It's everywhere. The two ends of the seesaw are at odds with
each other. But these terms are not incarnational. I mean, is God *up there*
or *down here*? The answer is he's both. Transcendent and immanent. Omnipotent and hugely intimate. Paradox is resolved by two things being
one, which the North American intellect has not mastered the art of.
Eventually, any religious person worth his or her mystical beans figures
out that two things are one, and they learn to live as if two things are
one."

How does di Cicco himself live this fusion? If you guessed that art is the
answer, you're right. "What I do to express twoness in one, the true
alchemy of religion, is to write poetry," he said. "Finally, art and poetry—
including liturgy, which is or ought to be poetry—is the only fit way to
talk about religion without doing it a disservice."

When I asked di Cicco about personal prayer, the individual's address
to God, I wasn't surprised when he talked in poetic terms about it too—
but what he emphasized was the immediacy, concreteness, and emotion-
ality of the poetic act. "Prayer should be as real as the most concrete
poetry that you can find," he said. "Prayer should have the immediacy of
any urgent thing that you say to a loved one or want to hear from a loved
one. And prayer should include your fantasies—in the sense that there is
nothing so fantastic that God won't give it to you. We're afraid of seem-
ing foolish in our requests. We're afraid of looking silly to ourselves. It's a
great gift to God to let yourself look silly to him. I'm not talking about
something fanciful. I'm talking about the most outrageous fundamental
need you might have, but maybe you don't feel like it's noble enough to
ask for, or universal or humane enough. Our prayer lives are constantly
self-censored by the fear of looking ridiculous. But before God, your
smallness is your greatness—your simplicity begins in your smallness.

"And God is a good deal simpler than people think. A good deal more powerful than people think but simpler. He has the heart of a child when it comes to wanting to hear what you have to say. You can give him the most complex things, but finally, he wants to hear your most basic and primal sentiments, which are not really very complex."

Churches have done little to encourage intimate conversation with God. As di Cicco succinctly put it, "The language that one uses *with* God should be the standard for the language that you hear *about* God." Instead, a flat kind of "Worldspeak" has disconnected church talk from talk about life, love, and desire. "Church bulletins and homilies include words like *inclusivity* and *stewardship,* these wonderful, universal, valid ideas that we all agree on," he said. "But when you talk to God, I don't think you use the word *inclusivity* in your prayer. You don't tell God you've been a *good steward* today. If you do, you're out to lunch. We have to talk about ourselves and talk to God in much more personal terms, more intimate terms, and use words that are fleshly words. *I need you* isn't the same thing as *Please don't disenfranchise me.*

"The church should have been sensitive a long time ago to the truth that the word was made flesh. They took the flesh out of the word and replaced it with an abstraction, like *steward* instead of *shepherd.* You have to find a fleshly, concrete, corporeal language that speaks to the body and not just the mind because the mentalistic will alienate the religious person from God."

· · ·

Di Cicco believes that one must pray with love and passion. "Love of a cause, love of people, love of everything. The trick is to feel that kind of passion in one's prayer life. To do that you've got to *talk*. You can't be in love with someone you don't talk to. You talk to them of love. And you can do the same with God. Use your vocal cords; this brings a real presence not an abstract presence. It conjures God. Prayer is not the rendering-present of God. Prayer is the conjuring of God! Even the word *invocation* is too abstract. And no, you're not an all-powerful magician who, with a stroke of the wand, brings the deity down; to conjure here means to flesh out the apparitions, the ideas of God. God is in the flesh."

And then, just as it seemed as if di Cicco were tipping the spirit-flesh dualism seesaw too far over toward the fleshly side, he added "And also not of the flesh. But how those two come together will only make sense when he is in the flesh."

In fact, the particular sense that the Incarnation makes is so crucial to the Christian faith that it takes the place of intellectual understanding for di Cicco. He baldly declared that he found questions about God to be, not difficult, paradoxical, mysterious, but useless—and at this point, I felt we had returned to the insights of Richard Rohr with which this book began: You can't think God—you can only be in God's presence, and that is prayer.

"Nothing makes sense unless one prays," said di Cicco. "Do you know how many people come to me and ask me questions about God? I say something to them that stops them dead in their tracks because it's never occurred to them: The question you just asked me—have you asked it of God? Bright, intelligent people have never done it! Questions about humanism, justice, faith, the good—they think their way into the answers, they don't pray their way through the questions. Thinking is what we do when we don't have God. Answers don't come by thinking. Illuminations come by praying. Yes, thinking about God is useless. Talking to God, living with God, teaching with God, doing with God—in those things is real awareness of God."

All well and good, but prayer can be strangely difficult, I said.

"Yes, it's difficult to pray," di Cicco agreed. And then he set out a way of prayer that surprised me by its frank aestheticism. "What seduced me to prayer is that I need beauty. That which is gentle and beautiful is the lexicon of God. So find beautiful prayers, and if you can't find them, make them up."

And where does this beauty come from for di Cicco? From gentleness. "A beautiful prayer is a sequence of words that disarms you in its simplicity and its gentleness," he said. "Find words that refer to the gentleness in your life. Find words that might have been said by someone who was gentle with you. Use those words on yourself. Hold them up in the palm of your hand when you talk to God, and pretty soon, you'll see that those words are actually not words of your invention. They're words *from* God. This is how I discovered prayer. I used gentle words not aimed at God but aimed at myself. And then I realized that they were donations—those gentle words were packages brought by the angels, brought by the Holy Spirit."

AFTERWORD

It would knit this book up nicely if I were able to report that, after sharing the spiritual lives of thirty-four believers across North America, I had come to understand exactly what a modern faith in God and Christ is. I would especially like to be able to report that my interviewees solved my intellectual problems with the Christian faith—that I now had a solid idea of how to think about the virgin birth, the resurrection, and the dual nature of Christ. I'd love to say that I learned exactly how to worship God, how to pray, and how to live in accord with Gospels.

But these things didn't happen, at least not in the straightforward way I've sketched them above. I still have plenty of questions—and that makes sense because the subject of God is inexhaustible and because life presents new problems every hour. But what I am quite sure I learned from my interviewees is a new set of *attitudes* toward the questions I have. A lot of my categories were shaken up.

To begin with, I learned that there is no such thing as *the* Christian faith if we understand faith as something that is lived and pondered by individuals as well as something articulated by churches. Of course, the various denominations have their differences of emphasis, but even on the bedrock articles of faith shared across the denominations, individuals differ in major ways.

The Christians I spoke with nearly all accepted the Trinity as a core doctrine, for example, but most seemed to have a favorite member of the Trinity, one of the Three who has meant the most to them over the years. For James W. Jones, the all-creating Father is the primary spark of his imagination. To Mary Forsythe and Cyndi Dale, Jesus came in visions and visitations. Helen Hansen's eyes light up when she talks about the flow of the Holy Spirit in and through her life. For Jim Rigby, Christ is first of all a great teacher of justice; for Chuck Robison, he is most significant as an eternal cosmic principle. Everyone in this book plays the music of faith with somewhat different instrumentation, at different tempos, and following his or her own different drummer as well as the musical score they have inherited from their traditions. I learned that a faith that you do not make your own is not a living faith.

The issue of individual differences became crucial for me when I considered the left-right split in the churches, an issue I didn't wish to emphasize but could not in good conscience avoid. It's been noted that this split has come to be more significant for many than differences between the denominations themselves. In other words, a conservative evangelical Baptist today is likely to feel more in accord with a Catholic traditionalist—at least on issues like abortion or homosexuality—than either of them would with more liberal members of their own denominations.

Though I have no desire to soft-pedal my own convictions, which mostly can be labeled liberal, I wanted to see if paying close attention to the concrete stories of real people, including some real people who are much more conservative theologically than I am (I didn't ask about politics), might unsettle some of my own "certainties" about the spirituality underlying the split and make a contribution toward healing it.

I was certain, for example, that conservative evangelicals were mainly institutionalists and moralists, always emphasizing externals, such as membership in the right church and the careful observance of rigid rules of behavior. But, thank God, I was led to evangelicals like Mary Forsythe, Victoria and Allen Queen, and Tina and Tom Engstrom, who expressed to me a vision of passionate, personal relationships with others and with God and Jesus Christ that transcends churchiness and mere moralism— and unsettled me by revealing the thinness of my own relationships to the human and the divine.

Thanks to these believers and many others in the book, I discovered that one of the ways I hide or hold back from relationship is to place too much emphasis on purely intellectual questions, thinking that if I get the questions answered and thus satisfy my left brain, that's enough to turn me into a faithful believer and a good human being. Going into this book project, I believed that faith is mainly a matter of assent to ideas.

I don't think I'm alone in this; both Christian fundamentalism and secular neoatheism as represented by popular writers such as Richard Dawkins assume that religious faith is mainly cognitive and is entirely based on what actually exists or doesn't exist "out there" in the objective world and what actually did or didn't happen in historical time. Either a humanlike, fatherlike Creator set the world in motion and guides it according to humanlike, fatherlike values, or the world's origin and continued existence are utterly random and essentially meaningless. Either Christ literally leaped out of his tomb, walked with his disciples, then flew off into the sky (presumably finding heaven someplace in the ionosphere, where he orbits today), or the resurrection and the ascension are absurd fables.

My intuition when I began this book was that I had to find a way between these two extremes, a way of believing religious doctrine and story without sacrificing my intellect and what that intellect knew about the world we all live in. It was, I think, the right impulse with which to begin my journey. The intellect is by no means to be thrown away when you follow Christ and believe in God; another lesson I learned from the people in these pages is that real faith involves the whole person and to cut away great chunks of one's brain in order to be faithful to fables is to misrepresent yourself to God and thus be stuck in what can only be called a bad-faith relationship.

People such as Aiden Enns, John Shelby Spong, James W. Jones, Pier Giorgio di Cicco, and Richard Rohr came to my rescue here by helping me to discover new ways to use mind and language to approach God. Enns and Jones suggested that religious language and religious story are, not statements of fact to be evaluated, but ways, via language, of opening the mind and heart to truth that goes beyond language. Rohr and di Cicco stunned me by flatly declaring that, where God is concerned, thought simply doesn't work. God is too enormous, too far beyond our categories of the thinkable to be thought. So the mind needs to go elsewhere: into contemplation and prayer.

That was a breakthrough for me. Now when my mind finds itself approaching God, I try to humble it by pulling it back from some pure left-brain activity like trying to figure out why God permits evil or how, exactly,

Jesus could be fully human and fully divine. I pull my mind back to a place where it can *contemplate* these things—that is, dwell upon them peacefully without trying to solve them. And when I read the Gospels or Genesis, I try for that same wise passiveness, that same contemplative attention.

Lo and behold, I have discovered that when the "unbelievable" elements of religious story and doctrine are freed from the literal, yet still held to be true, they actually expand in truthfulness, a truthfulness of a different and richer kind. Freed from the slavery of literal, one-time truth, Christ's resurrection becomes an eternal recurrence, a principle that holds true forever, a symbol of all the miraculous rebirths we know, from human reconciliation to the return of spring to the recovery of some poor alcoholic screwup.

And yet—here's where it gets really interesting—the resurrection is more than a symbol. It is an event that stands, as I see it, at the border between fact and imagination, just as it stands on the border between life and death. It is too strange to be literally true and too compelling, too charged with meaning, too transformative, to be a falsehood. (After all, it was enough to change a ragtag group of disciples, frightened and uncertain of their faith, into apostles who would willingly die for Jesus.) Something happened after Jesus's death, and it is a deep mystery. To linger in its special kind of truth is to deepen our idea of truth and to transform our consciousness bit by bit.

The idea that there is a higher truth than the literal, toward which language, ritual, and church can point but cannot fully comprehend, is mystical. Mysticism has had a hard time in the Western churches for centuries. Catholicism has preferred legalism. Despite the great tradition of mysticism in the church, the good Catholic has been most often defined as a keeper of church rules, whether they're enshrined in canon law or the catechism or the Pope's latest pronouncement. Protestantism has, by and large, opted for a rational approach to faith—again, despite mystical or charismatic countercurrents from Anabaptism to Pentecostalism.

But there is a revival of mystical consciousness going on in many Christian churches, and many of my interviewees bear witness to it. It thrills me because it carries the seeds of what I see as a return to the fountainhead of religion—conscious contact with God—after centuries of obsession with what Richard Rohr calls "membership issues"—how to be a good Catholic or Lutheran or Methodist, how to do the right things according to the various holy rules. Many Christians are finding common ground with Asian transcendental traditions like Zen Buddhism and Vedanta as they explore the ways of union with God.

But by far the most transforming message I received from my interviewees—and they all contributed to it—was that faith is more a matter of doing than of thinking. The *relationship* that the evangelicals emphasized—and many of the others spoke of too—is inconceivable as a mere idea. It's born of, and sustained by, will and work—going among people, staying with them, listening to them, aiding them, loving them even at their most unlovable.

Again and again as I worked on *How to Believe* I encountered people—Kosuke Koyama, Matt Helling, Peter Gardiner-Harding, Joan Kirby among them—for whom the intricacies of doctrine and theology were either secondary or just not a problem. They knew, and they reminded me, that the phrase used most often by Jesus in inviting someone into discipleship was "follow me." And by that, he seems to have meant do what I do: Go among people, heal them, tell them the good news of God's unconditional love, which he called the Kingdom of God and which he located in each human heart. Urge them to stop sinning—that is, stop doing things that cut them off from conscious contact with the God who loves them. Stand up and partner with God in the slow, steady creation of a better world.

It may be that no one will ever fully understand Jesus, but anyone can follow him, starting this very moment. This was a hard thing for me to hear because I am selfish and lazy; but it was also a hopeful thing to hear because it means I can be a Christian without having any certainty other than that God is love and I am called to love God and my neighbor. I then must get to work, or the love will turn theoretical and die.

Now, it is perfectly possible for an atheist to cultivate loving and giving relationships with his or her neighbors and even with a higher ideal or power of some kind: humanity, science, or the Good. An atheist may be as active and benevolent, as dedicated to helping others and building a better world as a Christian, a Jew, or a Muslim. An atheist may be just as committed to a great cause; in fact, unbelievers have often forged far ahead of the churches on issues of human dignity, gender equity, and economic justice. So where do God or Jesus come into the picture?

I think that the answer to that, at least as far as this book is concerned, lies in the personal stories that my interviewees tell, and it is in these stories that you, as a reader, can find the truth of our title. How to believe? Well, first, open yourselves to mystery, as these people did. Everyone in this book followed up on a hint, an intuition, or a revelation of something greater than the world of the five senses and the three dimensions.

Just as importantly, everyone in this book opened themselves up to the fact that this greater something had been sensed, loved, and communed with by people long ago, and that the records they left of this opening—in the case of Christians, the Holy Bible—were authentic revelations of this truth. There is wisdom in this second kind of openness; it says that the individual shouldn't go it alone. The individual is far too wayward, willful, and selfish not to need the steadying hand of a tradition, and far too prone to discouragement not to need the inspiration of the great stories that scripture tells.

The Bible, to be sure, needs to be approached contemplatively and with an eye on its great themes rather than a reverence for every detail in it. By focusing too minutely on short Biblical tags and "proof texts" picked to support free-market capitalism, homophobia, the war in Iraq, or the "natural" dominance of the male in the family or the church, fundamentalism and Biblical literalism can turn the great, overarching Biblical story—God's rescue of the human being from the bondage of his own selfishness and willfulness—into something very small indeed.

My interviewees also opened themselves to what is sometimes contemptuously called "organized religion." They opened to it, not because organized religion is the only way to experience the great mystery, but because organized religion, like scripture, can be a bearer of wisdom and a steadier of the inconstant, vacillating human mind. And organized religion provides community, without which spirituality nearly always withers into eccentricity or obsession. For the Christian, of course, community is not optional. Love of neighbor is Christ's second great commandment; it is bound up with and sustains the commandment to love God.

Organized religion has, as we well know, been both a gift to humanity and a blight on the face of the earth—comforting, exalting, brutalizing, and murderous. But let's be honest: it shares this two-faced quality with every institution that has been proposed to replace it, from science, which produced Galileo and the H-bomb, to capitalism, which produced intellectual freedom and wage slavery.

Finally, at the core of all my interviewees' openness to the divine was human need, the need we nearly all feel to fill the God-shaped holes in our souls. In some of my interviewees' lives, this need expressed itself with great drama: Allen Queen and Larry Lee found God in the depths, where most of us are too scared to go. Matt Helling was driven by a quiet and persistent dissatisfaction with life as he knew it. Cynthia Williams hit bottom when she realized that her corporate life was a living death. I tried filling the hole with booze, but the booze eroded the hole until it was as wide as my life.

I believe that this need goes beyond the need for meaning or purpose. It is a metaphysical need, a need rooted in the very structure of reality: We need to be who we truly are, and until we connect with what is profoundly greater than ourselves, we will continue to feel a kind of reality deficit, a sense that our very existence is false in a way that we can't quite put our finger on.

There's no need to list all of the ways we try to "get real" in modern culture: we get a car, we get a partner, we get a prestigious job, we get a flat-screen TV, we get a self-help book. These things, which in themselves are good, make lousy substitutes for what we are really missing. Work, love, and capitalized abstractions like Humanity or Freedom make better pseudo-Gods, but all of the stories in this book suggest that there is a deeper and more mysteriously magnetic, fulfilling, demanding, and joyful place to go.

You may have turned to this book for some really new ideas about faith and how to get it. But the experiences I recount here, and the experience I had writing *How to Believe,* suggest that only the most basic, traditional truths about faith are fresh enough to be contemporary. How to believe? Take a look at yourself. Acknowledge your need. Surrender, if only experimentally, to the mystery that you may soon call God.

This book isn't intended to convert anybody to Christianity, only to explore some of the intricate, beautiful, challenging aspects of that faith in order to suggest how anyone's faith may be deepened. But I'd still like to recommend Jesus because I believe his life and death show that he understood to a superlative degree our woundedness, our frailty, and our deep need to be loved. He poured out love upon us, and in a mysterious way, he still does. In so doing, he rescues me from myself. I'm still not quite sure how he does it, but I am very, very open to the idea.

ACKNOWLEDGMENTS

Reviewing a list of people who helped me with this book, I was amazed by the power of generosity. The interest of my family and friends in the project, and their belief in my ability to complete it, makes them co-authors. Over certain stretches of time, they had more faith in this book than I did; their repeated queries about the progress of the book made it too embarrassing not to finish it. And without the willingness of scores of people to respond to e-mail and phone inquiries that came out of the blue from a writer they didn't know, this book would still be a memo at Random House.

Speaking of co-authors: the people profiled in *How to Believe,* who opened the deepest parts of their spiritual and emotional lives to me, have given the book whatever value it possesses. My interviews with them were, in every single case, so absorbing for me that I had to take time afterward to "return to earth" and to everyday consciousness. I can only hope that I have been able to capture some of the energy of these encounters in my writing.

My travels in pursuit of interviews introduced me to wonderful cities that were new to me: Springfield, Missouri; Winnipeg, Manitoba; Ashland and Medford, Oregon; Ashland, Wisconsin; Dallas–Forth Worth and Austin, Texas; Charleston and Columbia, South Carolina; San Ramon and Santa Rosa, California; Atlanta, Georgia; Long Branch and Morris Plains, New Jersey. They allowed me to return to places where I have lived—Iowa City, Boston, San Francisco, and New York—and to places I have come to know through my wife and her family: Telluride, Colorado, and Toronto, Ontario. And they gave me glimpses of the rich spiritual life of my current home, the Twin Cities of Minneapolis and St.

Paul, Minnesota. In mysterious ways, geography and faith coalesce, and every place is holy ground.

The debt of gratitude I have incurred to my wife, Laurie Phillips, through twenty-five years of friendship and a decade of marriage is unpayable; but that's why there's love. A dedicated public artist, introvert, personal coach, and unconventional spiritual seeker, she is the most dedicated and skillful helper of other human beings—and, therefore, the most truly religious person—I have ever met. She thinks I can do things, and that's enough for me.

My old *Utne Reader* colleague and boss, Jay Walljasper, has been inspiring me for a quarter century with his absolutely unique blend of good sense, social and spiritual insight, and progressive politics that go way beyond "red and blue." If we would listen to Jay, we would have a country as decent as the majority of its people. Long discussions with him in the Mexican restaurants of Lake Street clarified and enlivened this project in many ways.

Thanks as always to the Tracy's Tertulia, that durable gang of free spirits who meet on certain Tuesdays at Tracy's Saloon in Minneapolis for comradeship, chatter, neo-Surrealist pranks, tarot readings (with a deck of our own design), stereopticon slideshows, and mutual support. Special thanks to members Matt Helling (who agreed to be interviewed for *How to Believe*) and to Carolyn Crooke. It's not Carolyn's fault that the work plan she devised for me fell apart—she had no idea how scattered I really am.

Adam Gordon taught me how to survive the real but challenging blessing of spending a couple of years on only one project, with no boss but myself. My dear Manhattan pal and fellow freelancer Vicki Brower and her partner, Michael Gottsegen, connected me with the rich Jewish-Christian interfaith world in New York, to which Michael is an important contributor. Another New York friend (long since fled to Austin, Texas), Elaine Robbins, alerted her network of friends to my project with great results. (She also took me to Threadgill's for grits and gravy.) Cliff Smith provided some wonderful referrals just when I needed them most. Tim Morgan, formerly of *Utne Reader,* connected me with evangelical Christians who rattled my prejudices (permanently, I hope).

Gratitude to Father Matthias Wahba of Saint Antonius Coptic Orthodox Church, Hayward, California. Thanks also to the gifted New York music critic, biographer, and all-around maestro of the life of the mind, Gene Santoro, who happens to be an old grad school pal, for his customary high-bandwidth generosity. And to my dear mother-in-law, Lorna

Phillips, who introduced me to Ekklesia and Fr. Bill Atwood; his help added balance and vividness to this book.

Scott Edelstein, who probably knows more about the book game than anyone else in America, handled the business end of this book to perfection. The inimitable Mike Fraase gave me some sage advice that worked. Grant Pound gave me a month's worth of quality time at his innovative artist/writer retreat, Colorado Art Ranch, which allowed me to finish the manuscript. And my Random House editor, Will Murphy, made everything happen from the start. Thanks for giving me a shot, Will, and for a sharp and graceful editing job.

Others I want to thank include various friends, helpers, agents, book editors, brief acquaintances who were generous with ideas, journalists who gave me leads, interviewees whose profiles didn't make it into the book for one reason or another, and a number of people who agreed to be interviewed but whose schedules (or mine) didn't allow it to happen. They include, in no particular order: Chris Dodge, Karen Hall, Chip Pearson, Faye Williamsen, Naomi Lewin, Michael DeMark, Sharon DeMark, Christa Tippett, Kate Moos, Karen Olson, Marlene Tupy, Elaine Anderson, Dorothy Greenaway, Jill Wilson, Greg Lockert, Mother Raphaela, John Longhurst, Francis V. O'Connor, Will Braun, Retta Blaney, David Schimke, Joseph Hart, Anne O'Connor, Heather Lee, Richard Mouw, Michael Gartland, Marjorie Hoyer Smith, Courtney Dukelow, Shelley Boyd, Greg Boyd, Cheryl Price, Mayor Joseph Riley of Charleston, South Carolina, Rita Donato, Mary Cayan, Kathy Mahoney, Bill Mahoney, Errol Castens, Toni Weingarten, Mike Mullen, Jon Goldstein, Deirdre Baker, Karen Jostad, Thomas Ciesielka, Linda Leicht, Shirley Ragsdale, Mike Miller, Linda Taylor, Paul Seebeck, Tim Townsend, Alecia Stevens, Louise Derrick, Victoria Smith, Terry Dosh, Colman McCarthy, Tiffany Compan, Chip Blake, Debra Bendis, Teri Seipel, Jim Comer, Right Reverend Dr. B. A. Kwashi, Fanny Howe, Aaron Wallentine, Marcus Borg, Fred Brown, Martin Delaney, Kate S. Warner, Anne Czarniecki, Matthew S. Diener, Damaris Moore, Richard Cimino, Susan Doubet, OSB, and Mary Jude Jun, OSU.

If you helped with this book and I missed you, let me know so I can at least apologize.

ABOUT THE AUTHOR

Jon Spayde is a former editor at the *Utne Reader,* where he wrote about personal growth, arts, spirituality, and many other subjects. He is the co-author of *Visionaries: People and Ideas to Change Your Life* and *Salons: The Joy of Conversation.*

About the Type

This book was set in Garamond, a typeface originally designed by the Parisian typecutter Claude Garamond (1480–1561). This version of Garamond was modeled on a 1592 specimen sheet from the Egenolff-Berner foundry, which was produced from types assumed to have been brought to Frankfurt by the punchcutter Jacques Sabon.

Claude Garamond's distinguished romans and italics first appeared in *Opera Ciceronis* in 1543–44. The Garamond types are clear, open, and elegant.